TO
Dean, Joan, and Marcia

Preface

This book presents a philosophy of political inquiry—a philosophy of science applicable to political science. In this context *philosophy* denotes, most briefly, thought about thought. Somewhat more broadly, it denotes general conceptions of ends and means, purposes and methods, in scholarly inquiry. Still more broadly, it includes an effort to spell out and clarify both the meaning of crucial words that are employed in scholarly inquiry and the meaning and implications of various assumptions and premises on which such inquiry is, or should be, based.

Though in part descriptive of the ends actually pursued and the means actually employed, the book is in larger part prescriptive or normative. What should political scientists be attempting to achieve? What standards of judgment should guide them in choosing what to do? What criteria should be employed in deciding what to teach and to write—and in appraising what others teach and write? What sorts of inquiry are to be regarded as worth while, and what sorts of accomplishments as satisfying? How should the ends that are chosen be pursued? Many of the words used in answering these questions are vague, making it necessary to devote considerable attention to their meaning. Thus much of the book is designed to enhance conceptual clarity. In addition, the book aims to be both analytical and logical: analytical in identifying the elements that go together to make for high-quality scholarship and logical in identifying relationships among those elements.

The main purpose of the book is thus to contribute to the development of good scholarship in political science. The ingredients of good scholarship that are treated have to do with the choices that scholars make. The assumption is that these choices are likely to be wiser if they are made deliberately and self-consciously, after due consideration of possible alternatives. The issues dealt with relate to the selective learning and teaching of what is already known as well as to efforts to discover or develop new knowledge; they relate to study, to teaching, and to research.

The book is divided into four parts.

Part I treats purposes in the study of politics, reflecting the assumption that immediate, intermediate, and ultimate purposes are more likely to be achieved if they are clearly identified. The identification of purposes—whether those that are pursued or those that should be pursued—is not easy. Graduate students attempting to write term papers and dissertations are commonly plagued by the problem of clarity of purpose. Aspiring authors at the post-doctoral level frequently give evidence of the same difficulty, e.g., by stating purposes so vaguely that they are left without clear criteria for the inclusion and exclusion of data. To start out on a clear line of thought and develop it cogently and coherently is a very difficult task. Even some published works create the impression that the authors did not quite know what they were doing—that they had no clear conception of purpose beyond the immediate and the obvious. This impression coincides with an observation made many years ago by R. G. Collingwood in *The Idea of History* that "the extent to which people act with a clear idea of their ends, knowing what effects they are aiming at, is easily exaggerated." He added that "to a very great extent people do not know what they are doing until they have done it, if then." Perhaps others who have written books and who have then tried to write a preface describing what they have done will join in testifying to the truth of the observation! In the absence of a clear sense of purpose—and a sense of logic which indicates what is relevant to the purpose—learning, teaching, and writing are likely to consist of a potpourri of miscellaneous information or a robot-like imitating of a conventional pattern. Conventional patterns are sometimes quite good, of course. Purposeful and cogent thought may lead to their deliberate endorsement. The point here is that choices regarding purpose, whatever they may be, should be discriminating and not automatic or unthinkingly imitative.

The argument in Part I is that the purpose should be to explain and predict political behavior, mainly with a view to contributing to the rationality of political decisions.

Part II focuses quite explicitly on a series of words commonly employed in explaining and predicting: fact, abstraction, classification, concept, generalization, hypothesis, rule, principle, law, theory, and model. Most of these words denote a form in which knowledge is expressed; e.g., it is expressed in the form of facts and generalizations. Most of them also denote, or are related to, a process that is important to the acquisition and expression of knowledge, e.g., abstracting, classifying, theorizing. Many of the choices that political scientists make rest on their understanding of the meaning of these forms and processes. What are "the facts" of political science? What is the difference between a specific fact and a general fact? What difference does it make whether a fact is regarded simply as true information or as evidence? What are the functions of concepts? What pitfalls are there in defining concepts? What dangers exist in reifying abstractions? What are hypotheses, when can they usefully be employed, and what is meant by their testability? When argument develops over the question of the extent to which political behavior is lawful, what various possible meanings are involved? When one writer speaks of "the decline of political theory" while another points "toward a theory of international politics," what does or might each one mean by the word *theory*? What is involved in the process of theorizing, and what role may theories play? What do facts, rules, laws, theories, etc., have to do with explanation and prediction?

Part III dwells mainly on approaches to the study of politics, with some attention also given to methods and techniques. In brief, the word *approach* is here defined to denote the criteria employed in selecting the questions to ask and the data to consider in political inquiry. Political scientists employ a wide variety of approaches. Some identify an approach with an academic discipline and take, say, a historical or a psychological approach. Some identify an approach with a salient feature of political life and take, say, an institutional approach or any of several varieties of decision-making approaches. Some take a behavioral approach or an analogical approach called general systems theory. Some identify an approach with an explanatory hypothesis or a causal theory; such approaches fall into any of several categories depending on the relative emphasis given to environmental, psychological, and ideological data and considerations. For example, those attempting to explain and predict on the basis of Marxist theories stress economic data and considerations; those attempting to do so on the basis of the ideas or belief systems of political actors stress ideological data. The principal purpose in cataloguing and describing these various approaches is, again, to encourage deliberate, self-conscious choice concerning them—whether the choice be to adopt just one approach or to employ two or more of them in attacking the same problem. There is considerable risk of fruitless work when an approach is adopted more or less blindly and unthinkingly, perhaps because of an unawareness of alternatives.

The treatment of methods in Part III is brief. The word *methods* is made to denote processes for acquiring and treating data. The focus is on the meaning of analysis, on the characteristics of quantitative and qualitative methods, on the difference between inductive and deductive methods, on comparative methods, and, finally, on the meaning of the term *scientific method*. The purpose is to clarify meanings rather than to give practical instruction in the application of methods.

Finally, Part IV asks whether political science is or can be a science. The question concerns the study of what is and not the study of what ought to be. The answer depends, of course, on the definition of science that one chooses to adopt. In brief, the definition adopted here is that a science consists of knowledge that is verifiable, systematic, and general. The problem for political scientists is that the more they insist on verifiability the more difficult it is to develop generalizations, and the further they go toward high levels of generality the more difficult it is to verify what is said. Roughly, the dilemma is whether to put the stress on saying what is important or saying what is true. Some political scientists respond in one way and some in another. This is not to say that no significant scientific studies of politics have appeared, for in some areas the dilemma is much less serious than in others. But the obstacles to making all descriptive studies scientific are very great.

Stimulation for the writing of the book has come from various sources. I have long felt a personal need for a rationale which would guide my teaching and research, and a graduate seminar that I have conducted has necessitated the articulation of a

rationale. (The seminar, incidentally, is of the kind usually en-
titled "Scope and Method in Political Science"; I entitle it "The
Philosophy of Political Inquiry.") The factor precipitating the
decision to write the book was my experience in directing post-
doctoral summer seminars on the teaching of international politics
in 1955 and 1956—seminars for which the Ford Foundation is to
be thanked. One of the objects of these seminars was to develop
a philosophy applicable to teaching and research in the international field. Though rewarding, the experience was also unset-
tling. It was not always clear what kinds of questions were worth
asking; and for some fundamental but simple questions answers
did not seem to be available. Following the seminars I started a
reading program along lines suggested by Richard C. Snyder and
Harold Sprout, with the book as the eventual result.

At crucial stages in the writing of the book others made suggestions without which it probably could not have been completed. My colleagues Edward Lane Davis and Robert Boynton
and my former colleague Arnold A. Rogow, now of Stanford University, were especially helpful. Robert Salisbury of Washington
University and Fred Sondermann of Colorado College likewise
gave invaluable aid. Charles Hyneman and others offered such
devastating criticisms of one chapter that I liquidated it completely—to the undoubted improvement of the book. Lee Lendt,
now pursuing his doctorate at Columbia University, made many
suggestions; and my research assistant, W. Hayward Rogers, saved
me from many errors and contributed significantly to the clarity
and precision of a number of passages. Gustav Bergmann, professor of philosophy and psychology at the University of Iowa,
helped more than he realized simply by the encouragement he
gave. If these and other persons did not make the book perfect,
it is not their fault.

Finally, I am pleased to acknowledge special assistance from
the University of Iowa in the form of a very drastic reduction of
my teaching load during the final semester of work on the manu-
script.

VERNON VAN DYKE

University of Iowa
Iowa City
March 1960

Contents

PART IV. SCIENCE?

Part I
PURPOSES IN THE STUDY OF POLITICS

Introduction

Those who teach and write about politics necessarily select and arrange the data they present, and sometimes they seek new data—new knowledge. These activities require the making of choices. One fact is chosen rather than another, one pattern of organization rather than another, one line of research rather than another. Of course, the choices could be random, but obviously they are not. Principles of some kind come into play. Standards of judgment guide action. There is a rationale for what is done.

It may not always be necessary for scholars to be articulate about the rationale of their activity. Those possessed with a good intuition or inspired by the right example may make good choices regularly even though they are no more than dimly aware of the criteria of judgment which they employ. In the main, however, it seems probable that choices will be better if they are made thoughtfully on the basis of explicitly formulated standards of judgment.

What standards come into play? What criteria do scholars employ, and should they employ, in deciding what to teach or write and how to get it organized sensibly?

The response can be the truism that scholars should make choices so as to serve desirable purposes. This may sharpen the focus of inquiry, but does not provide an answer.

What purposes of scholarship should be regarded as desirable?

The theme to be developed in answer to this question reflects the elementary proposition that the study of politics is the study of an aspect of human behavior in an environment. Quite apart from the scholarly purposes of political scientists, human beings have purposes (goals, ends, values) which they pursue under various conditions by various methods. Some of the purposes and some of the methods are called political.

These propositions suggest the purposes that political scientists ought to pursue. Their aim should be to gain and impart reliable knowledge of the purposes that are or might be pursued in political life and of the means that are or might be employed—knowledge of ends and means, and of interrelationships within and among ends and means.

Essentially the same thought can be expressed differently if the choice of ultimate ends is assumed to reflect something other than scholarly inquiry—an assumption that will be discussed in Chapter One. We can say that the purpose of scholarship is to account for and, in so far as possible, predict political conditions and events. This amounts to saying that the purpose should be to explain and predict—to establish relationships between thought and action, means and ends, cause and effect, conditions and consequences. Put in Hobbes' words, the purpose should be to gain and impart "knowledge of consequences, and dependence of one fact upon another."[1] Or, as John Stuart Mill said, the part of the "scientific observer and reasoner" should be "to show that certain consequences follow from certain causes and that, to obtain certain ends, certain means are the most effectual."[2] The meaning and implications of these statements will be spelled out through the chapters of Part I.

But why seek knowledge of ends and means? Why explain and predict? Various answers are possible. Such knowledge can be regarded as self-justifying—as an end in itself; or, to put it somewhat differently, it can be regarded as desirable because it helps to satisfy curiosity. At the same time, it may have practical effect and manipulative value. Knowledge of consequences permits the making of choices in terms of the desirability of the consequences. The scholar may seek such knowledge so that his own choices will more surely contribute to the consequences which he desires. More commonly, he seeks it so that others can be informed of the probable consequences of their choices, the hope being that they will use the knowledge for good rather than for evil ends. In truth, the desire to influence the decisions of others so as to promote the achievement of what is regarded as the good life may be the guiding purpose.

The above references are to "desirable" purposes. Sometimes the issue is discussed in terms of "significance." Those who engage in teaching and research naturally want their work to be worth while or significant, though many are chronically depressed by gnawing doubts about the value of their achievements—or disdainful of their professional associates for indulging in trivialities. The point here is that the criteria of desirability advanced above can serve equally well as criteria of significance.

Linked with the notions of desirability and significance is the notion of rationality, for to contribute to knowledge of ends and means in the sense described is to contribute to the potential rationality of action. This conception of the nature of rationality is important enough that it deserves to be stressed. As Dahl and Lindblom put it,

An action is rational to the extent that it is "correctly" designed to maximize goal achievement. . . . Given more than one goal (the usual human situation), an action is rational to the extent that it is correctly designed to maximize *net* goal achievement.[3]

Simon adopts a similar definition; and he goes on to suggest that since rationality can be judged from differing vantage points the word should be qualified so as to indicate the standard employed.

A decision may be "objectively" rational if *in fact* it is the correct behavior for maximizing given values in a given situation. It is "subjectively" rational if it maximizes attainment relative to the actual knowledge of the subject. It is "consciously" rational to the degree that the adjustment of means to ends is a conscious process. It is "deliberately" rational to the degree that the adjustment of means to ends has been deliberately brought about. . . . A decision is "organizationally" rational if it is oriented to the organization's goals; it is "personally" rational if it is oriented to the individual's goals.[4]

In sum, scholarship is significant when it contributes to the potential rationality of a political decision. Its significance varies with the importance of the end to which the decision relates, with the importance of the decision to the achievement of the end, and with the extent of the contribution to potential rationality.

Obviously, a clear conception of the characteristics of desirable or significant scholarship is not enough. The scholar needs to be guided by something more. The suggestion here is that he should be guided by explicitly stated questions or problems. He should seek answers to questions or solutions to problems having to do with thought and action, ends and means, cause and effect, conditions and consequences. The study of politics should thus be conceived as a question-posing and question-answering activity.

There are alternatives, of course. Many speak of teaching a subject or investigating a topic, the assumption apparently being that the title of the subject or the name of the topic is a sufficient criterion for the inclusion and exclusion of data. In addition to naming a title or topic, some go on to say, to themselves at least, that all they want is the facts. If they are a little more sophisticated, they may say that they propose to advance some propositions or, better, hypotheses.

Such ways of thinking about scholarly pursuits are not wrong, but they skip one or more steps. As will become clear later, the data relevant to most subjects or topics are mountainous; the facts are endless. And the mere statement of a subject or topic does not provide clear criteria of selection. In many cases it leads to a potpourri of miscellaneous information which makes the reader or listener shrug his shoulders and ask, "So what?" When this danger is avoided, it seems likely that the teacher or writer has supplemented the subject or topic with some implicit questions. Otherwise, how would he know what to include and what to exclude?

The point here is that questions should be made explicit. Scholarly inquiry should be guided deliberately by a question or series of questions. If questions are made explicit, they can be examined with a view to determining whether the answers are worth pursuing. Given a significant question, criteria of relevance can be adopted and data can be selected and organized in such a way as to provide an answer.

The questions raised in the study of politics are commonly divided into questions of fact and questions of value. The first chapter of Part I will be devoted to a clarification and discussion of this distinction. Answers to questions of fact are said to be descriptive, and answers to questions of value—at least if the value is "ultimate"—are said to be normative. Once this distinction has been made, our focus will be largely on description. Thus the second and subsequent chapters in Part I will be devoted to an examination of various ways of selecting and ordering descriptive knowledge. The second chapter is logically incomplete and is designed simply to provide stepping-stones to the third. It provides a classification scheme for descriptive questions according to whether they are developmental or cross-sectional and according to the level of generality of the answers sought. The third chapter—the heart of Part I—is an introduction to the notion of explanation: the selection and ordering of data with a view to accounting for conditions and events. The fourth concerns prediction and its relationship to explanation. It also asks, why predict? The answer has been given above. We predict in order that decisions can be made rationally—on the basis of knowledge of consequences.

CHAPTER ONE

Questions of Fact and Value:

THE "IS" AND THE "OUGHT," MEANS AND ENDS

The distinction between fact and value calls first for a discussion of the grounds of knowledge—the basis for asserting a belief to be warranted or true. Given some understanding of the relevant issues, we can proceed to a discussion of means and ends, examining the meanings of these concepts and the relationships between them.

FACT AND VALUE: THE DESCRIPTIVE AND THE NORMATIVE

The questions that political scientists ask call sometimes for a study of what exists or happens, and sometimes for a study of what ought to exist or happen. Questions of the first sort are questions of fact, whereas those of the second sort are questions of value, though, as we will see, there is some ambiguity here. The same distinction can be made by saying that some questions call for descriptive statements and others for normative statements.

Descriptive statements, being factual, assert alleged truths about reality. They deal with what is, and not with what ought to be. Among other things, they identify relationships, e.g., the efficacy or the consequences of the employment of given methods or means. Or they may indicate what people do or believe or desire.

Normative statements express conceptions of the desirable. They indicate value preferences. They concern not what is but what ought to be, endorsing ends, purposes, or norms.

In connection with each type of statement the question is, what are the grounds of knowledge? Upon what basis can we sensibly accept statements of each type as warranted or true? In answering this question, political scientists and others divide into two groups, the one endorsing positivism and the other endorsing rationalism. There are subdivisions within each group. The position taken in this book might be described as common-sense positivism.

Common-sense positivism calls not only for a distinction between fact and value but also for a distinction between the definitional or logical, on the one hand, and the empirical, on the other. Definitional and logical statements (sometimes called *analytic*) are designed simply to assign meanings to words and to clarify the meaning and logical implications of language, whereas empirical statements are designed to indicate what happens in the world.

So far as definitional and logical statements are concerned, the principal point is that they should be recognized as such. The definition of a word (e.g., justice) should not be construed as the description of either a physical or a metaphysical reality. Thus if the question is asked, "What is justice?" it ought to be reformulated in any of several possible ways, e.g., "What meaning is it useful to assign to the word *justice*?" The revised phrasing is preferable because it is less likely to suggest that justice has a form or essence which men have the opportunity to discover and describe and is more likely to suggest that justice is what men define it to be.[1]

So far as empirical statements are concerned, the principal point of the positivist is that they be either verified or verifiable through observation—through the use of one or another of the senses. They are supposed to be descriptive of reality.[2]

Positivists see no way of establishing what ought to be by observing what is. They see no way of verifying normative statements by empirical methods. They see no logical way of proceeding from the realm of fact to the realm of value. From their point of view, values or conceptions of the desirable stem, ultimately at least, from will and emotion, and are thus volitional rather than being dictated by empiricism or logic. Thus, ultimate values must be regarded as self-justifying; they are simply postulated.[3]

The implication of this position is that political inquiry of a positivist sort provides no basis for choice among ultimate values. If liberals, fascists, communists, and others choose different sets of ultimate values, the positivist can react emotionally along with others, but he cannot demonstrate that one set is to be preferred over the others—except perhaps in terms of a still more ultimate set of values which in turn is simply postulated.

Rationalists express different views, of course. As the label suggests, they give far more emphasis to right reason as a source of knowledge. "The fundamental tenet of rationalism is that thought is an independent source of knowledge, and is moreover a more trustworthy source of knowledge than experience."[4] The difficulty is that, even within the same culture and still more between different cultures, the thought or right reason of different individuals leads to different results; and none of the rationalists can prove through right reason alone that his views are true and contrary views false. Anyone can endorse the alleged dictates of right reason as an act of faith, of course; but this amounts to postulating their truth.

ENDS AND MEANS: THE PRESCRIPTIVE

The distinction between fact and value is not quite as sharp and obvious as the above suggests, especially where means and ends are involved. We referred above to ultimate values, which suggests that values constitute a series, like links in a chain or rungs on a ladder. The same suggestion is conveyed by the term *goal-value,* which seems to imply the existence of one or more instrumental values leading to the goal. This raises the question whether the problem of truth or correctness is the same for each of the values in a series.

The same question can be posed in a different way. We noted above that *ought* (or *should*) statements are sometimes ambiguous. For example, "The study of politics ought to be scientific." Does this sentence express a postulated, self-justifying value — a goal-value? Or does it come closer to being a factual assertion that the study of politics ought to be (should be, must be) scientific *if* some more remote value is to be served most effectively?

Obviously, the problem concerns ends and means. Herbert Simon describes the situation as follows:

The fact that goals may be dependent for their force on other more distant ends leads to the arrangement of these goals in a hierarchy—each level to be considered as an end relative to the levels below it and as a means relative to the levels above it. . . .

A means-end chain is a series of anticipations that connect a value with the situation realizing it, and these situations, in turn, with the behaviors that produce them. Any element in this chain may be either "means" or "ends" depending on whether its connection with the value end of the chain, or its connection with the behavior end of the chain, is in question.[5]

This suggests that all (or nearly all) ends can alternatively be means, and that all means can alternatively be ends. It depends on where one chooses to break into the means-end chain. The link where one breaks in becomes, for current purposes, an "ultimate" or a "goal" value; links leading up to the ultimate one become instrumental values or means.

As intimated above, the question whether a specified means will serve a postulated end—and whether it will do it "better" than any alternative means (e.g., more reliably, more quickly, more cheaply)—is a question of fact, calling for description.

The problem can perhaps be clarified by the use of another illustration. Suppose the proposition is made that the independence of the state should be preserved. Obviously, the statement could designate either an end or a means. If it designates a means, however, there must be an assumption that the preservation of the independence of the state would serve an end, e.g., the welfare of its inhabitants. Thus, the full thought requires two statements. The first would be that the welfare of the people is the end to be postulated. The second would be that the welfare of the people will more probably be promoted by preserving the independence of the state than by abandoning it in favor of any available alternative status. Now the first of these statements is obviously normative, and the second asserts a finding of fact—a descriptive finding.

The problem of classifying ends and means suggests that the two categories, normative and descriptive, are not entirely adequate and that a third category is needed. Statements belonging in it are called prescriptive: on the basis of an assumption concerning the end(s) or value(s) to be promoted, they prescribe a method or course of action that ought to be pursued. Prescriptive statements thus reflect a combination of a normative postulate with a descriptive finding. Once identified, the two elements can be classified differently and treated accordingly.

Prescriptive statements seem to be most common when the normative postulate is thought to be so generally and thoroughly accepted that it can simply be taken for granted. But the short cut has fairly obvious hazards. Assumptions concerning the general and thorough acceptance of values may be incorrect. Even if correct, the values may be accepted only out of habit and remain acceptable only so long as they are not articulated and examined. Moreover, what is initially endorsed as a method of promoting tacitly accepted values may come to be regarded as an end in itself. Especially since prescriptive statements employ words like *should* and *ought,* they may tend to be accepted as statements of the normative. Explicit statements that are clearly normative, on the one hand, or clearly descriptive, on the other, are less likely to reflect ill-considered value judgments and less likely to reflect confusion between fact and value.

The fact that the same event or state of affairs may be either an end or a means gives the scholar some choice. If he wishes to spell out values in great detail, he will thereby be broadening the realm of ethical postulates—the realm of the normative. By the same token, he may be broadening the realm where emotion, faith, fervor, and, perhaps, fanaticism operate, for these phenomena are associated primarily with values or ends. If the scholar chooses to regard all or virtually all events or states of affairs as means, he will thereby be broadening the realm of fact—the realm of the descriptive. By the same token, he will be broadening the realm of empirical and logical inquiry, enlarging the opportunities and potentialities for the use of reason.[6] There is some basis for the view that the scholar should regard very little as self-justifying and that, conversely, he should seek a situation in which he and others judge nearly all events and circumstances as means requiring justification.[7] The positivist should especially desire this, for by making the realm of the descriptive very large and the realm of the normative very small he minimizes his major failure—his inability to demonstrate the truth of ultimate value judgments.

The positivist has another possibility open to him in seeking to minimize the weakness of his position regarding values. Unable to build a logical bridge from the *is* to the *ought,* he may attempt to build a factual bridge. That is, he may ask about the extent to which people agree on the values that they postulate. The greater the degree of agreement through time and space, the more impressive the claim becomes that the values provide a desirable if not necessary basis for social life.[8]

CHAPTER TWO

Selecting and Ordering Descriptive Data

Descriptive questions can be classified roughly as developmental and cross-sectional. Developmental questions call for a description of the historical background of a condition or event and thus for a chronological ordering of data. Cross-sectional questions call for a description of phenomena at a given time or without regard to time, e.g., for a description of the organizational arrangements under which Congress operates and of the process by which it enacts laws.

Descriptive questions can also be classified (or, more strictly, ranged along a scale) according to the level of generality of the answers sought.

These categories will now be examined.

DEVELOPMENTAL OR HISTORICAL QUESTIONS

A person who enters a theater when the play is half over is likely to have difficulty understanding the rest unless someone can give him background information, orienting him to the plot, the characters, and their roles. Some bits of background will be much more important than others in providing an adequate orientation.

There is an obvious analogy to political life. The world can be considered a theater in which political dramas are played— dramas that began in the more or less remote past and that will presumably extend into an indefinite and uncertain future. People cannot avoid entering one or more political theaters, and cannot avoid doing it long after the play has begun. The choice, if they have any, is between taking a place in the audience or striving to secure a role on the stage; and this choice calls for others relating to the degree of interest to be shown or the kind of role to seek.

The political drama differs in many ways, of course, from plays for which actors are selected and trained to act out predetermined parts, their lines being written in advance. The political drama is commonly much more confused. The distinction between the audience and the actors is not always clear, and so it is not always clear what actions and what lines are part of the play. The plot is ordinarily much more complex; or perhaps it should be said that many different plots are being acted out at once in such a way that the relationships among them, if any, are far from clear. Moreover, the various plots have not been written out; we do not know precisely either what belongs in them from the past or what is to be included in them in the future. As the play develops, some scenes from the past seem to gain and others to lose in the light which they shed on the present. Denouements remain obscure.

To carry on the metaphor, the political scientist enters the political theater as an interested member of the audience and as a student of the play. And he spends his life trying to orient himself to the play, or to parts of it. At the same time, by teaching and writing, he is trying to orient others in the audience and, perhaps, to advise and train some of the actual or potential actors. For his own satisfaction, and for the benefit of those whom he tries to assist, the questions he asks and the answers he seeks must be those that will provide orientation most adequately, guide actual and aspiring actors most wisely and effectively, and, perhaps, affect one or more of the forthcoming scenes in a desirable way.

Among the most obvious and elementary kinds of orienting questions are those that lead to a chronicle: which actors did what, and in what sequence? Chronicles simply recite events in chronological order. Their usefulness will be greater than otherwise if the events selected for inclusion are related not only in terms of time but also in other ways, e.g., causally. It will also be greater for those who have a fund of knowledge—mainly knowledge of human behavior—which helps them to see the relationship.

Generally, those seeking to gain or to give orientation are not satisfied with a simple chronicle of the manifest events of the past. The next step beyond a chronicle is probably a story, in which there is an effort to convey an understanding of present and future scenes in the political drama through a narrative account of what has gone before. The items of a chronicle of selected events provide the framework, but supplements and interpretations are made so as to provide "a smooth narrative in which every event falls as it were into its natural place and belongs to an intelligible whole."[1] The process of developing such a narrative has been called col-ligation. The individual attempting colligation is said to look "for certain dominant concepts or leading ideas by which to il-luminate his facts, to trace connections between those ideas them-selves, and then to show how the detailed facts become intelligible in the light of them by constructing a 'significant' narrative."[2]

The term *story* connotes an intuitive, impressionistic effort to get events related to each other in a coherent way—to fit them to-gether in coherent contexts. The terms *colligation* and *significant narrative* connote a more thorough and determined effort to achieve approximately the same objective; i.e., they connote the use of more careful and reliable methods. Full-fledged *historical* or *genetic explanation* is probably the end point—the opposite of a chronicle of haphazardly selected events. What this may mean will be discussed more fully below in connection with explana-tion and, in Chapter Ten, in connection with an analysis of the notion of a historical approach to politics. It should be said here, however, that it has to do with the reasons for, and the causes of, action.[3] This implies that as change occurs in knowledge of human purposes and in knowledge of the causes and consequences of action, historical narratives and historical explanation need to be changed accordingly. It also implies that history may, in a very real sense, be oriented to the present and future. That is, the questions that are asked and answered may be those that are deemed most likely to be helpful in connection with current or anticipated problems and events. The following statement may help clarify the point.

New consequences flowing from past events change the significance of the past, of what has happened. Events which before had been over-looked, because they did not seem "basic" for anything that followed, now come to be selected as highly significant; other events that used to seem "basic" recede into the limbo of mere details. . . . In this sense, we understand any history-that-has-happened in terms of the future: our principle for selecting what is basic in that history involves a refer-ence to its predicted outcome.[4]

Obviously, the above implies that political scientists may engage in the same kind of activity as many historians. That this should occur is not surprising, for the history of politics is as much a part of political science as it is of history.

Perhaps it should be noted that as we proceed up the scale from chronicles through stories and significant narratives to genetic explanation, change occurs in the criteria for selecting and ordering data. Criteria for selecting the data to be included in a chronicle are likely to be rather vague, and the data included may or may not be interrelated; the ordering device, i.e., the notion of time, is, of course, clear and explicit. In stories and significant narratives the criteria of selection are likely to be clearer. The purpose is to clarify given conditions or events by selecting and ordering background data that somehow seem relevant; data that do not contribute to an understanding of the conditions or events in question are omitted. In genetic explanation, the criteria for selecting and ordering data are even clearer and more explicit. The purpose is to identify the historical sources or origins of the events or conditions in questions and thus to construct a causal sequence. Data are included if they shed light on the reasons for, or causes of, the developments under scrutiny; and all other data are omitted.

Perhaps it should also be noted that as scholarship goes up the scale from chronicles toward genetic explanation it is likely to become increasingly significant. Chronicles may well contain some information about means and ends, cause and consequence, but it is likely to be fragmentary and inchoate. Thus the writing of chronicles is not an especially desirable kind of scholarship, under the definitions advanced above. Colligation and genetic explanation, however, are bound to contribute to knowledge of ends and means, and, in the degree to which they do, the scholarship that is involved becomes desirable or significant.

CROSS-SECTIONAL QUESTIONS

Many of the questions taken up in political science, though assuming an instant or a period of time, have little or nothing to do with the passage of time. If we ask what induces people to vote as they do or whether war can be limited, the passage of time does not ordinarily have much to do with the answer. Such questions are here called cross-sectional.

In terms of the selection and ordering of data, cross-sectional questions cover a considerable range. At the one extreme, specific and narrow questions are raised, giving little or no freedom to select data and little or no opportunity to order it. At the other extreme, very general and broad questions are raised, often requiring the use of considerable imagination and intelligence in selecting and ordering the data that enter into the answer.

Cross-sectional questions of a specific and narrow sort can be illustrated by citing such publications as the *World Almanac*, the *United States Government Organization Manual*, and the *Statesman's Yearbook*. For the most part, these publications give specific, detailed information. By looking in one or another of them it is possible to find the name of the Minister of the Interior in Bulgaria, the population of Thailand, the principal subdivisions of the Department of State, and thousands of other items of specific information. The arrangement of the data reflects a classification scheme; like or related items are placed together. But each item is there for its own sake. Each item is presented simply as information in answer to a specific question, and not as evidence in answer to a broad question. For the most part, at least, questions are avoided if they require a marshaling of evidence in support of an answer. The realm of the doubtful and controversial is eschewed. No interpretative scheme is advanced. No theses are presented. No explanations are offered. No preferences are expressed. No conclusions are reached. Explicit and direct contributions to knowledge of ends and means are minimal. There is simply a recording of isolated bits of information on various topics. Such publications are for reference purposes. Each item of information, taken by itself, is trivial, achieving significance only when it proves useful in answering a broader question which itself has significance.

Some "scholarly" works in political science are not entirely dissimilar to such publications as those cited above, being devoted to the compilation of answers to masses of specific, narrow questions. The authors make little or no attempt to select and order their data so as to answer broader questions. They simply collect and classify information. The products of their "scholarship" may appear to be quite distinct from reference works like those cited, but sometimes the difference is only one of form, e.g., the alphabet may not be used as an ordering device, and tabular styles of presentation may not be so common.[5]

Of course, in the early stages of work on a new subject, specific and narrow questions may be the only ones that can be answered. The collection and classification of data for informational purposes may be the only activity possible and may become highly important. More advanced (i.e., significant) types of scholarship are likely to be impossible until a considerable supply of raw data has become available. Thus, knowledge of what might be called the anatomy of government is prerequisite to an understanding of at least some aspects of its physiology. Nevertheless, the point already made remains true, i.e., that the answers to specific, narrow questions are in themselves trivial, acquiring significance, if at all, as they are useful in answering questions of a broader and more general sort which are themselves significant. It is not the isolated fact that counts, but the "dependence of one fact upon another." "The object of all inquiry is the discovery of significant relations within the subject matter studied."[6]

Though some scholarship in political science is guided by a conception of purpose no more significant than that which guides the editing of the *World Almanac,* most scholarship is fortunately above this level. The usual situation is one in which questions of some breadth are asked, and evidence is then marshaled to contribute to (or to provide) an answer. The crucially important feature of such questions—the feature that gives them importance— is that they somehow concern ends and means. They somehow concern the identification of political actors, or the methods that the actors employ in the political struggle. Even broad questions will be trivial unless they have this quality. If one asks about the nature of federalism, one is asking about a method of allocating functions and powers of government in the pursuit of certain ends. A similar statement applies to questions about democracy, dictatorship, monarchy, etc. The guarantee of certain civil rights is a means to ends. So are war and peace, and the very existence of the state. If one were to ask about the relative frequency with which statesmen blink their eyes, the question would be broad. Conceivably an answer might satisfy someone's curiosity and so be significant in this sense. But since, for all we know, the answer would have nothing to do with ends and means, contributing nothing to the rationality of decisions, it would otherwise be trivial.

LEVELS OF GENERALITY

Though the main discussion of "generality" and "generalization" will be found in Part II, a statement concerning levels of generality must be made in connection with the subject of this chapter—the characteristics of questions calling for description. Before we generalize, we classify. We put items possessing shared attributes into one category. A generalization is a statement that is true of two or more items in the category. When a statement is true of only a very few items in the category, it is said to be at a low level of generality; the more items to which it applies, the higher the level of generality. If an item is in a class by itself, a statement concerning it would be particular rather than general.

For example, the statement that the American colonies won independence from the British is at a low level of generality when compared with the statement that sooner or later all colonies seek independence. The statement that Jack Sprat voted for Eisenhower in 1956 is a particular. But the statement that 75 per cent of the men like him (e.g., 75 per cent of the urban male Protestant voters with incomes over $8,000) voted for Eisenhower is a generalization at a fairly high level.

What is the relationship between levels of generality and the significance of scholarly work? Implicitly, the answer has already been given. If significance is measured in terms of the contribution made to knowledge of relationships between thought and action, means and ends, cause and effect, or conditions and consequences, true statements about any one category of items are likely to increase in significance along with their level of generality. To put the same thought differently, if the significance of knowledge is measured in terms of the degree to which it helps us to understand or account for conditions and events, it is to be expected that general statements will ordinarily be more significant. The fact that the American colonies became restive may help us understand the current behavior of some other colony, but the general proposition that all colonies sooner or later seek independence is likely to help still more (assuming that the generalization is true). Similarly, knowledge of the voting habits of all men in the same class with Jack Sprat will be more significant in explaining or predicting the outcome of an election than knowledge which pertains to Jack Sprat alone.

Many significant statements at a high level of generality are simply taken for granted, being expressed rarely if ever. Suppose that it is said, for example, that Puddinhead Jones, running for election, alienated a voter by spitting in his face. The statement rests on an unspoken high-level generalization: that candidates who spit in the faces of voters are likely to alienate them. The unspoken general statement asserts a causal relationship, holding true within the country or culture under consideration if not universally. As an assertion of cause and consequence it is, by definition, more significant than the statement that a specific candidate spit in the face of a specific voter, thus alienating the voter.

Just as the articles and books that command respect in the field are ordinarily those addressed to broad rather than narrow questions, so are they ordinarily addressed to questions calling for answers at high rather than low levels of generality. If questions are asked at a low level of generality (e.g., in writing a biography, where the focus is on one man), they will have little significance in their own right. But if the answers contribute to higher levels of generalization (e.g., to an understanding of the behavior of many or all men like the subject of the biography), then greater significance is acquired.

CHAPTER THREE

Explanation

In the preceding chapters we said that questions of fact and questions of value are raised in the study of politics, and that questions of fact call for descriptive answers. We further said that questions of fact can themselves be subdivided; they can be either developmental or cross-sectional, and they can be ranked according to the generality of the answers sought.

In describing what is done in the study of politics we have also been prescribing. The prescription is that those who want to do desirable or significant teaching or research, thus contributing to the rationality of decisions, should state and answer questions. The questions should concern ends and means. The object should be to identify ends and means and to clarify conceptions of them; it should further be to identify and clarify relationships within and among ends and means. These will be relationships having to do with thought and action, purpose and method, cause and effect, conditions and consequences. We have said that answers to developmental questions are likely to be more significant the further they go up the scale from the chronicle to genetic explanation, that cross-sectional questions are likely to be more significant if they are general and broad than if they are narrow and specific, and that statements about any one category of items are likely to increase in significance along with their level of generality.

As we shall soon see, this amounts to saying that description becomes increasingly significant the more it contributes to explanation. Thus the prescription advanced is that the explanation of political conditions and events should be considered the purpose (or, at least, a major purpose) of political scientists.

This calls for an analysis of explanation. The analysis in this chapter will be incomplete, for some of the features of explanation will be more understandable if we wait to take them up in Part II. But enough can be said to provide a fairly good grasp of the elements involved.

A brief preview may be helpful. The main subdivisions that follow will deal with explanation in terms of reasons, causes, and functions served. The behavior of a person, for example, might be explained by citing reasons for the behavior. War might be explained in terms of causes. Either might be explained in terms of functions served. In addition to discussing these types of explanation, we will discuss both the approaches and the levels of discourse that may be employed in explanation. Further, we will describe measures that can be employed in judging the relative importance of factors entering into an explanation. A few other less important subtopics will also appear.

EXPLANATION IN TERMS OF REASONS

The basic point about political phenomena is that they consist of or result from the actions of human beings. An effort to explain these phenomena is thus an effort to explain certain kinds of human behavior. The problem thus differs from most of those confronted in the natural sciences. So far as is known, at least, the entities or forces or organisms that are studied in chemistry, physics, and botany do not have conscious desires or purposes which help account for their behavior. Given certain conditions, they act in a certain way. Necessary relationships exist. Events are interrelated in a fixed pattern. A nuclear explosion can be explained without reference to desires or purposes motivating the various atoms or parts of atoms. The failure of a wheat crop or the production of a bumper crop is never explained in terms of the attitudes of the seed or of the plants.

The action of human beings, however, usually relates somehow to their desires. Human beings are purposive. They are goal-oriented. And where desires or purposes exist, it is helpful to know them if the related behavior is to be explained. The rule is that the purposes of an actor (or his reasons for action) are included in the explanation of his behavior, and sometimes knowledge of them appeases curiosity and in this sense provides a quite satisfying explanation. The reasons may or may not be avowed and the actor may or may not be conscious of them.[1]

Explanation in terms of reasons is akin to, if not identical with, what Karl Popper calls explanation in terms of the "logic of the situation."[2] The assumption is that explanation can be achieved by giving attention to the dispositional premises or attitudes on the basis of which the actors make their decisions with regard to ends and means, to the cogency of their thought processes, and to their estimate of the situation, i.e., to the image of reality on the basis of which they choose. Given data of these and perhaps other types, actions taken can be explained in the sense that the knowledge revealed makes them appear intelligible or logical.

Suppose, for example, that the problem is to explain the outbreak of war between the United States and Japan in 1941. This was the work of human beings. The human beings who comprised or influenced each government had desires and purposes; and, figuratively, we can say that the governments themselves came to pursue certain purposes. Further, the individuals and governments acted on the basis of certain images of reality. We can thus explain the outbreak of the war in terms of the conflicting desires or purposes of the two governments and in terms of their effort to achieve these desires in a situation that was perceived in a certain way. Each government (each actor) had reasons for what it did, and knowledge of them helps account for what happened. In truth, unless we take into account the attitudes or purposes of people involved and their conception of the problem confronting them, we cannot explain the outbreak of war.

Not only are human beings purposive. They are also rule-following. Purposes are pursued according to certain rules, mostly of a very commonplace sort. The rule is that if one government wants to force the submission of another, it will resort to coercion (and not, for example, to witchcraft or incantations). Further, in certain kinds of situations the coercion must take the form of a military attack (and not, for example, an effort to poison the head of the other state or, still less, an effort on the part of the head of one state to defeat the head of the other state in personal combat). When the actions that are taken conform to the expected rules, the reasons that the actor avows are likely to seem quite credible and may be taken as a satisfying explanation of the behavior in question. When the actions transgress the rules, the avowed reasons are likely to be suspect and the explanation unsatisfactory. In other words, behavior is sometimes said to be explained when we see the rule according to which it was to be expected or when we see that it should not have caused surprise.[3]

The rules in question relate generally to the rationality or effectiveness of the action in light of the purpose pursued and to its appropriateness in light of social norms. If the government in Tokyo had ordered its fleet to sail around Oahu seven times, giving as its reason the expectation that this would sink the American fleet in Pearl Harbor, the reason would have appeared incredible; the action would have seemed irrational and ineffective, and thus to be explained on some basis other than by reference to Tokyo's avowed reasons. Or if the government in Tokyo had said that its reason for bombing Pearl Harbor was not to start a war but rather to emphasize a desire for an exchange of visits between the American President and the Japanese Emperor, the explanation would have violated rules of social appropriateness and would not have been believed.

Even when the reasons given for an action are quite credible, the explanation they provide is bound to be incomplete. After all, there are reasons and causes for reasons, and there are causes of causes. The search for explanation can lead one far in a number of different directions. The explanatory chain (or, more accurately, network of chains) is endless. For example, even if we find the reasons given by the leaders of the Japanese government for the attack on Pearl Harbor completely credible, there are other questions that might be asked to get a fuller explanation. Why did the leaders develop the purposes that led to Pearl Harbor? Why were men pursuing these purposes in power rather than other men pursuing other purposes? And so on.

Though an actor's avowed reasons sometimes provide a credible and satisfying explanation for what he does, it is a commonplace that this is not always the case. Very often people act—in politics and in other spheres—without being willing to avow the actuating reasons, in which case the scholar may make it his object to ferret out the unavowed reasons. Frequently people are not themselves entirely aware of the reasons that are operating. To a

considerable extent they act unthinkingly on the basis of a rule
that has not been articulated or on the basis of habit or impulse
and would find it difficult to express a reason for what they do.
Sometimes they become dimly aware of reasons for action which
they do not want to admit, even to themselves; and so they may
repress thought of these reasons, perhaps pushing it into the unconscious. Freud maintained with some cogency that influences
flowing from the unconscious are of great importance in guiding
behavior.

Illustrations of the thought that the unavowed and perhaps
unconscious reasons may differ from the avowed reasons are perhaps superfluous, but we might revert briefly to events leading up
to Pearl Harbor. The Japanese leaders who talked publicly in
terms of a Greater East Asia Co-Prosperity Sphere may also or alternatively have been inspired by the secret expectation that con-
quests would bring riches to Japan or to its ruling class or to themselves. Those who talked publicly in terms of the glory of the
Emperor may have been sick personalities goaded on by a lust for
power; or they may have been drawn unconsciously toward foreign
adventure to reinforce patriotism at home. Similarly there are no
doubt reasons why the United States acted as it did which differ
from those that Roosevelt and others avowed or even grasped.

Avowed reasons for action are normally purposive. This may
or may not be true of unavowed or unconscious reasons. Sometimes the latter seem to relate more to traits of character than to
purposes. For example, we sometimes cite lust or greed—or trust-
worthiness, honesty, fairness, and saintliness.

EXPLANATION IN TERMS OF MOTIVES, ATTITUDES, BELIEFS, OR DISPOSITIONS

What are called reasons above are sometimes given other labels.
Thus, explanation is sometimes offered in terms of motives, attitudes, beliefs, dispositions, etc.

Motives are reasons, but we speak of motives instead of reasons
in certain kinds of circumstances. Especially where behavior de-
parts from the expected, where it is somehow unconventional, we
art apt to ask about motives rather than reasons; and in everyday
usage the implication often is that we are engaged in an effort not
only to explain the behavior but also to assess it. Beyond this,
motives always relate (as reasons usually do) to behavior that is

directed toward some goal. Further, when we ask about a motive, we are always asking about what we think of as the real reason, whether or not it coincides with the actor's avowed reason.

If we ask for a man's reason for doing something we expect an answer in terms of the rule-following purposive pattern which is relevant to this sort of action. But when we ask for his motive we just want to know the goal towards which his behavior is directed. The implication usually is that his behavior is directed towards an end but that the means do not conform to any stereotyped, habitual pattern, or to any conventional canons of appropriateness. What he does is to be explained entirely by reference to the end which it seems to be directed towards.[4]

It seems unnecessary to attempt a precise definition of attitude, belief, predisposition, or dispositional tendency. Common-sense conceptions of their meanings will do for present purposes. The principal point is that they all have to do with reasons, just as motive does. Explanation in terms of attitudes or beliefs is thus approximately the same as explanation in terms of reasons.

EXPLANATION IN TERMS OF CAUSES

Knowledge of the reasons for action may or may not provide a satisfying explanation. When it does not, or when the purpose is to explain a condition or a state of affairs rather than an action, there is likely to be an effort to identify the cause or causes that are relevant.

The distinction between a reason and a cause is rather nebulous. It seems to turn largely on the presence or absence of elements that are personal to the actor and that, at least potentially, are under his conscious control. (Though this statement, taken literally, applies only to individual persons, it can be applied figuratively to a group considered as an actor.) More particularly, reference to reasons for action usually connotes the notion of an actor who is purposive and rule-following, whereas reference to causes of action (or causes of reasons or attitudes) connotes the notion of conditions or events and their consequences. Whereas reasons are usually personal, causes are usually social or environmental.[5] In relation to cause, the idea is that the presence of a certain condition or the occurrence of a certain event may or will bring about, or help to bring about, a certain consequence. Further, the consequence occurs predictably according to a regular pattern, not being subject to capricious desire or purpose. Sometimes it is said to occur mechanically or automatically, given the causal conditions. These words may be useful, but they may also be misleading in that they suggest that the consequence is always necessary or certain. Actually, consequences follow from causes with varying degrees of probability rather than with certainty.

The above distinction obviously involves difficulties. For example, how is a neurotic compulsion to be treated? Is it to be classified as a desire associated with a reason for action, or as a condition associated with the idea of cause? Since the neurotic compulsion is suffered, and since something beyond control is happening to the person who suffers it, it probably should be classified as a cause rather than as a reason for action, but the basis for decision in such matters is not always clear-cut.

Consider again the explanation of the outbreak of war between the United States and Japan in 1941. An explanation of American behavior in terms of reasons may well be satisfying, for the behavior reflects purposes and rules to which we are accustomed; in truth, the reasons may seem cogent and compelling enough to make the action appear to be entirely natural and unavoidable. An explanation of Japanese behavior in terms of reasons is not so likely to be satisfying. If we are unfamiliar with Japanese culture, and thus with the purposes and rules of the Japanese, the reasons influencing them are likely to seem alien and puzzling, perhaps incredible. For this and other reasons, we may attempt a more thorough explanation of their behavior and so look for causes, i.e., for the conditions that brought about the consequences in question. Perhaps we will attach significance to Emperor worship, thinking of it as a neurotic and irrational religious obsession. Perhaps we will attach significance to the political system under which a small elite could rule and under which the military elements in the elite had a special position of power. Perhaps we will attach significance to economic circumstance, explaining attitudes and reasons for action in terms of the class struggle and class interests. Perhaps we will inquire into the accuracy and comprehensiveness of the information available to the decision makers in Tokyo, and this might lead us to conclude that bad intelligence work was one of the necessary conditions or causes of the decision to launch the war.

Again we should remember that each cause has one or more

causes. If Emperor worship was a cause, what political, economic, sociological, or psychological—or biochemical—conditions explain the development or persistence of such worship? If the political system was such as to increase the probability that militaristic influences would come to dominate, how did it happen that such a system developed and survived? And so on, *ad infinitum*, for each of the causes identified.

EXPLANATION IN TERMS OF END STATES

In psychology human behavior is sometimes explained not so much in terms of reasons or causes as in terms of needs or end states. This type of explanation calls attention to purposes or goals, but they are purposes or goals of a different sort from those associated with reasons for action. Thus they are called end states rather than ends. The end states in question are designated by such terms as satisfaction, need reduction, tension reduction, and homeostasis. Explanation in these terms is sometimes helpful. People act as they do not simply or always to achieve the more specific types of purposes connoted by reasons; a general state of satisfaction may be the goal. Usually, however, such end states as satisfaction, need reduction, tension reduction, and homeostasis are more the by-products of activity than the immediate purpose or goal. And when they are by-products it is questionable whether they should be considered as either reasons or causes.

The above discussion of explanation gives attention first to reasons, then to causes, and then to end states. The order has no special significance. More specifically, there is no intention to recommend that explanation should be sought first in terms of reasons, then in terms of causes, and then in terms of end states. Nor is there an intention to convey the impression that one kind of element in explanation is necessarily more important than another. Both the problem of assigning relative importance to explanatory factors and the criteria employed in selecting explanatory factors will be discussed below.

EXPLANATION IN TERMS OF THE FUNCTION SERVED

Functional explanation or functional analysis is somewhat similar both to explanation in terms of end states and to explanation in terms of causes.

The meaning of the term *function* can best be understood by reference to its use in other disciplines. When biologists speak of the function of an organ, the reference is to the role the organ plays in some system of which it is a part.[6] To sociologists, the function of an activity is "the part it plays in the social life as a whole and therefore the contribution it makes to the maintenance of structural continuity." Anthropologists speak of explaining activities "by their function, by the part which they play within the integral system of culture, by the manner in which they are related to each other within the system."[7]

This suggests that, within a political system, any institution, practice, activity, or pattern of behavior can be said to be functional if it helps to preserve the system. And if it has a tendency to undermine or destroy the system it can be said to be dysfunctional.[8] The finding that an activity is functional does not necessarily mean that it is morally good, nor are dysfunctional activities necessarily bad. Such value judgments might go one way or the other, depending on the value attached to the system that is being served or undermined.

Functional explanation may be attempted in relation to any operating system, whether or not organic. For some purposes, perhaps the reference could be to a world or international political system. For other purposes it might be to a national political system, or to subdivisions thereof. Each unit and agency of government is, in a sense, a system of action; so are armed forces, political parties, and pressure and propaganda groups. An individual person is a system of action. Applied to any such system, a desire to engage in functional explanation calls for an identification of internal activities and conditions that actually or potentially affect its operations. These activities and conditions must then be described and appraised in terms of their effects on the system. Thus, judgment must be exercised in relation to the question of the extent to which a given activity or condition has system-sustaining effects. The procedure may, of course, be reversed. That is, given a system on which to focus, the initial effort might be to identify imaginatively the activities that ought to be carried on or the conditions that ought to exist if the system is to operate in a desired way. Then existing activities and conditions can be examined and judged in terms of the standards thus fixed; and perhaps new activities can be inaugurated.

Functions are either manifest or latent. Manifest functions consist of those objective consequences for a system "which contribute to its adjustment or adaptation and were so intended," and latent functions consist of "unintended and unrecognized consequences of the same order."[9] The distinction is significant mainly in that it calls attention to the fact that latent functions exist. It thus suggests a search for them—a search that might not otherwise occur. And the search may be very important. Karl Popper, for example, takes the view that "the main task of the social sciences [is] to analyze the unintended social repercussions of intentional human actions. . . . An action which proceeds precisely according to intention does not create a problem for social science. . . . "[10] The possible significance of latent functions can easily be illustrated. Take, for example, the not uncommon desire of underdeveloped countries to develop a steel industry, whether or not the necessary raw materials are at hand. If consideration of the desire is confined to the manifest function of a steel mill, i.e., the production of steel, the conclusion may quickly be reached that the development of the industry is unjustified. But there are potential latent functions, among them the stimulation and development of national consciousness and national pride. Such latent functions may or may not justify the project, but they obviously deserve to be looked for and considered. Similarly, the manifest functions of war may be supplemented by various latent functions; e.g., war may serve to curtail the growth of population, to stimulate or retard scientific or technological development, etc. Political parties have latent functions such as the recruitment and training of future governmental leaders. If a member of the United Nations has taken a position that threatens to bring on unwanted war, and if it cannot back down without loss of face, the United Nations itself may serve the latent function of making the retreat appear to be a virtuous and noble act, reflecting deference to the principles of the Charter. A congressional investigation may serve the latent function of providing a national reputation for individuals conducting it. When intended and recognized, such functions become manifest, of course.

Activities or conditions thought to be associated with a system may, of course, be found to be nonfunctional, i.e., to be without bearing on the operation of the system. Or they may be found to be either functional or dysfunctional, manifestly or latently.

Perhaps the activity or condition examined in relation to one operating system may also figure in another. Behavior that is dysfunctional for a combat soldier in that it leads to his death may be quite functional for the country for which he fights. Activity that is functional from the point of view of a political party may be dysfunctional for the government. Thus findings with regard to the effects of activities or conditions in one system of action should presumably be supplemented by analogous findings in other relevant systems before any general conclusion is reached. Where an activity is functional for one system and dysfunctional for another, a more or less serious dilemma obviously arises.

Once reliable findings have been reached concerning the nonfunctional, dysfunctional, or functional consequences of a given activity or condition in various systems, the obvious next question concerns the action, or alternative sets of actions, that might be taken. The question can be resolved, of course, only on the basis of a value judgment concerning each of the systems—a judgment on the question whether it is desirable to maintain or to subvert the system in question. For conditions or activities that are found to have nothing but functional effects in all "good" systems to which they are relevant, the problem is to find ways by which they can be maintained or by which they can be altered to increase their desirable effects. For conditions or activities that are found to be dysfunctional in all "good" systems, the problem is to find ways of terminating them. In relation to "bad" systems, these statements can be reversed. Nonfunctional activities may be either terminated or ignored. Where the same condition or activity has contradictory effects in different systems, action would have to be predicated on a judgment of the relative importance or value of the systems in question.

It should be apparent that functional explanation is essentially causal; if it is concerned with the effects of a given activity or practice on a system, its purpose must be the establishment of cause and effect relationships. The difference between causal and functional explanation is "quite comparable to the difference between saying that B is the effect of A, and saying that A is the condition (or cause) of B."[11]

Explanation is sometimes called teleological, meaning that it rests on reference to purposes. Causal explanation, as defined above, is nonteleological. We have not used the term teleology because of its ambiguity, but should at least take note of it. Sometimes purposes are identified with desires and intentions, in which case teleological explanations are approximately the same as explanations in terms of reasons or motives. Sometimes they are identified with functions, in which case teleological explanations consist of functional analysis. In each case the difference between the kind of explanation that is called teleological and the kind described above, if any, is one of emphasis and perspective.[12] Sometimes, however, teleological explanation takes the form of an argument or assertion that all change or growth is to be explained in terms of purposes fixed by nature, by morality, or by God. A predetermined destiny thus controls and, in a sense, causes the events of the present. Agreement on the shape of the predestined future and proof that it controls the present are difficult to obtain.[13]

The stress above is on the view that if scholarship is to be desirable or significant it must explain conditions and events, and that in explaining scholars must make choices. They choose the question to ask, and where the answer is a general one, they must further decide how to divide it into questions that are more specific. This means that they must choose the data to consider in seeking an answer, for the subdivisions of the general question specify the data to be employed. So many different elements enter potentially into explanations that no one person is likely to be able to identify or even to understand them all. The sociologist and the psychoanalyst who look for the reasons that explain voting behavior are sure to come up with very different sets of reasons. Similarly, the historian and the economist (or, for that matter, two different historians, or two different economists, or even two different political scientists) who look for the causes of war are sure to ask different subordinate questions and come up with different lists of causes.[14]

The differences that crop up in the types of questions asked and the types of data considered in developing the answer reflect choices among approaches, on the one hand, and among levels of discourse, on the other.

The meaning of *approach* and the types of approaches employed in the study of politics will be examined in Part III. In brief, the word approach is made to denote the criteria by which questions and relevant data are selected.

Approaches are sometimes identified in terms of academic disciplines. Thus students of politics employ historical, economic, sociological, psychological, geographic, and philosophic approaches. The assumption is that certain kinds of explanatory data go with each discipline.

Alternatively, approaches are sometimes identified with a focus on what is regarded as a central or salient feature of politics. The prominence of governmental and related institutions suggests an institutional approach. The importance of law suggests a legal approach. Some adopt a power approach or an interest-group approach. In recent years considerable attention has been given to approaches focusing on the process of making decisions or on the decisions themselves, i.e., on the ends and means chosen.

At least two approaches seem to belong in classes by themselves. Thus there is the so-called behavioral approach, distinguished by its stress on a scientific purpose, i.e., by its stress on developing knowledge that is verifiable, systematic, and general. And there is an analogical approach, called general systems theory, characterized by an effort to develop knowledge of systems of various types (including political systems) by comparing them with each other.

Finally, approaches are often identified with explanatory hypotheses or causal theories. And these hypotheses or theories fall into three main groups depending on the relative emphasis that they put on environmental influences (geographic or economic), psychological data and considerations, or ideologies.

We will not try to anticipate what is said about these various approaches in Part III. Obviously, however, the asking and the answering of questions about politics is bound to be affected significantly by the approach, or the combination of approaches, that one adopts. Different people taking up the same general question (e.g., "Why do wars occur?") are likely to treat the question very differently, emphasizing very different types of data. And the reasons for or causes of most political phenomena are so complex that different treatments of the same question may be equally sound.

LEVELS OF DISCOURSE EMPLOYED IN EXPLANATION

In addition to choosing an approach in developing explanations, the student must choose a level of discourse. This term is perhaps unduly pretentious. It denotes the degree of care and thoroughness with which a subject is discussed. The levels employed are variously described as ranging from the superficial to the fundamental; or from a focus on immediate, precipitating factors to a focus on underlying conditions that permit those factors to be precipitating; or from the microscopic (molecular) to the macroscopic (molar); or from "explanation in principle" to "explanation in detail"; or from an "explanation sketch" to the remote ideal of complete and thorough explanation.[15]

At the level of the superficial, one might explain the election of a president by saying that he secured a majority of the votes in the electoral college. At the level of precipitating factors, one might explain the American declaration of war in 1941 by citing Pearl Harbor. At the microscopic (molecular) level one might look only at what are, relatively, the minutiae, ignoring major factors that are operating; e.g., something called "international relations" might be discussed in terms of current "hot spots" over the world. An "explanation in principle" might, for example, rest on presumed knowledge of the typical dispositional premises of various categories of people, knowledge being lacking of the dispositional premises of the specific persons whose behavior is being explained; thus we might explain the distribution of the presidential vote in a given county, even though we have no direct knowledge of the thoughts of the individual voters, by citing the fact that 75 per cent of them are farmers. An "explanation sketch" is a tentative suggestion of the various factors that are thought to comprise an explanation, advanced in the absence of some necessary knowledge but in the thought that the suggestion would be sustained if only the missing knowledge could be obtained.

The level of discourse that is appropriate will naturally vary in different circumstances. One would scarcely explain the outcome of a given election in precisely the same way to a ten-year-old boy and to political scientists who specialize in the study of voting behavior. The level of discourse employed in discussing a political issue at a dinner party where the guests have varied interests and knowledge is likely to differ from the level established at a meeting of a small group of experts. The level employed in mass news media is likely to differ from that employed in more specialized news media, and a still different level is likely to be employed in serious scholarly journals and monographs. No one level is necessarily right and all others wrong; the selection of the level can properly depend on the purposes at hand and the circumstances confronted.

Going from one level of discourse to another (e.g., from the superficial toward the fundamental, or from the precipitating toward the underlying factors) frequently means going back through a sequence of reasons or causes. The point at which to stop in identifying the links in the chain is rarely, if ever, foreordained. Rather, it is selected, whether arbitrarily or on some more or less rational basis; perhaps the needs or purposes that the person is seeking to serve, or his skills or interests, will determine the level that is desirable.

THE RELATIVE IMPORTANCE OF EXPLANATORY FACTORS

We have noted that explanation reflects a series of choices concerning relative emphasis on reasons and causes, concerning approaches, and concerning levels of discourse. Obviously, then, explanation is highly selective and therefore incomplete. Obviously, too, a number of different factors influence the choices that are made, e.g, the circumstances confronted, the curiosity of the scholar, his training and skills. Assuming all this, the question may yet be raised whether there are any measures of the relative importance of explanatory factors on which agreement might be obtained. What basis may there be for saying that one factor is more important than another in explaining the condition or event in question?

Statements of this sort are common, of course. That is, those who teach and write about politics very commonly assert that a reason or a cause they have selected has special importance. It may be described as chief, principal, basic, root, strategic, primary, fundamental, crucial, key, sole, true, real, etc.

Ernest Nagel has identified five possible meanings of such statements, and thus five bases for claiming greater importance for one factor than for another. His discussion focuses on the statement that A is more important than B as a determinant of C.[16]

— If B is relatively constant while A varies, and if variations in A are followed by variations in C, A is sometimes said to be more important. For example, Japanese aggressiveness might be said to be a more important cause of war than the determination of the United States to defend its territory.

— If both A and B vary, but if the variation in A has a greater proportionate effect than the variation in B, A is sometimes said to be more important. Thus, increases in the amount of money that a political party spends for TV during a campaign may be said to be more important in influencing the outcome of the election than a proportionate increase in the amount spent on printing and distributing pamphlets.

— If additional elements combine more frequently with A than with B to cause C, A is sometimes said to be more important. For example, money in the campaign chest may combine more often with a popular candidate than with a good platform to capture the presidency. In connection with this meaning and this test of relative importance, as in connection with the next one, it is obviously assumed that "the joint presence of A and B is not necessary for the occurrence of C."

— If A occurs and causes C more frequently than B does, it is sometimes said to be more important. For example, pressure from the President may be more important in getting Congress to enact bills than pressure from college professors.

— Finally, if A contributes to a generalization which, though explaining C only when coupled with B, explains other phenomena quite independently of B, it is sometimes said to be more important. To illustrate this meaning, Nagel cites the claim made by some "that the social relations that govern the production and distribution of wealth constitute a more basic determinant of the legal institutions of a society than do the religious and moral ideals professed in that society."

When such meanings as these are intended, it is quite possible that reliable data will be available to support the claim advanced, in which case a finding concerning the relative importance of different explanatory factors may have great significance. But often supporting data are inadequate; and when the comparison is not only between A and B but also between A and a whole series of additional factors, the reliability of assertions about relative importance becomes increasingly doubtful. It is rarely possible to place reasons or causes in a hierarchy on the basis of their relative importance, and to do it reliably. It is even more rare that a reason or cause can properly be designated as the sole one. No doubt those who describe causes as "true" or "real" are frequently using the words simply to indicate a judgment about relative importance. If the meaning is that other causes are false or unreal or nonexistent, the assertion is likely to be highly questionable.

REASONS, CAUSES, VARIABLES, NECESSARY AND SUFFICIENT CONDITIONS, GENERAL LAWS, AND THEORIES

We have discussed explanation in terms of reasons, motives, causes, end states, and functions and in terms of approaches and levels of discourse.

We might have spoken, instead, of explanation in terms of variables and constants, for often these are the terms that are employed. Naturally, factors that change somehow in different times or circumstances are called variables, whereas those that do not change (or that are treated as if they do not) are called constants. When a change in one variable is associated somehow with a change in another, the two are said to be related, and related variables may be classified as independent or dependent. A variable is said to be independent when a change in it precedes and presumably causes the change in a related variable; and, obviously, a variable is said to be dependent when a change in it is contingent on change in another.

Philosophers of science, who usually write with the natural sciences in mind, rarely speak of reasons, and they may or may not speak of variables or of causes. More commonly they speak of conditions. Thus it is said that "the search for explanation is directed to the ideal of ascertaining the necessary and sufficient conditions for the occurrence of phenomena."[17] The term *condi-*

tion can, of course, be defined broadly; the presence of a condition can be made to mean the presence of a reason, a motive, an attitude, a variable, a cause, etc.[18] As the quotation indicates, conditions are ordinarily classified as necessary and/or sufficient.

This terminology might have been employed above. All of the types of explanation described might have been treated as explanation in terms of necessary and sufficient conditions. The attack on Pearl Harbor was a condition of the American declaration of war; so was the purpose and rule of the United States to defend itself when attacked, and so were many other factors.

Conditions are said to be necessary when their presence is essential to the occurrence of the phenomenon in question—when their absence would preclude its occurrence. They are said to be sufficient when their presence is enough to assure its occurrence. Conditions classified as necessary to a phenomenon may exist without actually bringing it about, which means that necessary conditions may not be sufficient. And conditions classified as sufficient may have alternatives, i.e., there may be disjunctive sets of sufficient conditions any one of which is enough to bring about the phenomenon in question; and this means that the sufficient conditions that operate may not be necessary.[19]

We have seen that the search for explanation commonly involves choice—choice among types of explanation and among approaches and levels of discourse—and that explanation is therefore commonly incomplete. Since the search for explanation is also the search for necessary and sufficient conditions, the statement concerning choice and its consequences applies again. Moreover, the classification of conditions as necessary or sufficient, or both, requires further judgment and choice. What were the necessary conditions of the election of Eisenhower to the presidency in 1952? Where is the boundary line between conditions that were helpful and those that were necessary? Obviously, it was necessary that he meet the constitutional requirements for eligibility; tradition prescribes, too, that a candidate shall be male. His campaign had to be financed, but who can say how much money was necessary? Many other conditions may well have been helpful— his war record, his smile, his platform, his Protestant background, his apparent health and energy, the long tenure of Democrats in the White House, and, perhaps, mistakes by the Democratic Party or its candidate — but were any of these conditions necessary?

Would the absence of any one of them have precluded Eisenhower's election? Perhaps the voters were influenced more by a combination of helpful conditions than by the few that can surely be classified as necessary.

Similar problems arise in relation to the problem of identifying sufficient conditions. Where a multitude of factors were operating, as they were in 1952 and as is usually the case with complex political events, which ones were sufficient? Different people would surely render different judgments.

In connection with efforts to identify the necessary and sufficient conditions of natural phenomena, it is often possible to run experiments and to include or exclude or alter variables in each instance until the variables that are necessary and/or sufficient have been identified. That kind of check is obviously impossible in connection with efforts to identify the conditions of election to the presidency and to classify those conditions as necessary and/or sufficient; it is also impossible in connection with a high proportion of the developments that political scientists study.

Perhaps because of the difficulties and uncertainties involved, political scientists rarely attempt to classify conditions or causes as necessary and/or sufficient. They are more inclined to speak of influencing conditions or factors, and perhaps to rate them according to presumed degrees of influence, e.g., "very" influential. They are also inclined, as indicated earlier, to describe causes as important, major, "real," etc., and we have noted some of the meanings and some of the vaguenesses that such words reflect. Precise and reliable explanation, as well as complete explanation, is difficult to achieve.

Along with their references to "conditions," philosophers of science who discuss explanation are also likely to refer to laws (or, less frequently, to rules) and to theories. These terms will be examined more thoroughly in Chapters Eight and Nine, but a brief comment on them may be helpful here.

The role and importance of rules, laws, and theories in explanation can be illustrated by reference to the question why the United States declared war against Japan after the bombardment of Pearl Harbor. The connection between the two events may seem obvious. *Naturally* the United States declared war when it was attacked. But what makes this reaction seem so natural? The answer might take either or both of two forms. On the one hand, the reference might be to a rule that American statesmen, or statesmen in general, are known to follow; or it might be to a broader rule that peoples of the world generally follow. And the rule is, of course, that those who are attacked fight back, especially when they think that they have some chance of doing so successfully. On the other hand, the reference might be to a descriptive law, i.e., to a finding that states regularly fight back when attacked. In truth, on all, or virtually all, occasions when states have been attacked in circumstances like those surrounding the bombardment of Pearl Harbor, they have reacted by going to war. It thus becomes possible to combine knowledge of what states regularly do when attacked with the fact of an attack and get a satisfying explanation of the reaction. The truth is that most or all explanations rest on knowledge of the rules that guide behavior or the laws that reflect it, though these rules and laws are frequently so obvious and trivial that it is absurd to cite them. Thus it is a rule and a law of American politics that the county, state, and national chairmen of a political party shall be, say, more than twenty years old.

Explanation by reference to a rule or a law is ordinarily incomplete. Among other things, it is incomplete in the sense that we are likely to want to know why the rule is observed or why the law holds. For this purpose we seek a theory. Having explained the event by reference to a rule or a law, we seek to explain the rule or law by reference to a theory.

Though these statements concerning the role of rules, laws, and theories in explanation are obviously inadequate, we will not elaborate on them at this point. A fuller discussion of the topic will be found in Part II.

We might note that the difference between the conditions that explain an event and the conditions that produce it is simply a difference in time and the perspective of the observer. After the event has occurred they are the reasons and causes that explain the occurrence. Before it has occurred, these same reasons and causes indicate the means or methods of bringing it about. If one side of the coin gives knowledge of causes, the other side gives knowledge of means. It is this consideration that leads to the following prescription: "The social sciences must be pure and applied at the same time. They must formulate their problems not only in terms of cause and effect but also in terms of means and ends."[20]

CHAPTER FOUR

Prediction

Why explain? Why should it be a major objective of scholars to identify relationships that are explanatory? One reason, usually considered self-justifying, is to satisfy curiosity. Another reason, and probably the more common one, is to provide a basis for prediction. And prediction in turn is prized as a basis for making choices.

THE PREVALENCE AND IMPORTANCE OF PREDICTING

In discussing explanation—and in other connections, too—we have mentioned choices. Scholarship reflects choices. We have argued that the choices should be such as to make the scholarship of a desirable sort, i.e., significant, or contributory (at least potentially) to rationality in decision making. Assuming agreement on this, suppose that the scholar faces a choice. He has two alternative lines of action before him. How does he go about deciding between them? Obviously, he makes one or more predictions. He may predict that one alternative is surer to lead to significant results than the other, or that one will lead to more significant results than the other. Having made his prediction(s), he makes his choice. The choice turns on the prediction(s), considered in terms of the goal being pursued.

These statements can be made more general. Whenever anyone makes a rational choice, he is predicting. Those who chose rationally to vote for Eisenhower rather than for Stevenson in 1956 were presumably predicting that in some sense Eisenhower would make a more desirable President. A Congressman who votes for a bill and a President who signs the bill are making predictions about the outcome. Likewise, when a judicial decision is rendered or when a treaty is concluded or when a state arms or when a municipality adopts or drops the council-manager system or when money is appropriated for one purpose rather than for another, there is a prediction that, among the courses of action considered and open, the one chosen is more likely than any of the others to produce the desired result or results. In other words, the rational choices that people make among alternative courses of action in all spheres of life reflect their expectations or predictions concerning the consequences.

THE BASES FOR PREDICTING

Now the question is, on what bases are predictions made? The answer is that they have approximately the same bases as explanations. Predictions, like explanations, are based on knowledge of relationships—relationships between thought and action, means and ends, causes and effects, conditions and consequences. (The qualification should perhaps be noted that predictions may be based simply on knowledge of correlations, whereas by definition explanation calls for knowledge of the why of the correlation.) We know that certain kinds of actions go with certain kinds of thought—i.e., reasons, motives, attitudes. Similarly, within limits that we seek to expand we know what kinds of ends go with given means, what effects follow from given causes, and what consequences ensue from specified conditions.

If knowledge of these relationships can provide explanation of past events, why can it not serve as a basis for predicting future events? If on the basis of hindsight we can say with assurance what the reasons and rules were that led to an action, then it is reasonable to infer that had we known the reasons and rules prior to the action we could have predicted it; and likewise if we can say what the causes of an event were, it is reasonable to infer that had we identified the causes prior to the event we could have predicted it. If we explain an existing state of affairs by identifying certain antecedent conditions together with the applicable general law(s), then it is reasonable to think that awareness of the conditions and law(s) prior to the development of the state of affairs would have permitted us to predict it. Obviously, if we are fortunate enough to know the sufficient conditions of an event, we can use the knowledge either to explain or to predict, depending on whether or not the event has already occurred. If on December 8, 1941, the declaration of war against Japan was explained by the attack on Pearl Harbor, then on December 6, 1941, one could have safely predicted that such an attack would bring about the declaration.

In other words, prediction is often based upon approximately the same elements as explanation. The combination of factors that permits explanation also permits prediction. This means that the capacities and limitations of political scientists for explanation apply also to prediction.

Both the capacities and the limitations are considerable, as has already been suggested in connection with the discussion of explanation. Rarely is an event completely unintelligible; almost always an explanation of sorts can be advanced. The counterpart of this is that events are rarely unpredictable; almost always there is some basis for making at least a vague estimate of the probability that an event or state of affairs will occur or can be brought about. Some events can be explained, and therefore some predictions can be made, with a considerable degree of assurance.

At the same time, however, we should recall that explanation is almost always more or less incomplete and more or less uncertain and imprecise. The same limitations therefore apply to prediction. We are perhaps more conscious of them in the latter connection than in the former. Knowledge that a certain action has occurred may make us bold in thinking that we can identify reasons that operated, and knowledge of an event is apt to lend credence to the claim that we know its causes. But in advance of the action, we are less likely to be sure of the reasons that will be controlling, and in advance of the effect we are more likely to be conscious of the frailty of the conception of cause. Further discussion of the problem will be found in Part II.

We might sum up by citing a statement by Herbert Simon.

Knowledge is the means of discovering which of all the possible consequences of a behavior will actually follow from it. The ultimate aim of knowledge, in so far as it is part of the process of choice, is to discover a single unique possibility which is consequent on each behavior alternative, although in practice this aim is of course only imperfectly attained.[1]

PROMOTING RATIONAL DECISION MAKING AS THE
PURPOSE IN PREDICTING

Scholars sometimes hold that gaining and imparting knowledge of relationships is their ultimate end, and that the use made of the knowledge is not their concern, at least in their capacity as scholars. This is a defensible point of view. Just as some people climb mountains for the fun of it or because the mountains are there, so may other people answer questions and solve problems for the fun of it or because the questions and problems are there. But it is doubtful whether society would support scholarship much more extensively than it supports mountaineering if the only purpose were to give personal satisfaction to the intellectually inquisitive and vicarious thrills to others. Obviously, other purposes operate—social purposes. Many statements concerning these other purposes have been made.

The "training of citizens" is sometimes advanced as "one of the major goals" in studying and teaching about politics;[2] and, especially at the graduate level, training of a professional sort is an obvious purpose. Both of these conceptions of purpose have elicited rejoinders or reservations. The view has been expressed that "complete absorption in the goal of 'citizenship education,' as that term is generally interpreted, would . . . be fatal for political science . . . "[3] and that

the job of the political science teacher is not to produce a good citizen but to produce an intelligent man. It is not to give a student values but to develop his talent for valuation. If education contributes to citizenship, then it does so indirectly, and not as the central goal of its effort.[4]

Professional training is generally considered a proper purpose when it "is primarily concerned with the development of the intellect, the comprehension of general principles, the inculcation of methods of thought, the proper approach to problems, and a systematic view of the subject."[5] But training of a technical sort designed to equip a person for the public service is sometimes condemned. "A university ceases to be a university when it trains for the public service."[6]

Many make statements that coincide with those quoted above, rejecting "the training of citizens" as the goal. As Robson puts it, "the purpose of political science is to throw light on political ideas and political action in order that the government of man may be improved."[7] According to Gunnar Myrdal, the purpose is "to make policy more rational by ascertaining relevant facts and bringing them into their true perspective and by clarifying the causal relations between means and aims."[8] Quincy Wright suggests that "political science should seek to devise formulae to predict those aspects of group behavior centering about tension, struggle, and conflict" and that it should do whatever it can "to increase the probability that the political struggles going on in the world will utilize only methods consistent with human dignity and human progress."[9] Louis Hartz suggests that "inquiry into the Aristotelian good life . . . can never become outdated."[10] Harold Lasswell has abandoned an earlier reluctance to express preferences among values.[11] Along with Kaplan he regards political science as one of the policy sciences whose function "is to provide intelligence pertinent to the integration of values realized by and embodied in interpersonal relations." They describe political science as the policy science "which studies influence and power as instruments of such integration."[12] On various occasions in recent years Lasswell has stressed the view that political scientists should pursue such purposes as, on the one hand, the identification and clarification of goal values and, on the other hand, the appraisal of alternative courses of action that relate to the achievement of these goal values.

I postulate that the goals of fundamental policy in this country (ideally conceived) can be expressed in terms of human dignity. Under the crisis conditions now prevailing and in prospect, it is of the utmost importance for political scientists to take timely and continuous action in their behalf. Our problem is to combine national security with individual freedom, in order to bring about the largest net result in terms of human values.[13]

These statements are in accord with the assertion of Alfred Cobban that, if there is a right way of considering political problems, "it might possibly be the way of all the greater political thinkers of the past. . . . "

They all wrote with a practical purpose in mind. Their object was to influence actual political behavior. They wrote to condemn or support existing institutions, to justify a political system or persuade their fellow citizens to change it: because, in the last resort, they were concerned with the aims, the purposes of political society.[14]

The above comments suggest that the main social purpose of political scientists is and should be to influence choices, to contribute to the rationality of decisions. When we ask or answer questions, whether in teaching or in writing, we are contributing to the potential rationality of policy decisions. The decisions in question may range from those of the individual citizen who decides to pay no attention to politics to those of prime ministers and heads of state. They may relate to either purposes or methods, ends or means. Efforts to contribute to the rationality of decisions may be either direct or indirect. The possibilities have actually been presented earlier, but repetition in a different framework may contribute to clarity and understanding.

Direct efforts may be made in either of two overlapping ways. In the first place, there can be an effort to reveal and invite attention to the possible range of choice, i.e., the list of alternatives, open to the decision maker in the realms of ends (values) and means.[15] Decision makers themselves do not always attempt to identify the possible alternatives, and when they do attempt it their success is sometimes incomplete. Many decisions are made unthinkingly, or on the basis of very careless and inadequate thought, or on the basis of incomplete information. Decisions may be made impetuously or intuitively or out of habit or in conformity with tradition or to please God or the gods. Very commonly decision makers do not clearly articulate the values that their actions reflect, and they may not really be aware of some of them. Nor are they always clear on the question of the extent to which their own values are coherent and mutually reinforcing and the extent to which they are contradictory. Ignorance about the values of others whose activities may have a bearing on the wisdom of decisions is likely to be all the greater. What people endorse which values, and with what intensity or order of priority? Why do they think as they do, and under what conditions might their views change? To what extent and for which persons or groups is a given practice or condition a value, perhaps to be sought or maintained as a matter of nonrational, emotional faith, and to what extent and for whom is it a method or instrument concerning which there can be rational discussion and appraisal? For some people, for example, the idea of the sovereign independence of the state inspires fanatical devotion, and suggestions that it be qualified or abandoned are treated as treasonable or sacrilegious; for others, sovereignty is designed to serve practical purposes, e.g., the welfare of some or all people directly involved, and should be dropped when and if it ceases to serve those purposes as satisfactorily as they could be served under an alternative arrangement. Democracy, too, may be either a fetish or an instrument judged to be good or bad depending on the extent to which it serves given purposes. Fervent dedication to both democracy and sovereignty may lead to a dilemma in cases where the two are incompatible. Just as decisions are sometimes made without full consideration being given to questions about values, so are they sometimes made without awareness or full consideration of possible methods. And just as the political scientist may contribute directly to the rationality of decisions by examining and calling attention to value problems, so may he do it by identifying and appraising alternative methods or courses of action that might be adopted.

The above discussion of direct methods of promoting rationality assumes that the political scientist will himself take up approximately the same problem that actually or potentially confronts a decision maker and that he will then make statements pertaining to the problem, probably in writing, in the hope that they will influence action.

The concern above is with the *descriptive* statements that political scientists make and the purposes that they serve. Normative postulates, of course, may also be advanced.

Indirect methods of influencing decisions in the direction of rationality are also employed. Most textbooks and teaching should probably be classified as involving indirect efforts. For the most part, they are not aimed at specific problems which a decision maker does or will confront, and, for the most part, they are not aimed at individuals in their capacity as responsible decision makers. Rather, they are designed to promote the various aims cited in the statements quoted above: to provide a fund of information, to provide knowledge of principles and descriptive laws, to provide explanation and some sensitivity to the requirements that must be met if explanation is to be at all satisfactory, to stimulate inquiry into ends and means and into relationships within and among them, to stimulate inquisitiveness, and to inculcate some appreciation of the standards of serious scholarship, etc. Indirect methods are thus general rather than specific, aiming generally at decision makers and generally to provide types of knowledge, skills, and attitudes that will make for rationality in decision making.[16]

Earlier in this chapter we noted that political behavior, like all human behavior, is purposive and rule-following. Obviously, then, the objective of political scientists must be to identify the purposes that are pursued and the rules that are followed by various actors. Further, the identification of purposes and rules must be accompanied by an effort to discover interrelationships among them and to discover the consequences of pursuing or applying them in varying circumstances. The discovery of interrelationships and consequences can scarcely help having direct or indirect effects on policy.

A NOTE ON OBJECTIVITY

The statement that the social purpose of political scientists is to contribute to the rationality of decision making raises the question of objectivity. The question as discussed here relates only to descriptive statements and to the descriptive element in prescription. From a positivist (as distinct from a rationalist) point of view, normative statements express preference or volition and are necessarily subjective. Uniformly, objectivity is thought to be good in connection with descriptive studies. But what are the characteristics of objective inquiry?

Assuming both that objectivity is desirable and that the study of politics is a question-answering activity, it follows that objectivity must be defined in such a way as to permit question answering to be compatible with it. In other words, objectivity must not be so defined that it precludes answers or conclusions. It must not be equated to the collection of facts and the avoidance of judgment. As someone has said in another context, if objectivity were defined to bar conclusions or answers, objective study would be study without object. It would be pointless.

Sometimes the assumption seems to be that, to be objective, one must allow the facts to speak for themselves. From what has already been said, it should be clear that this involves deception, perhaps self-deception; and the deception is facilitated by the figurative language employed. Whatever "facts" are (and the meaning of the word will be discussed in the following chapter), they do not speak. Scholars do. The scholar asks the question, selects or ferrets out data that he considers relevant to it, and seeks an answer on the basis of the data. His selection and arrangement of the data may point toward or lead to an answer; out of expediency he may stop short of expressing the answer, but, still, if any speaking is done, he does it. He does not become objective simply by refraining from expressing the answer that his selection and arrangement of the data suggest. In some cases, an absolute and extreme conclusion may be thoroughly supported by the evidence, in which case a statement of the extreme conclusion may be entirely compatible with the requirements of objectivity. The judgment of a doctor that the patient is dead may be quite objective, even though extreme.[17]

Objectivity, relevant only to empirical inquiry and to subsequent descriptive statements, has to do with attitudes and practices that are generally accepted within the profession and that lead different scholars to approximately the same answer to the same question. The attitudes and practices concern the criteria by which data are judged to be relevant and reliable, the thoroughness with which data are located or developed, the criteria by which degrees of importance or significance are assigned, and the logic employed in determining what answer the data will support. A scholar who addresses himself to a question calling for description is being objective if he employs generally accepted criteria in judging data to be relevant and reliable, if he is thorough in locating or developing such data, if his criteria for weighting the data are generally accepted, and if he is logical in deriving his answer from the data. In short, he is being objective if replication by other scholars would lead to approximately the same result. Under this definition, of course, an answer might be wrong even though arrived at objectively.[18]

The words *thesis* and *polemic* are sometimes used in connection with scholarly writing, and the question of objectivity comes up in connection with both of them.

The answer to a question is sometimes called a thesis. The word scarcely applies, of course, to answers that are universally accepted as true. If someone asks in ignorance where the White

House is, the answer that it is in Washington is not likely to be called a thesis. But if someone asks in doubt whether the President was wise in signing a given bill, the answer is likely to be a thesis; this means that an argument supporting a particular conclusion will be developed, the argument resting on testimony, evidence, and reasoning. The adjectival form of *thesis* is not much used, but will be convenient for our purposes later. Just as *hypothesis* can be changed to *hypothetical* and just as *antithesis* can be changed to *antithetical*, so *thesis* can be changed to *thetical*. So, writing is thetical when it argues in support of an answer and seeks to resolve doubt. It may be thetical when the question is at a very low level of generality, for details are sometimes in doubt; it is likely to be thetical when the question is at a high level of generality, for doubt is then to be expected.

The distinction between a thesis and a polemic, and thus between the thetical and the polemical, is not very clear. Both words are associated with doubt, argument, and controversy. The distinction is probably to be found in the care with which relevant data are adduced and the fairness with which they are considered. When a piece of writing is called *polemical*, the connotation is that the author was trying above all to make a case for a controversial point of view, that in this effort he went to extremes, and, perhaps, that his purpose and outlook affected his perception and judgment in such a way as to lead him to fail to see or give fair consideration to relevant data. The zeal of a polemical writer for his point of view is thought to make him guilty of violating the standards of good scholarship. Almost certainly polemical writing will be lacking in objectivity. But when a piece of writing is called thetical, there is no implication that the author's desire to make a case has led him to abandon scholarly standards. He is credited with an outlook and purpose that, in principle, can be combined with objectivity and other qualities to make his work trustworthy; whether he actually succeeds in supporting his thesis convincingly is another matter.

Part II

THE EXPRESSION OF KNOWLEDGE: FORMS AND PROCESSES

Introduction

The chapters in Part II focus on a series of words: fact, abstraction, classification, concept, generalization, hypothesis, rule, principle, law, theory, model, and doctrine.

Most of these words designate a form of knowledge; e.g., knowledge is expressed in the form of facts and theories. Alternatively or in addition, some of them refer to processes that are important in the development of knowledge, e.g., classification and generalization.

Several purposes are served by discussing these words. One is simply to elucidate the meaning(s) given them in the literature of political science, or to suggest meanings. A second and related purpose is to identify types of definitions, the purposes they serve, and the possible sources of confusion relating to definitions. The achievement of these two purposes should contribute automatically to a greater degree of clarity of thought and communication among political scientists. Finally, a major purpose of the chapters in Part II is to further develop the thought advanced in Part I, i.e., to describe the role of these words (or of the meanings and processes they symbolize) in thetical teaching and writing designed to convey knowledge of relationships between thought and action, ends and means, cause and effect, conditions and consequences.

CHAPTER FIVE

Facts

"It is Facts that are needed," Bryce once declared, "Facts, Facts, Facts!"[1]

But what are facts? What is meant by a "specific" or a "general" fact? Which facts are "the facts" of political science? And what do facts have to do with theses about ends and means?

DEFINITIONS OF *Fact*

A number of definitions of *fact* have been advanced which may help to confer meaning on the word. Goode and Hatt define it as "an empirically verifiable observation" — a definition that is quite acceptable if both direct and indirect verification and observation are contemplated.[2] Wilson says that "facts are situations or circumstances concerning which there does not seem to be valid room for disagreement"—a definition that is useful, especially if the terms "situations" and "circumstances" are interpreted broadly and loosely.[3] Easton defines a fact as "a particular ordering of reality in terms of a theoretical interest"—a definition that should be clearer after we have discussed the meanings of the word "theory";[4] it may be better now to think of an ordering of reality in terms of a question that has been posed. Another possibility is that we might define a fact as a finding or a statement about reality, arrived at by a reliable method. A method is reliable when it produces the same result for all those who employ it. Thus, the definition just offered can be translated to read that a fact is a finding or a statement about reality on which universal agreement is, in principle, achievable.

THE RANGE OF DATA ORDERED BY FACTS

Facts are sometimes described, at the one extreme, as specific or narrow or detailed and, at the other, as general or broad. The difference is in the quantity of data that is ordered or summarized or somehow drawn upon to provide a basis for the fact. The greater the quantity of data symbolized by the fact, the broader or more general it is.

The possibilities can easily be illustrated. Suppose that we enter the Senate Chamber in the Capitol in Washington, D.C. We note that a presiding officer is at his place, that a Senator is speaking, and that one or more other Senators are at their desks. All others who check on these observations confirm them. We can say, then, that what we have noted are *facts*, the word *fact* in this case denoting direct sense perceptions. Suppose that, having established the above sense perceptions as facts, we go on to say that the Senate is in session. In this case we would be inferring a fact from the others already established; or, to put it differently, we would be interpreting the established facts, and the interpretation, if confirmed, would itself be a fact. If we observed the Senate long enough, or if we talked to the right persons, we might discover a third fact: we might learn that bills and resolutions are invariably declared passed by the Senate when, in specified circumstances, a certain vote is obtained; in other words, a proposition that truly asserts "an invariable sequence or conjunction of characters" is called factual. Further, the word *fact* can denote something still broader. It may apply to general conclusions reached after study of other facts. The general conclusion might be that the Senate has been devoting an increasing proportion of its time to foreign affairs, that over the years influence and power in the Senate have come to be concentrated in fewer and fewer persons, etc. If the evidence supporting such general conclusions is sufficient, they are statements of fact. Otherwise, the statements, if made at all, should be regarded as hypotheses, which will be discussed below. The line between a fact and a hypothesis is not fixed.[5]

Other sorts of examples can be added. After a national election we can state the outcome by precincts, by counties, by states, or for the country as a whole, and each statement might be factual. It may be a fact that an individual civil servant has made a decision and also that a government has done so, perhaps by ponderous constitutional processes. Oligarchical control of political power in a given precinct and a universal "iron law of oligarchy" might both be facts. Similarly it may be a fact that a person learns how to shoot a carbine, that he receives military training, and that a government has brought about these and a multitude of other actions to avoid being compelled by hostile power to give up precious rights. That statements of fact may embrace or encompass or rest upon vastly different quantities of data is further suggested in the following:

Darwin's essential contribution was twofold. By his patient accumulation and analysis of *facts* he made it clear that plants and animals could not possibly have been created in their present form but must have undergone a long process of development—in other words, that evolution was a *fact*.[6]

The word *fact*, then, may designate anything from the most minute detail to the most general truth.

WHICH FACTS ARE "THE FACTS" OF POLITICAL SCIENCE?

Perhaps it is clear from the above that "the facts" of political science and, for that matter, of any other subject are not foreordained. As Hallowell puts it, "facts do not present themselves to individuals (certainly not with neat labels already attached to them). . . ."[7] To start out to learn or to teach the facts of even a subdivision of political science would be to start out on an endless and nearly aimless quest, for the facts are infinite and varied. "The facts" about the House of Representatives, for example, might include statements on innumerable topics and reflect vastly differing quantities of data. They might include physiological data about the members—the condition of their hearts, their metabolic rates, the pigmentation of their skin and hair, the keenness of their sight and hearing, etc. Also included might be data about the physical environment in which the House works—the size and shape of the Chamber, the style and type of furnishings, the degree of cleanliness of the floors at different times, etc. It is presumably a fact about Congressmen, too, that they have somewhat different habits of dress, make somewhat different grammatical errors, enjoy somewhat different foods, and are influenced by somewhat different backgrounds. These and many other types of facts might be compiled, but the mere fact that they relate somehow to the House and its members does not necessarily make them facts of political science. Otherwise, political scientists might be reduced to an attempt to determine how many of the socks worn by Congressmen (or by voters) have holes in the toes.

Far from being foreordained, the facts of political science are selected by political scientists.[8] A fact belongs in the field when a political scientist considers it helpful in answering a question he has posed. As old questions cease to be considered important, or as old approaches to questions cease to be considered useful, the old facts drop out of the field. Conversely, new questions and new approaches call new facts into the field.

It follows from the above that facts vary greatly in their significance.[9] They become significant to the political scientist only when they relate to a question he has asked, and then their significance may vary considerably in degree. Facts that are very helpful in answering a number of important questions derive great significance from the role they play, whereas facts that give only minor help in answering a petty question are rather insignificant.

FACTS AS TRUE INFORMATION AND AS EVIDENCE

Implied in the above is the fact that there are alternative ways of thinking about facts.[10] On the one hand, they can be regarded as statements of true information, as established truths, as conclusions; once a fact in this sense has been expressed, there is nothing more to be said. Thus, the statement that evolution is a fact can be regarded as a statement of true information, the culmination of a question-posing and question-answering process. Similarly, the statement that the United States and Britain are parties to the North Atlantic Treaty is a statement of true information, which implicitly or explicitly answers a question. On the other hand, facts can be regarded not so much as true answers to questions as evidence relevant to questions that remain unanswered. Thus, the fact of evolution can be treated as evidence on the question whether plant and animal life came into existence in substantially its present form by a single act of creation, and adherence to the North Atlantic Treaty can be treated as evidence of intended behavior in certain kinds of future contingencies.

Both these ways of looking at facts have their place. True information needs to be summed up and kept available; as suggested before, reference books like the *World Almanac* and the *United*

States Government Organization Manual serve useful purposes. It is perhaps inevitable, too, that some textbooks and teaching will consist of little more than an effort to convey facts in this sense. But knowledge is not enhanced, and little intellectual satisfaction is gained, simply by reciting or memorizing what is known, particularly when the facts are specific and narrow and thus count as minutiae. The purpose of scholarship is not so much to conserve as to expand knowledge. And this can be done only if facts are sought and treated as evidence in relation to questions that are as yet either unanswered or answered in an inconclusive or unsatisfactory way.

Another way of expressing approximately the same thought is that the scholar deals not so much with a series of isolated, individual facts as with relationships among facts. He seeks to use facts as evidence in a process of reasoning so as to derive new knowledge from what he already knows. Given a question, what facts fit together in what way to provide what answer? It is said that "the value of original historical work largely lies in bringing to light connections between well-established historical facts."[11] *Mutatis mutandis,* the statement also applies to political science. This means that scholarship calls for the development of theses— that scholarly writing should be thetical in that it should demonstrate connections between facts and arrive at conclusions.

Once again this means that the good scholar does not simply find or assemble facts in the expectation that the process will lead him somehow to significant knowledge. The starting point, as indicated before, is a problem or a question.

It is an utterly superficial view . . . that the truth is to be found by "studying the facts." It is superficial because no inquiry can even get under way until and unless *some difficulty is felt* in a practical or theoretical situation. It is the difficulty, or problem, which guides our search for some *order among the facts,* in terms of which the difficulty is to be removed. . . . It is idle to collect "facts" unless there is a problem upon which they are supposed to bear.[12]

CHAPTER SIX

Concepts

When we speak of the White House or of Khrushchev or of the bomb dropped at Hiroshima, our words are specific and designate the concrete. They identify things or persons or events, and have only one application. Such specific, concrete words are, of course, indispensable. At the same time, if we were limited to such words, we would suffer a handicap that might well be fatal to the development of knowledge. We could make remarks about one or a few specific and concrete items, but the more of them we tried to comment about, the more of our time we would have to spend simply in naming the items. No remark about human beings in general would be possible without naming all of them individually.

We handle this problem by an obvious but fundamentally important process. That is, we note likes and unlikes, similarities and differences; we see patterns or groups or classes or combinations of items. And then we name or otherwise identify what seem to belong together, and talk about the items named collectively. Thus we can speak of men and women without naming them individually; and we can speak of states, politicians, voters, purposes, and so on. We can think in terms of classes or categories or types rather than in terms of the multitude of separate items involved.

Four words are important in describing and understanding this process and the benefits derived. They are abstraction, classification, concept, and generalization. Our purpose now is to explore their meaning and significance, and the interrelationships among them.

Robinson defines abstraction in the following way:

Abstraction is becoming aware for the first time of a new general element in one's experience and giving it a name. A general element is a form or pattern or characteristic, as opposed to a particular or individual. To become aware of a particular cow in a field is not called "abstraction." But it is called "abstraction" to become aware of the form cow as opposed to the form bull or the form sheep.[1]

Similarly, abstraction occurs when one becomes aware of other general elements in experience, like governments, parties, pressure groups, war, justice, democracy, authoritarianism, etc. In defining abstraction we have had to use concepts. A concept is the name given to any general element in one's experience. In the above quotation, *cow, bull,* and *sheep* are emphasized as concepts, though the quotation contains a number of other concepts as well.

When similar events are placed in the same class and the class is given a name, we have made use of a concept. . . .

A concept is a mental construction, an abstract idea that refers either to a class of phenomena or to certain aspects or characteristics that a range of phenomena have in common. . . . Concepts . . . are abstractions from reality, designating types of movements, persons, behavior, or other classes of phenomena.[2]

Obviously, the above statements involve the ideas of classification and generalization. When we classify, we sort elements into classes or categories on the tentative assumption that it will be useful to consider them together. The very act of naming what we have abstracted or classified is itself an implicit generalization (i.e., a concept is itself an implicit generalization), for it asserts that the items named belong together somehow—that they have shared characteristics. More broadly, a generalization is "a proposition that describes some attribute common to two or more objects."[3] Presumably it is derived from an examination of these objects and can be judged to be true or false.

Though abstraction, classification, concept, and generalization are interrelated words, we cannot talk about all of them at once. It will be best to focus in this chapter on concepts, and to deal with abstraction in relation to concepts. Then in the next chapter we can discuss classification and generalization.

THE LEVEL OF ABSTRACTION OF CONCEPTS

Concepts vary in their level of abstraction. That is, they vary in the number of phenomena to which they relate and, frequently, in the ease with which they can be identified with something that is observable—with empirical referents. The greater the number of phenomena to which a concept relates, and/or the further removed it is from empirical referents, the higher its level of abstraction is said to be.

Cow is a concept at a fairly low level of abstraction; *animal* is higher, for the concept applies to more phenomena. *Legislator* is at a lower level of abstraction than *political actor*. *Democracy* and *collective security* are concepts at a high level of abstraction, for they relate to very numerous phenomena, many of which are rather problematic and difficult to identify.

Concepts at every level of abstraction are useful, no one level being necessarily and always better than the others. By definition, high-level abstractions assert a likeness among greater numbers of phenomena. On the one hand, this makes them potentially more significant in reflecting relationships and, on the other, it involves the danger that they may be so very broad and vague that they carry no clear meaning; they may mean so much that they mean nothing.

THE REIFICATION OF ABSTRACT CONCEPTS

One is said to reify an abstraction if one treats it as concrete. The word *state*, for example, is an abstraction. It is not something that can be seen, felt, heard, touched, or smelled. No one could take a picture of a state acting. Yet it is common in practice to speak of the purposes or functions or actions of the state. Sometimes this amounts to no more than the use of a figure of speech, and figurative language is often very convenient. Sometimes, by a slight extension, it amounts to treating the state as a corporate body—an admittedly fictitious person; and, again, the practice is convenient. But sometimes reification seems to be involved. That is, some references to the state seem to predicate the real existence of an entity quite apart from the human beings (the officeholders and others) who are the visible actors; perhaps it will be called an organism with a life and will of its own, existing independently of the life and will of the human beings who compose it. In view of the distinction of some of the writers who have seemed to reify the state in this way, it is perhaps better not to call the practice obvious nonsense. Yet there is nothing to say in support of the view, and there are many dangers in it.[4]

Usages associated with many other words present similar problems. *Government* is used in much the same way as *state*. *History*, too, is sometimes personified—whether purely figuratively or as a fictitious person or as a reified entity. "History will not excuse our failings." Some use the word *interests* in such a way as to suggest that they have real existence. And so on. Reification is very common. The suggestion has even been made that to speak of a human being is to reify, the assumption being that what political scientists are really concerned with is not a human body but activity.[5]

THE FUNCTIONS OF CONCEPTS

Concepts are of fundamental importance both in seeking knowledge — in guiding inquiry — and in expressing knowledge. There is an interaction, of course, between perception and conception. Our perceptions provide a basis for conceptions, and once conceptions have been developed we are more likely to see what they name. As William James said,

> The intellectual life of man consists almost wholly in his substitution of a conceptual order for the perceptual order in which his experience originally comes. . . . Every new book verbalizes some new concept, which becomes important in proportion to the use that can be made of it. . . .[6]

It is always the case that patterns or classes of phenomena exist unobserved, perhaps for very long periods of time. No one sees them in a distinct way; no one sets them apart and gives them a name. After all, people do not ordinarily look for something without having some reason to think that it exists. But when someone finally does perceive a new pattern or a new class of phenomena and gives it a name, thus creating a new concept, many others become aware of its existence and are likely to perceive it. Concepts thus alert us to the existence of what is named, and in their absence we may allow phenomena to go unobserved. They may even act as blinders; once we have developed a set of concepts, we are likely to see only what they alert us to see. We may fail to see new phenomena, or, if we do see them, we may force them into the old conceptual framework even though they do not quite fit. Some imagination and boldness must usually be added to perceptivity to provide an adequate basis for conceptualization and reconceptualization.

Conceptual problems can briefly be illustrated, though the development of new concepts is not the purpose here. We speak, for example, of the location of political power within governmental systems. In doing so, should we think in terms of rule by political parties? by a dominant class? by an elite? by pressure groups? or by the Establishment? The *public interest* and the *national interest* exist as concepts, but to what extent, if at all, do these concepts blind us to practices that serve private interests? For that matter, precisely what does the concept *interest* mean? By calling something an *interest* do we make it less likely that it will be perceived as either an end or a means and judged accordingly? Some political scientists have used the concept *administration* in such a way as to suggest that administrators are aloof and removed from policy and politics, but the general view seems to be that this concept did violence to the facts. We commonly classify governmental activities as *legislative, executive,* and *judicial,* but might ask to what extent the concepts distort or falsify our thinking; obviously, people in each of the three so-called branches of government exercise functions and powers that seem to belong conceptually in one of the other branches. Perhaps we should scrap the concepts legislative, executive, and judicial, or supplement them with others that more usefully and significantly classify and name governmental activities. In the international field the concepts *sovereignty, nation, imperialism, free world, satellite, balance of power, limited war,* and many others are employed. Whether some of them name combinations of phenomena that belong together in reality is a moot question; some of them, instead of being useful in analyzing behavior and developing knowledge, may be obstacles to realistic thought and understanding. And who knows what classes or combinations of phenomena belong together without having been perceived, analytically differentiated, and named?

THE DEFINITION OF CONCEPTS

To be useful, concepts must, of course, be defined. The statement is obvious, but its implications are not. Untold years of intellectual labor have been wasted and in all probability the course of human events has in many ways been altered because of mistakes and misconceptions relating to the definition of words. The problems have been cogently explored by Richard Robinson, and what follows is drawn almost entirely from his work.[7]

Our concern is with the purposes served by definitions and not with the methods employed in the defining process. On the basis of their purposes, definitions are divided into two categories, nominal and real. The purpose of a nominal definition is to indicate the meaning of a word or symbol, and the purpose of a real definition is to indicate the nature of a thing—to identify features of what is defined. "The failure to distinguish all the time between the analysis of things and the nominal definition of words has been the cause of most of the common errors in the theory of definition."[8]

Nominal Definitions: Lexical and Stipulative

Nominal definitions divide into the lexical and the stipulative. Lexical definitions record or report the fact that the word has in practice been assigned the specified meaning(s). Stipulative definitions are predictive rather than historical. They legislate meaning, giving notice that when the word is used in the future it will have the meaning specified. It is appropriate to ask whether lexical definitions provide a true and correct reflection of usage, but from a positivist point of view it is nonsense to ask whether either lexical or stipulative definitions are true in the sense of coinciding with some mystically determined, foreordained meaning. According to positivists, words have the meanings that human beings give them; they do not have unknown, foreordained meanings that remain to be discovered. Both types of definition may be appraised in terms of their usefulness; or, more accurately, the words or concepts to which the definitions relate may be appraised in terms of usefulness. And they may be useful in various ways, e.g., in heuristic quality, as alerting devices, or as tools of thought and communication. Stipulative definitions may, of course, become lexical.

Concepts that are common currency and that therefore have lexical definitions frequently have so many different connotations and meanings that their usefulness in scholarly work is impaired.

Where clarity and precision are desired, the scholar then faces a dilemma. If he stipulates a meaning, whether or not a new meaning, there is danger that other meanings will still affect his thought or distort the understanding that others gain. If he abandons the old concept and adopts a new one, stipulating its meaning, there will be some who will object to the development of jargon and some who, whether or not they object, will not understand.

In stipulating new meanings for old concepts, some limitations must be accepted if scholarly integrity is to be preserved and confusion avoided. The writer who employs a word having strong emotional connotations will be suspected of intending to evoke these connotations even if he stipulates a definition that omits them; it would not do to classify voters as patriots or traitors depending on whether they voted for the party in power unless emotional implications were intended. Stipulated meanings should not be deceptive, either; and they may be deceptive if familiar words are given meanings that differ drastically from those normally conveyed. One might stipulate, for example, that lines of action that contribute to the survival of a going system are conservative, whereas lines of action that tend to undermine it are radical. But then the New Dealers of the 1930's might be called conservatives, and those who opposed the New Deal might be the radicals. The confusing nature of the stipulation is obvious. Similarly, even if a communist author were to stipulate clearly that "proletarian democracy" means "dictatorship of the proletariat," it is still probable that his use of the word democracy would turn out to be deceptive.

Real Definitions: Meaning and Types

Real definitions, we have said, are designed to indicate not the meaning of a word but the nature of a thing—to identify features of what is defined. (After Robinson, the word *thing* is here used very broadly and loosely to designate an object, an event, a process, a characteristic, an institution, or anything else that can be symbolized by a word.) Actually, a number of different kinds of activities are said to comprise real definition, and it is important to distinguish between them; some of them reflect seriously mistaken or confused thought.

Socrates and Plato were seeking real definitions when they

asked such questions as, "What is justice?" They reified an abstraction, and then sought a definition for the concrete thing. The assumption was that justice and many other concepts had a foreordained essence or form which men should seek to discover. The implication was that, once the essence of justice and other virtues was known, men would be in a position to establish a truly good society. Further, the notion that essences or ideal forms existed encouraged the thought that persons who gained the appropriate knowledge should see to it that the good society was actually created and evil made to disappear. Some have thought that repressive and bloody dictatorship was justified if it was necessary to realize true justice and to make other virtues triumph. But no one has ever succeeded in validating the assumption that essences exist in the sense intended. Robinson's conclusion is that essence "is just the human choice of what to mean by a name, misinterpreted as being a metaphysical reality."[9] In other words, those who thought they were defining a thing were, instead, simply stipulating the meaning of a word. The essence of justice was what the defining person declared it to be. Confusion on the point has cost untold years of wasted intellectual effort. More seriously, it has undoubtedly affected the course of political events, for people seem to be able to devote themselves more wholeheartedly to a foreordained essence than to a man-made meaning. The feeling that they are fighting on the side of the Lord gives them courage and strength. Moreover, the notion of essences reinforces authoritarianism especially, for it implies Truth that exists independently of the majority will.[10]

A real definition is sometimes nothing more than a recommendation concerning values. What is ostensibly a descriptive definition is actually a normative appeal. A real definition of this type "is a moral or evaluative appeal misrepresented as a statement of fact, and gaining force from its pseudo-scientific character."[11] Thus the dictator is likely to define justice as what the law provides. Those who would like to change the law, whether by peaceful or violent action, are also likely to define justice in such a way that the definition incorporates their preferences. The statement that politics is "the art of getting men to live together and cooperate in matters of common interest" is really an exhortation, though ostensibly a definition, and the same can be said of the assertion that "the state is a fellowship of men aiming at the enrichment of the common life." The value preferences of the person clearly show in the definition of the "democratic faith" and of the "democrat" implicit in the following statement:

The democratic faith is not tied to any political or social system. It regards all systems (including "democracy") as instruments for the self-realization of human nature; and if representative institutions are shown to be no longer useful for that purpose, then the democrat must look elsewhere for other instruments and better institutions.[12]

The thought is one that few people who think of themselves as democrats are likely to accept, yet it is offered as a matter of definition or of fact. The following statement contains the same kind of deception.

The democratic or anti-democratic nature of public life of a state, of a government's policy, is determined not by the number of parties but by the substance of the policy of this state, of these parties—by whether this or that policy is carried out in the interests of the people, in the interests of its overwhelming majority, or in the interests of its minority.[13]

This statement concerning the nature of democracy is by a communist. Communists take the view, of course, that they alone can determine the "true interests" of the people, so the existence of democracy comes to be equated by definition with the rule of the leader(s) of the Communist Party. As Robinson says, to offer such a definition is "at best a mistake and at worst a lie, because it consists in getting someone to alter his valuations under the false impression that he is . . . correcting his knowledge of facts."[14]

This book urges a conception of desirable or significant scholarship, and at times comes perilously close to the error in point. That is, it comes close to treating a recommendation concerning values as simply a matter of fact. But the recommendation is contained in a definition (of "significance") that is nominal and stipulative rather than real.

Real definition sometimes consists simply of an analysis of the thing defined, i.e., an identification of the parts, and perhaps a statement about interrelationships among the parts, which go together to comprise the whole. Thus, the concept *state* has been defined as designating a body of people located on a given territory under the jurisdiction of a government that is independent or sovereign.

Given the fact that a number of different purposes or processes are associated with real definition, and given the fact that some of these purposes reflect considerable confusion of thought, it is doubtful whether the term should be retained. Clearly, what is advanced as a real definition is not always definitional. Terms that are more accurately descriptive of what is designated would lead to less confusion.

In talking about concepts and their definition, we have been assuming that a concept is an individual word. The term is also sometimes used to designate a general notion or scheme, in which case *concept, conception,* and *conceptual scheme* become virtually synonymous. General notions or schemes are often theories, and we will discuss them later in relation to theories rather than here in relation to words.

In sum, concepts express knowledge, reflecting perceptions of reality. At the same time they have heuristic value, alerting scholars and others to the existence and significance of the things named. Usage gives them meanings that are lexical and scholars may give them meanings that are stipulative. In any case their definitions are man-made. It is not good scholarship to attempt to inculcate values by advancing definitions that seem to be statements of fact.

CHAPTER SEVEN

Classification, Generalization, Hypotheses, Rules, and Principles

The discussion of the level of generality of questions which appeared in Chapter Two necessarily included some statements about classification and generalization, and the words have been mentioned at other points as well. But a more extended and coherent discussion of them will be helpful. Moreover, in this chapter the notion of *classifying* will be supplemented with the notion of *ordering;* and three kinds of generalizations—hypotheses, rules, and principles—will be discussed.

CLASSIFYING AND ORDERING PHENOMENA

Classification consists of grouping items or phenomena on the basis of their shared characteristics. Whether or not a class of items is named (i.e., whether or not they provide a basis for the formulation of a concept), the process of classification is tremendously important. "This ability to order things into likes and unlikes is, I think, the foundation of human thought."[1]

The basic purpose of classification is to simplify the handling of a great number of individual items by putting them into a smaller number of groups, each group consisting of items which act more or less alike in relation to the problem being studied.[2]

Classification may involve a series of steps. For some purposes it is enough to divide items into very broad and general categories, as when we classify political actors as governmental and nongovernmental. For other purposes sharper differentiations are desirable, in which case, for example, governmental actors might be subdivided into federal, state, and local. For still other purposes the differentiations need to be sharper yet, in which case each of the three categories (federal, state, and local) might in turn be subdivided. The end point is reached when each political actor is in a category by itself. A classification scheme involving a series of steps is said to be articulate.

Classification also involves logic. A scheme of classification is said to meet the requirements of logic when, at each of the articulated steps, the categories provided are exhaustive and mutually exclusive. They are exhaustive when there is a place for every item; and they are mutually exclusive when no item fits in more than one of them.

Quite apart from matters of form and structure, classification schemes must meet a vague but important requirement: they must be apt. For one thing, this means that they must lend themselves to the purposes of the scholar in relation to the problem he is attacking. He must look for and identify the particular kinds of shared characteristics that are significant for his purposes, and must devise categories accordingly. Characteristics of the data may, in a sense, be heuristic, suggesting appropriate categories. At the same time, thought about the question or problem being attacked may alert the scholar to the types or categories of data that might be useful. Thus, data stimulate thought in the development of an apt scheme of classification, and thought stimulates the search for data. If it should occur that no data are available for a category that thought suggests, the fact may be as significant as if data for the category were abundant.

Classification occurs in virtually every intellectual activity in which we engage. This book is a reflection of the fact. The division of the subject into parts is itself a scheme for classifying the data and the considerations involved. Further classification occurs within each part. In Part II, considerations relating to "facts" made up the first chapter. The second chapter related to concepts. The third, the present one, deals with classification itself. And additional categories of subject matter will follow. The classification scheme employed was not at all obvious when work on the book began; in fact, several alternative schemes were explored, and it is quite possible that someone else might devise a classification scheme—or a pattern of organization—that is better than the one here employed. The point is that the development of a desirable classification scheme often requires insight or perceptivity; creative and imaginative thought, and even a sense for the aesthetic, may well be very helpful.

Data do not always divide into distinct categories. Sometimes there are simply variations in degree rather than differences in kind. We could, for example, divide human beings into two categories on the basis of age; all of those below twenty might go into one category and all those over twenty into another. But this would be very arbitrary and might or might not be helpful. For many purposes it would be more helpful to range people along a scale, i.e., to engage in a process of ordering the data rather than classifying them. Lasswell and Kaplan suggest that the difference between classifying and ordering is the "difference between a science of species and a science of functional co-relations," and they point out that "once concepts are formulated in terms of order, of variations in degree, scales and methods of measurement can be developed to suit the needs of particular problems."[3]

GENERALIZATION

We have already noted that a concept is an implicit generalization in that it asserts the existence of shared characteristics in different items. We further said that a generalization is "a proposition that describes some attribute common to two or more objects." This is tantamount to saying that the process of generalization is the passage from a statement true of one observed instance to a statement true of more than one instance of a certain class. Cohen and Nagel are much more extreme, for they define the process of generalization as "the passage from a statement true of some observed instances to a statement true of all possible instances of a certain class."[4] We will use the less extreme definition. Unless otherwise indicated, our concern is with generalizations that are descriptive rather than normative or prescriptive.

When we cite an example or say that something is typical, we are generalizing. A high proportion of our sentences, including this one, make use of concepts that are generalizations and link the

concepts together in such a way as to advance another generalization. The object in the study of politics can be said to be the development of "generalizations with both reliability and validity
for the understanding of political behavior."[5]

In Chapter Two we noted that the questions that political scientists ask vary in their level of generality. Some call for the identification of shared characteristics of very few particulars, whereas
others call for efforts to give order, structure, and meaning to considerable masses of particulars. Another way of saying the same
thing is that our generalizations are at different levels of generality—some applying to few particulars and some applying to very
many.

Various words are associated with the word *generalization*. A
generalization is also a *statement* or a *proposition*. When employed descriptively, all three of these words designate sentences
that are, in principle, either true or false. Postulates, assumptions,
premises, and principles may be generalizations. Hypotheses and
descriptive laws and theories are generalizations. The following
passage by David Easton serves both to illustrate the use of certain
of these and other words and to advance a thought that is important in the present context.

> In and of themselves facts do not enable us to explain or understand an
> event. Facts must be ordered in some way so that we can see their con-
> nections. The higher the level of generality in ordering such facts and
> clarifying their relations, the broader will be the range of explanation
> and understanding. A set of generalizations that orders all the kinds of
> facts we call political would obviously be more useful for purposes of
> understanding political activity than a single generalization that related
> only two such facts. It is for this reason, among others to be discussed
> later, that the search for reliable knowledge about empirical political
> phenomena requires ultimately the construction of systematic theory,
> the name for the highest order of generalization.[6]

The term *generalization* is thus broad enough to cover all of
the remaining subject matter in Part II, which means that the divi-
sions that follow reflect preferences concerning styling and emphasis rather than logic. We will examine three kinds of generalizations—hypotheses, rules, and principles—in the remainder of this
chapter, and will devote separate chapters to two other kinds of
generalizations, laws and theories.

Definitions of Hypotheses

The words *hypothesis* and *hypothetical* are given different meanings and shades of meaning.

Statements and questions resting on contingency are commonly said to be *hypothetical*. For example, "If he wins in New York he will win the presidency" is a hypothetical statement. In this same sense, empirical, descriptive generalizations are hypothetical, for general knowledge that is inductive is contingent on the prospect that observations in the future will coincide with those of the past.

Our concern is not so much with hypotheses involving contingency as with hypotheses involving conjecture. Thus, "propositions that assert the existence of relationships among phenomena . . . ," or propositions that state an answer to a question or a solution to a problem, are hypotheses, if they are in some sense conjectural.[7] They are put forward for consideration, judgment concerning their truth or falsity being suspended until the consideration is completed.[8] Usually they are expressed in affirmative statements, but can be contained within the question to be answered. For example, we might say, "The distribution of influence over decisions concerning the constitutional system in society tends to correlate with the distribution of control over military power." Or we might ask, "Does the distribution of influence over decisions concerning the constitutional system in society tend to correlate with the distribution of control over military power?" The same statement or question might be expressed on an if-then basis: "If there is a change in the distribution of control over military power, then there will tend to be (or, will there tend to be?) a corresponding change in the distribution of influence over decisions concerning the constitutional system of a society." Explicitly or implicitly, each of these various formulations expresses a hypothesis. The hypothesis is eliminated if the proposition is eliminated, i.e., if the sentence does not itself suggest a tentative answer. For example, "If there is a change in the distribution of control over military power, what happens, if anything, to the distribution of influence over decisions concerning the constitutional system in a society?"

As a variation on the above, hypotheses are sometimes expressed in models or in ideal types—devices that will be discussed below.

Occasions for the Use of Hypotheses

The answer to any question of fact first can be stated as a hypothesis and then be subjected to test or check with a view to confirmation or disconfirmation. The desirability of going through this procedure varies. Where a universally accepted answer is available, perhaps in a reference book, the simplest thing to do is to look it up without bothering to state a hypothesis; this situation often prevails in connection with very specific questions—questions at a very low level of generality. Further, where the answer is quite obviously obtainable by a recognized procedure, there is no point in trying to anticipate the answer by stating a hypothesis. For example, if the question concerns the extent of correlation between religious affiliation and participation in a given election in a given precinct, there would probably be no advantage in advancing a hypothesis; the answer could be secured through various accepted kinds of operations, perhaps including a door-to-door survey. Hypotheses are more likely to be useful where trial and error are involved—where there is an element of uncertainty or unavoidable conjecture; perhaps there is doubt about the kind of method or the kind of data that will lead to a trustworthy answer. If, for example, we ask not about the relationship between religious affiliation and participation in elections but rather about the factors that influence decisions to participate or to abstain, we create a need for a series of hypotheses—no doubt including the one mentioned above. Each hypothesis in the series might then be tested and rated as true or false, or probably true or probably false, and a summary generalization might be made.

The Testability of Hypotheses

As the statement just made indicates, to be immediately useful as guides to scholarly inquiry, hypotheses are supposed to be testable, which is another way of saying that the questions that give rise to them are supposed to be answerable. This requirement might be interpreted in a strict and extreme fashion to mean that no question should be considered unless the relevant hypothesis can be confirmed or disconfirmed with near certainty. Or it might be interpreted more loosely to permit the consideration of questions and hypotheses on which there is enough evidence to base probability statements, e.g., that there is some reason to think that the hypothesis is true (or false). Many important political questions would be excluded from consideration by the first of these interpretations; few, if any, would be excluded by the second. Of course, the requirement of testability rules out hypotheses that are normative, prescriptive, or rationalist, for by their very nature they cannot be tested. Prescriptive hypotheses, however, might be translated into their normative and descriptive elements, and the descriptive element might then be tested. Similarly, the requirement of testability rules out needless ambiguity or vagueness; precision is desirable whenever it can be obtained without excluding important questions from consideration.

At the risk of laboring a point unduly, let it be noted that hypotheses do not mysteriously appear, ready-made; nor are they likely to be formulated by the scholar who starts by looking at "the facts." The starting point is an act that frequently requires considerable insight: becoming aware of a question or problem. Once that awareness has developed, there may well be a call for further insight and imagination in getting the question or problem formulated properly. In many cases, "the difficulty is to state the question rightly; once that is done, it may almost answer itself."[9] If it does not answer itself, intuition and, hopefully, a spark of genius may come into play in suggesting one or more hypotheses that deserve to be checked. Once thought and imagination have guided the task of assembling evidence, it may be that in some cases the work can proceed in an unimaginative and mechanical way; even if this is possible, however, more or less rigorous thought is likely to be necessary, once the evidence has been gathered, before a judgment can be reached on the question of the degree of probability with which the hypothesis has been confirmed or disconfirmed.

A summary quotation may be in place:

A well-designed piece of research must start from an explicit statement of the major questions to be answered. These, of course, may and in fact are likely to be altered as the research progresses, but if the central propositions [hypotheses] at any stage are implicit or cloudy, the application or development of investigative techniques will be loose and the resulting research will be wasteful and inconclusive. Once the basic propositions [hypotheses] have been stated, however, it is possible to elaborate them almost indefinitely.[10]

RULES

In Chapter Three we described political actors as purposive and rule-following. Nothing more need be said here about the desires or purposes that are pursued, but there probably should be another mention of *rule*, even though political scientists have not so far paid much attention to the term.

The noun *rule* is given a number of different meanings. For our purposes a rule is a criterion that an actor follows in making decisions and that, if followed, leads him to do the same kind of thing on the same kind of occasion.[11] He may or may not be entirely conscious of the rule, or able to give verbal expression to it. But it is a feature of the concept that he and others should be able, at least in many cases, to know whether he has applied the rule correctly or whether he has made a mistake. Rules are prescriptive or normative rather than descriptive.

Under this definition there are many kinds of rules that guide human behavior. A definition is itself a rule for the use of the word defined. There are rules of grammar, of logic, of safety, of morality or ethics, of etiquette, of prudence, of efficiency, of organizational behavior, of leadership, of strategy, etc. There are rules of law—statutory or common. Voters and political parties follow rules in nominating candidates; candidates follow rules in their campaigning; officeholders follow rules in performing their duties; governments follow rules in conducting relationships with each other; the Secretary-General of the United Nations follows rules in his efforts to induce members to uphold and abide by the obligations of membership, and so on. They all follow hierarchies of rules, the more general rules being applied when a choice has to be made among those that are more specific. Knowledge of the general rules that are followed and, even more, knowledge of the specific rules that have been adopted will obviously go far in providing a basis for explaining or predicting political action.

Rules play an important part in policy. In fact they have been named as one of the two components of policy, the other component being action. The rules are guides to action. They may specify "the substance of response to some future situation," e.g., retaliation in kind for a nuclear attack. Or they may specify "the occasion for a response or the conditions under which a particular response will be made," e.g., give aid to any Middle Eastern government which is threatened by international communism, provided the aid is requested. Or rules may specify an "interpretation of future events and circumstances," e.g., regard any communist revolution as essentially the work of Moscow.[12]

Rules are more closely related to reasons for action than to causes of action, for they are associated with purpose and choice. Behavior that conforms to a rule consistently may appear to reflect descriptive law (defined in the following chapter), but the elements of choice and purpose are more fully recognized if the rules are treated as prescriptive and the behavior as rule-following.[13]

If it is a purpose of scholarship to explain and predict, it follows that it must be a purpose to identify the rules by which political actors guide their behavior. Some rules are so commonplace that they can be taken for granted. But by no means all of them are. The clear and reliable identification of distinctive rules of behavior can be a very significant scholarly achievement.[14]

PRINCIPLES

The word *principle* is often used as a synonym for *rule*.[15] Instead of referring above to the rules of grammar, of logic, of safety, of morality, etc., we might have referred to principles. The use of the term is illustrated in the United Nations Charter, in which the members bind themselves to act in accordance with a series of *principles,* e.g., the principle of the sovereign equality of members and the principle that international disputes shall be settled by peaceful means. Many principles are associated with democratic and constitutional government in the United States: that every man shall count for one and no man for more than one; that power shall be widely shared; that agencies of government shall not abridge freedom of speech; that no state shall deny to any person the equal protection of the laws; and so on.

If there is a difference between principles and rules, it seems to be in the scope of the statements made, the word principles applying to statements of the broadest and most general sort and the word rules applying to more narrow and specific guides to behavior; in other words, the most general rules may be called principles.

When principles state rules, they are normative or prescriptive. Of course, the fact that the principles are espoused may be reported descriptively. Thus there may be descriptive statements indicating that states follow a rule or principle calling for the balancing of power.

Sometimes principles assert causal relationships and thus are more akin to descriptive laws than to prescriptive rules. Such principles are found especially in the natural sciences. For example, a thermostat works on the principle that changes in temperature cause metal to expand and contract, thus establishing or breaking off electrical contact between given points. There have been efforts to develop principles of this type in political science, especially in the field of public administration. Thus, the principle is advanced that "administrative efficiency is increased by arranging the members of the group in a determinate hierarchy of authority."[16] Discussion of principles of this type, presuming to assert descriptive law, will be found in the following chapter.

Principles are derived from various sources, depending on their type. The positivist position is, of course, that normative principles are postulated. Descriptive principles are empirical, stemming from observation. Prescriptive rules or principles are a combination of the two; they combine a postulated end with an assertion concerning a way to promote its achievement. Whether normative, descriptive, or prescriptive, principles may also be definitional or logical statements. Postulating the desirability of democracy, for example, we also postulate certain normative principles that figure in the definition of democracy. Similarly, if we postulate the desirability of preserving the independence of the state, adherence to certain further principles is logically implied.

CHAPTER EIGHT

Laws

When we were discussing explanation in Chapter Three, we referred briefly to the role of laws. The statement was that explanations in terms of cause normally rest on one or more general laws, many of them so simple and obvious that it is absurd to cite them. We noted a law of international politics: that deliberate military attacks by one state on the territory of another commonly lead to war. But the reference to law in Chapter Three did not include a definition of the term; nor did it do much to clarify the role of law in the study of politics.

The problem of definition is crucial. The discovery or development of laws of politics can be regarded either as a major or as a very marginal pursuit, depending on the definition that one adopts. When political scientists disagree about the role of law, like as not the disagreement reflects no more than the acceptance of different definitions.

We are concerned here only with *descriptive* law. To put it negatively, we are not here concerned with the enactment or discovery or development or interpretation of prescriptive law; that is, we are not concerned with the kind of law, whether called jural, moral, ethical, or religious, that is accompanied by an alleged obligation of obedience.[1]

But what is descriptive law?

LAW AS INVARIABLE ASSOCIATION

Sometimes descriptive law is defined in terms of "invariable association."[2] There may be, for example, an invariable sequence between two specified kinds of events; when one of them occurs, the other always follows. Or it may be that when one condition is found to exist, it always happens that another also exists. Now it may or may not be true that laws of politics of this sort can be formulated. But few political scientists would want to risk their reputations by expounding such laws. *Invariable* and *always* are strong words. If *invariable* association is required, a single exception ·invalidates the law. And political behavior is commonly affected by such complex assortments of phenomena that somewhere or sometime exceptions to all "laws" are likely to occur.

It is perhaps this definition of law that has led many political scientists to deny (perhaps heatedly or scoffingly) that it is the task of the profession to discover or develop laws. Whether or not because of such attitudes, most political scientists avoid using the term *law*, or at least refrain from claiming that they have discovered or developed a law.

It is rather interesting that some unconventional students of politics are less hesitant than the conventional about the use of the word *law*. Joseph Stalin and C. Northcote Parkinson provide examples. Stalin felt that he commanded a science that revealed laws of historical development; and, naturally, he concluded that "the party of the proletariat should not guide itself in its practical activity by casual motives, but by the laws of development of society, and by practical deductions from these laws."[3] Parkinson likewise accepts the view, though puckishly, that there are laws of social development. What has come to be known as "Parkinson's law" not only asserts that expansion is a law of bureaucratic life but fixes the rate at which expansion occurs. It is a law of a more advanced type than those espoused by Stalin in that it is expressed mathematically.[4] It is a moot question whether Stalin's laws or Parkinson's are the more valid.

LAW AS A REGULARITY, UNIFORMITY, OR TENDENCY

The more conventional political scientists, eschewing the word *law*, are inclined to speak of *regularities* or *uniformities*. Thus David B. Truman, reviewing "The Impact on Political Science of the Revolution in the Behavioral Sciences," notes that "both groupings in political science [the institutionalists and the behavioralists] assume the existence and discoverability of regularities in political behavior" and, especially on the part of the behavioralists, he further notes "an increased and general commitment to the discovery of uniformities."[5]

In words, at least, some go further away from the concept *law* when they speak of a tendency. There is obviously less chance of being contradicted or refuted successfully if one says that men have a tendency to seek power than if one calls this a law of life. It is obviously correct that among Americans there is a tendency to love liberty; and it is equally correct that there is a tendency to love order. But though the statements are safe they are not very precise. They may be useful in connection with an "explanation sketch,"[6] but they are of questionable utility in connection with an attempt at full-fledged explanation.

LAW AS A STATEMENT OF WHAT HAPPENS

Actually, there is no need to avoid the use of the word *law*. It can be defined quite properly to carry virtually the same meaning as *regularity* or *uniformity*. Descriptive law can be regarded simply as a generalization indicating what usually or always happens.[7] The generalization may be a statement of probability or of relative chance. Obviously, such a law is not rendered invalid by its failure to provide a basis for predicting a special event; what might be thought of as exceptions are anticipated and provided for.

Statistical Laws

Statistical laws are in point here. They describe regularities and are at the same time probability statements. "A statistical law states that if each member of a class of objects has the character A then a certain fraction or percentage . . . has the character B."[8] For example, a statistical law might declare that if all persons under consideration are trade unionists, then under normal circumstances a certain portion of them are Democrats. Another might state that, out of every ten native white rural residents of Georgia whose annual incomes do not exceed $5,000, nine oppose integration. Still another might state the correlation between income, on the one hand, and attitudes toward income taxes and sales taxes, respectively, on the other. In principle, statistical laws are discoverable concerning many kinds of correlations; perhaps they might be developed to overlap or embrace most of the kinds of correlations to be cited below.

Empirical Sequences as Laws

Statements describing empirical sequences are closely akin to statistical laws. They can easily be illustrated. When one state builds up its military power, one or more other states commonly follow suit. When a depression occurs in a democratic country, it is likely that the party in power will lose the next election. In any political system significant changes in the distribution of military power are likely to be followed by corresponding changes in the distribution of political power. Electoral victory enhances a man's prospect of being nominated for some office again, and, conversely, defeat reduces the prospect. These laws are stated rather vaguely, of course; if knowledge were more precise and reliable, its expression in law could be altered accordingly.

General Facts as Laws

"Every general fact that can be authenticated can be regarded as a law."[9] By the same token, an empirical generalization may constitute a law.[10] Among the relevant illustrations already cited is the one concerning the relationship between military attack and the outbreak of war. It is currently a law of American politics that political parties commonly nominate candidates for the presidency whose names are well known, and that once the candidate of a party has served a term as President he is nominated for reelection. Probably it is a law of bureaucratic life that civil servants who have been assigned certain duties and powers seek to avert appeals to higher authority that would reflect on their integrity or competence. These laws could alternatively be called rules. Popper lays down the law that attempts to bring about political reform commonly arouse opposition, the intensity of the opposition roughly increasing with the significance of the reform; and he refers to the corollary that vested interests commonly develop around a status quo and want to preserve it. He formulates Lord Acton's law of corruption as follows: "You cannot give a man power over other men without tempting him to misuse it—a temptation which roughly increases with the amount of power wielded, and which very few are capable of resisting."[11] The statement that elections occur in the United States is a general fact; as such, it is a descriptive law, and, at the same time, the descriptive law correlates very closely with prescriptive law. In other words, what usually or always happens may happen on the basis of prescriptive regulations; but the fact that it happens may provide a basis for the formulation of a descriptive law.

Process Law

Gustav Bergmann has done much to clarify the concept of law.[12] Though he is concerned with law mainly in relation to psychology, and though some of the types of law which he describes seem unlikely to be developed in relation to politics, it may nevertheless be helpful to give attention to some of the distinctions he makes. Under the label *perfect knowledge,* he describes what he calls "process laws." They relate to dynamic or changing systems which develop through a sequence of stages or states. Each state is a consequence of the preceding one and, at the same time, is the necessary and sufficient condition of the succeeding one. A process law, then, is one that can be combined with knowledge of any state to give knowledge of a preceding or subsequent state. In other words, knowing the characteristics of state B and knowing the appropriate process law, one could, in effect, determine the characteristics of state A and predict the characteristics of state C. Of course, the system must be closed, i.e., relevant variables must remain unaffected by developments outside the system. The process is mechanistic or deterministic in the sense that no element in the system can do anything to alter it; the sequence of states is immutable. Obviously, process laws are bound to be rare in political science, if any can be developed at all. Within the field of politics, few systems are closed in Bergmann's sense, and presumably human choices do much to influence or determine what the next stage or state of a system will be.

Cross-sectional Laws

Bergmann deals with several other types of law under the heading *imperfect knowledge.* They are imperfect in that they do not provide an entirely reliable basis for prediction, holding "as a rule" or "under ordinary circumstances." Among the laws that express imperfect knowledge are what Bergmann calls statistical laws, cross-sectional laws, developmental laws, and historical laws. We have already mentioned statistical laws, quoting Bergmann's

definition in that connection, and so will now confine ourselves
to the other types.

Cross-sectional laws relate to any one state in a process; they
"state functional connections obtaining among the values which
several variables have at the same time." As an example of a cross-
sectional law, Bergmann cites a type referred to above in another
connection: " 'Whoever has personality trait A also has personality trait B.' " To use an example more specifically in the field of
politics, one might say that perhaps it is a law that free speech
necessarily goes with free elections; or, conversely, that free speech
and dictatorship are not found together.

Developmental Laws

Bergmann describes a developmental law as a "crude sketch or
anticipation of a process law." " 'If a system of a certain kind has
at a certain time the character A, then it will under normal conditions at some later times successively have the characters (go
through the stages) B, C, D, E, F.' " In principle, such a law might
state the stages through which a society will pass. Bergmann points
out that Comte and Spencer proposed laws of this sort. Stalin's
(or Marx's or Lenin's) laws of social development presumably belong in this category. Toynbee has sought developmental laws
relating to civilizations.

Historical Laws

To get at the meaning of the term historical law, Bergmann
uses an illustration. He cites the problem of determining why
plants grown from seed in one bag are better than plants grown
under the same conditions from seed in another bag. One solution
is arrived at by looking into the origins and background of the
seed. It is found that the poor seed came from a region in which
plants of the type in question were generally diseased, whereas
the good seed came from another region where the disease was
unknown. Thus a historical explanation is arrived at. Experience
of this sort has already demonstrated the law that if plants of a
certain variety are diseased, seeds taken from them will produce
a poor crop.

Under Bergmann's conception a historical law differs from a
developmental law. A historical law provides a basis for prediction when knowledge is available drawn from two or more tem-
porally distinct states, whereas a developmental law provides a

basis for prediction on the basis of knowledge of only one state. In connection with the illustration given above, if microbiological tests of the bad seed were to reveal traces of the disease, knowledge of the state or condition of the seed might be combined with a developmental law to permit prediction. And, in this case, the historical law would be expendable.

Perhaps analogous illustrations relating more directly to political science will be helpful. Suppose that an election turns out very differently in two precincts which in most respects seem very much alike. The person who asks why inquires into the origins and background of the voters; and he finds that the voters in one precinct are mainly of German ancestry, whereas those in the other are descended mainly from British stock. Moreover, he finds that an important issue in the election relates to the historic affinities of the two ethnic groups. Thus, he is led to a historical explanation. The relevant historical law is to the general effect that, when confronted with a certain type of issue, voters of German stock are inclined to react in one way, whereas voters of British stock are inclined to react in another way. So, again, knowledge of an existing situation can be combined with knowledge of the past to provide a basis for predicting the future.

In principle, such a historical law, like the one concerning the seed, might be displaced by a developmental law. Presumably ethnic backgrounds have left traces on the individuals just as disease left traces on the seed. The attitudes and personality traits of the two ethnic groups are likely to differ. Given reliable means of identifying the relevant attitudes and traits, knowledge of them might be combined with a developmental law to permit prediction. An illustration of this kind of analysis is to be found in a study of the "Foreign Policy of the German Federal Republic" by Karl W. Deutsch and Lewis J. Edinger.[13] Instead of looking into German history for whatever light it may shed on present and potential German behavior, they look at the results of public opinion polls, where traces of historical experience and knowledge of it are presumably revealed.

THE LAWFULNESS OF POLITICAL BEHAVIOR

As is perhaps already clear, there is little agreement among those who seek to identify types of descriptive laws, and students of the subject have so far made practically no effort to classify the

descriptive laws that are especially relevant to political science.
Nor has it been the purpose here to provide a coherent and comprehensive taxonomy. Rather the purpose has been simply to
discuss the meaning of the concept *law* and to show that, under a
quite acceptable meaning, political scientists commonly assume
the lawfulness of much political behavior and that they frequently
express knowledge of politics in the form of law. In truth, law is
normally either explicit or implicit in causal explanations. The
very definition of causal explanation calls normally for the establishment of a relationship between what is explained and a general law. As indicated earlier, the laws are often so obvious or so
trivial that no one bothers actually to cite them, but sometimes
they are neither obvious nor trivial.[14] More satisfying explanations of many political phenomena await the development of
knowledge of significant laws.

Laws explain our experience because they order it by referring particular
instances to general principles; the explanation will be the more satisfactory the more general the principle, and the greater the number of
particular instances that can be referred to it.[15]

Bergmann puts the thought somewhat differently in saying, "After
all, knowledge of causes and knowledge of laws and theories are
virtually the same thing."[16]

CHAPTER NINE

Theories

The word *theory* is full of ambiguity. Often those who use it do not themselves seem to know what meaning they intend to convey; and quite commonly those who do make their meanings clear disagree with each other. Just as with law, it therefore seems best to review various meanings.

THEORY DEFINED AS THOUGHTS, CONJECTURES, OR IDEAS

Theory is often employed as a synonym for thoughts, conjectures, or ideas. Thus political theory is political thought or political speculation, and all three terms involve the expression of political ideas or "philosophizing about government."[1] This general and vague meaning of the word shows up in various contexts.

In everyday usage we sometimes contrast theory and practice.[2] We say, for example, that in theory disarmament might be a good thing, but that we have doubts whether in practice it would turn out to be desirable. In this kind of context theory seems to denote conjecture or thought, and practice denotes action; and the further implication is that the thought would probably turn out to be false or inadequate or misleading if it were tested in action. In connection with expressions of this kind, we sometimes say "in principle" rather than "in theory."

By a slight variation of the above we contrast theory and fact. Thus we say that under democratic theory citizens are expected to be strongly motivated to participate in political life, to be informed, and to be rational, but that in fact relatively few citizens meet these expectations.[3] And we say that in communist countries the government "simply executes the will of the party, in fact as well as in theory."

Sometimes we extend the above usages by referring to any rather complicated or doubtful proposition as a theory and by treating a simple and obvious proposition as a fact or a practical observation. For example, we might cite the question of the relationship between the influence of the President of the United States over congressional actions and the number of seats controlled by his party. If the proposition were made that the President stands to lose influence when his party jumps from a majority of 55 per cent to a majority of 80 per cent, it would likely be regarded as a theory, whereas the proposition that the President gains influence when his party jumps from a minority to a majority position in each house is likely to be treated as a fact or a common observation.[4] In other words, theory is related to a presumed need for much thought and evidence—and to doubt.

Sometimes the word theory is used to designate a thought or an idea about how to solve a problem. Thus some proceed on the theory that one way to strengthen democracy is to induce more voters to participate in elections, regardless of the extent of their ignorance.

As is implied above, thoughts may be called theories whether they are normative or descriptive. To illustrate the point explicitly, we might recall the theory that each nation ought to be free to constitute itself as an independent state; and we might note the usage under which we say that relations with unfriendly country A are conducted on the basis of the theory that it has a secret alliance with unfriendly country B.

As is also implied above, we sometimes use the word theory to designate a conjecture about causal relationships or about the most effective means of promoting a given end. To make the point explicit we might cite the theory that proportional representation was among the causes of the weakness of the Weimar Republic; and we might note the theory that, given the objective of deterring a Soviet attack, the best means is to threaten massive retaliation.

Statements of what we call theory may range from a very low to a very high level of generality. Those who want to bring about the election of Smith for Mayor may operate on the theory that endorsement by the leading member of the local power elite will turn the trick. At a higher order of generality is the theory that within some or all political systems it is a power elite that really controls the governmental process.

Presumably it is usages such as the above that led Thomas P. Jenkin to note that

. . . a theory about anything is an abstracted generalization. As such it is primarily and initially a matter of mind rather than a matter of fact. . . . Such intellectualizations are not facts, no matter how closely they are related to or guided by facts. Theories, rather, are a kind of short-hand that may stand in lieu of facts.[5]

T. W. Hutchison makes an analogous distinction.[6] He speaks of "propositions of pure theory" and "propositions of applied theory." Both are theories in the sense that they reflect thought. "Pure theory" is said to consist of propositions of the type, "if p then q," and "applied theory" is illustrated by "since p therefore q." There is potential difficulty here in that the word *if* has different meanings. Sometimes it connotes *when* or even *since,* in which case Hutchison's distinction breaks down. Sometimes, however, no assertion of a factual sort is made; and this is the meaning of *if* which Hutchison intended. Under his meaning, the formulation "if p then q" implies "no empirical assertion as to the truth of p or q." Obviously, in the other formulation ("since p therefore q") the premise is declared to be empirically true. To illustrate the difference—and the ambiguity involved— we might cite the statement that "a group will have a higher rate of voting if its interests are more strongly affected by government policies."[7] Given a purely conjectural and hypothetical interpre-tation of the *if* clause, no assertion being made that differentially affected groups actually exist, the statement would be one of "pure theory" in Hutchison's sense. It might be called an axiom or theorem.[8] But those who construe the *if* to mean *when* must conclude that the statement expresses an "applied theory."

In most of the above usages, if not in all of them, what is called a theory might alternatively be called a hypothesis. Sometimes the choice between the two words seems to turn on nothing more serious than the difference in the number of syllables they contain. Sometimes, though, *hypothesis* seems to connote a greater degree of doubt than *theory*; thus, when a hypothesis is regarded as pretty well confirmed it may be called a theory, and when it is regarded as completely confirmed it may be called a fact or a law.[9] Jenkin adjures against such a usage in the statement quoted above.

POLITICAL THEORY

DEFINED AS A FIELD WITHIN POLITICAL SCIENCE

Students of politics have, of course, long employed the word *theory* in a special way by treating something called "political theory" as a subdivision of political science. Texts are written and courses are offered in political theory, just as in other subdivisions such as comparative government and international politics. The practice has an objectionable aspect in that it seems to suggest that all statements expressing theory belong in the subdivision labeled political theory; and, conversely, it seems to suggest that books and courses in other subdivisions go beyond their proper limits if any theory is included. If theory is taken to be synonymous with thought, this attitude becomes disastrous for the other subdivisions.

Considered as a subdivision of political science, political theory is not easy to define. The suggestion here is that it is concerned with two different kinds of knowledge. In the first place, it is concerned with political belief systems of a general and comprehensive sort; they can be called rationales or ideologies. In the second place, it is concerned with political philosophy—thought about political thought. These two kinds of "political theory" will be discussed in turn.

Theory as Knowledge of General Belief Systems

Political theorists are clearly concerned with the normative— with moral and ethical questions. They inquire into beliefs about ends or goals or values. They examine conceptions of the good and the right.[10] Moreover, the normative beliefs with which they are concerned are mainly of a general sort. If they inquire into immediate or intermediate ends, it is likely to be for the purpose of determining how they relate to broader ends that are thought of as "ultimate" or nearly so. Perhaps the purpose is to test or clarify or somehow develop conceptions of "ultimate" ends, or perhaps to see whether immediate or intermediate ends can themselves be clarified or adjusted in the light of the "ultimate."

Suppose, for example, that the political theorist concerns himself with the normative proposition that it is good and right to have a political system in which dignity and worth are accorded to the individual simply because he is a human being. It is quite possible that he will associate this proposition with the existence of democracy, and that he will associate democracy with widespread participation in decision making. This in turn may lead him to inquire into the extent to which participation occurs in a democracy and the conditions affecting it. He may want to know something as specific as why a given voter participated or failed to participate in an election, or what influenced the voter to support one candidate rather than another. This may seem to take him out of the subdivision of political science called political theory and into another subdivision called, for example, political parties, propaganda, and electoral behavior; and in a way it does. But his essential concern is not with electoral behavior in relation to the fate of a political party or even in relation to the operation of a given government; rather his essential concern is with the general normative proposition stated above concerning respect for the dignity and worth of the individual. Similarly, a political theorist might concern himself with the council-manager system of municipal government not with a view to assessing its efficiency or its chances of survival but rather with a view to determining how it relates to the general proposition that democracy is good.

Political theorists sometimes give personal endorsement to normative conceptions, recommending values to be promoted. Sometimes they simply describe the normative conceptions of others. In either case they ordinarily go on to examine in a descriptive way the conditions and practices that are associated with the values under scrutiny. The notion of democracy, for example, connotes not only values to be promoted but also the means of promoting them. A theorist who recommends justice or who simply reports that justice is commonly posited as a value is likely to go on to describe the conditions or causes that lead justice to be upheld or denied. The point is that, though political theory is concerned with the normative, it is an error to think of it as limited to the normative. It also includes substantial amounts of description and explanation.

The fact that political theory, so defined, overlaps with each of the other subdivisions of political science is a possible source of confusion and difficulty among different political scientists. The theorist who enters other subdivisions may seem to be abandoning his special field for another one. And the person in another subdivision who wants to get the beliefs pertaining to it related to broader and more general belief systems may likewise seem to be entering terrain that ostensibly belongs to others.

Confusion and difficulties of these sorts have been kept at a minimum so far by the very pronounced tendency of political theorists to confine themselves to general belief systems as expounded by great authors of the past. Thus, courses and texts in political theory are commonly histories of political thought, i.e., analyses of the political thought of a series of persons considered in chronological order—say, from Plato to Lenin. Under this practice, "theory" is distinguishable from other subdivisions not only in terms of the general and comprehensive nature of the belief systems examined but also in terms of the question whether the beliefs are set forth in writing regarded as classical.

But obviously the belief systems examined need not be those of the classical writers. They can be those of living persons, whether political leaders or the man in the street. Further, there is no reason why the focus cannot be on belief systems as such (e.g., on liberalism or communism) rather than on the thoughts of classical writers.[11] Even those who spend their lives determining precisely what it was that Aristotle or Aquinas or Machiavelli said or meant will probably grant that for many purposes it is less important to know which classical writer said what than to know how beliefs are interrelated. Greater emphasis on general belief systems may make it somewhat more difficult to distinguish theory from other subdivisions of political science, but the difficulty may have its compensations.[12]

Theory as Philosophy: Thought about Thought

The second kind of knowledge encompassed by the subdivision of political science called political theory is sometimes called political philosophy.

This book is called a philosophical analysis. We discussed the meaning of the word *philosophy* in the preface. The statement made in the preface is that *philosophy,* in the sense used here, denotes general conceptions of purposes and methods, ends and means, in a field of scholarship, e.g., in political inquiry. Theory in the sense of philosophy is thus addressed to such questions as the following: What should political scientists be attempting to achieve? What standards of judgment should guide them in choosing what to do? What criteria should be employed in deciding what to teach and write—and in appraising what others teach and write? What sorts of inquiry are to be regarded as worth while, and what sorts of accomplishments as satisfying? Thus, philosophy consists of thought about thought. Normative postulates, logic, and analysis are combined in an effort to develop a coherent rationale for the guidance of the scholar.

In somewhat less general terms, philosophy has been defined as "the study of the nature and implications of rational thought."[13] It calls for the clarification of thought, the elucidation of meaning, the reduction and elimination of confusion stemming from language. Used in this sense, the term political philosophy denotes the logical analysis of thought about politics expressed (implicitly or explicitly) either by political actors or by commentators on the political process. And the term logical analysis denotes an effort to identify the component elements of what is being examined as well as to determine whether these elements fit together in a way in which the actors or commentators assume.[14]

We might note that *philosophy* in this sense is sometimes called *theory*. Thus Arnold Brecht's book on *Political Theory* fits under this definition of *philosophy*. Further, we might note that *theory* in the sense of the analysis of belief systems is sometimes called *philosophy*. Thus, A. R. M. Murray says, "Political *philosophies* . . . may be provisionally divided into Moral and Naturalistic *Theories* of the State." But, though the terms are sometimes employed interchangeably, a distinction is permissible.

THEORY DEFINED AS A CONCEPTUAL SCHEME

To define theory as any conjecture, thought, or idea is to assign the word an extremely broad and loose meaning—so broad and loose that the word is of little utility in conveying precise meaning. To define it in terms of the subdivision of political science called political theory is somewhat more helpful, but a search for narrower definitions is still in place. Our search will relate mainly, if not exclusively, to descriptive theory.

Not far removed from the notion that theory is thought is

the notion that it is a conceptual scheme, i.e., a set of interrelated concepts. As we have seen, concepts reflect thought and convey it. They are the product of a discriminating intelligence, which puts things that are alike into a distinct category, and names them. The very process of developing a concept requires some insight into relationships—relationships among the things named and relationships between the new concept and others. And once a concept has been formulated there is likely to be a deliberate search for further relationships; perhaps the search will lead to the formulation of additional concepts naming things of the same general sort, perhaps to new and "higher level" concepts which themselves name other concepts that have been seen to belong together in the same general category.

These processes are identified with theorizing in different ways. Sometimes the very effort to analyze and clarify the meaning of a concept is called theorizing.[15] In other words, sometimes a definition is regarded as either a theory or a significant part of a theory. For example, the definitional statement that politics is a struggle for power might be regarded either as a theory or as a proposition that is important to the development of theory. For that matter, this whole book consists of an effort to clarify selected concepts and so, in this sense, might be said to consist of theory.

Whether or not theorizing is defined to include efforts to clarify meanings, it is sometimes defined as "essentially a set of propositions that assert that certain concepts are interrelated in certain ways."[16] Since so many sentences assert a relationship between concepts, this statement does not do as much as it might to narrow down the meaning of theory. But it suggests that we have a theory when, for example, we make a series of statements like the following: "The rulers of sovereign states generally seek to preserve the state. History shows that the existence of states is sometimes threatened by the aggression of other states. Thus rulers feel compelled to seek a relative power position for their state which will either deter or defeat aggression." What we have here is a series of concepts which are interrelated in a series of propositions. In other words, we have, in brief form, a conceptual scheme, i.e., a theory.

The above paragraphs reflect an assumption that we start with concepts and build conceptual schemes or theories from them.

This is true, of course, but it is scarcely the whole truth. The process sometimes goes in the other direction. That is, once we have a conceptual scheme or theory, it may lead us to look for new concepts that fit into the scheme; further, as we noted earlier when discussing concepts, it may lead us either to fail to see or to ignore data or concepts that do not fit. Thus if we start with the notion that rulers want to preserve the state we are likely to be alert to relevant data. We may see that technological developments make unrestricted war of questionable value as a means of promoting the desired end, and so we may develop the concept of limited war. We can relate this concept to others in ways we consider useful. It would be possible to develop a vast number of concepts, but we do not ordinarily develop them unless we see some way of using them; i.e., we do not ordinarily develop them unless we see some way of relating them to other concepts and using them to answer questions.[17] We might, for example, speak of *lanoceanatio,* making the concept designate the ratio between the distances covered by a state's land boundaries and its sea boundaries. But it seems highly improbable that this concept will be taken up and used, for there is no apparent way of relating it meaningfully to other concepts. It seems unlikely to be helpful in answering any question that interests us; it seems to be irrelevant to existing conceptual schemes, i.e., to be lacking in theoretical relevance.

It might now be recalled that Easton defines a fact as "a particular ordering of reality in terms of a theoretical interest"; we can now see that the reference is to an ordering of reality in terms of a conceptual scheme. It may be true that the lanoceanatio of country X is 2 to 1, but we do not treat this as a fact of international politics (or as a useful concept) because this particular ordering of reality does not fit into a conceptual scheme or theory. In short, theory in the sense of a conceptual scheme is both a result of conceptualization and a guide to further conceptualization.

Sometimes it happens, of course, that not just one but a great many facts or concepts clamor for attention which really do not fit into the dominant conceptual scheme; we must then suppress or distort them, or abandon the scheme in favor of another one. An example of this can be found in conceptual schemes relating to war and peace. One scheme can be briefly stated as follows:

States normally seek peace with each other. Statesmen and diplomats are virtuous men who act in behalf of peace, attempting through political action to resolve such disputes as arise. But sometimes through ignorance they fail, and sometimes they are manipulated or displaced by sinister conspirators, and so war occurs. Then political action is replaced by military action, and the diplomats are replaced by generals, until somehow peace and normalcy are restored.

Many facts and concepts fit into this conceptual scheme, and some have regarded the scheme as satisfactory. But others see a substantial number of facts and concepts that do not fit, and so abandon the scheme for another which runs more or less as follows:

Conflict is the essence of politics, including international politics, even if it be over the terms on which cooperation will occur. Within a variety of limits participants in the conflict choose the ends to pursue and the means to employ. Depending on the choices they make, the conflict ranges from the mild and verbal to the extreme and violent. At a somewhat arbitrarily selected point along this scale, the conflict comes to be described as war rather than peace. A comparison of the international political system with the system prevailing within the more advanced states suggests that international war can be expected to occur more frequently than civil war, regardless of the extent of the virtue and knowledge of the decision makers. In any event, those who act on behalf of the state are not necessarily made either virtuous or evil by the nature of the office they hold.

This type of conceptual scheme has substantially replaced the first type, for it accommodates many more of the facts and concepts of international politics. Possibly a third type of scheme can be developed which will perform the service still more fully.

THEORY DEFINED AS AN INTERPRETATION OR A POINT OF VIEW

Karl Popper offers a definition of theory that is somewhat similar to the notion that it is a conceptual scheme. He refers to theory, or to quasi-theory, as an interpretation or a "crystallization of a point of view."

Popper bases this conception of theory on a fact we discussed in Chapter Three: that a great many rather complex sets of conditions usually operate to produce the social and political events that we regard as significant, and that different types of explanation can be sought on the basis of various approaches and at various levels of discourse. Description and explanation, we said, are rarely complete; they must be selective. But on what basis do we choose the data to consider? Random choice is unlikely to produce a satisfying result, for it would likely lead to a number of unrelated statements. The alternative to random choice, as Popper sees it, is the adoption of either a point of view or an interpretation. Preferably the act should be conscious and explicit so as to minimize self-deception and maximize the prospect that the standards of selection will be critically and intelligently applied. Adopting a point of view is like selecting a vantage point from which to look at a landscape. It permits one to make a true report while granting that the scene may look very different when observed from another angle; in other words, differing reports reflecting differing points of view may all be correct as far as they go. A point of view may, however, develop into an interpretation; i.e., there may be a "crystallization of a point of view." In Popper's scheme a crystallized point of view or an interpretation amounts virtually to an explanation, the difference being that explanations can be refuted or established whereas interpretations always remain somewhat conjectural. In his view, though explanation may be possible in the natural sciences where replication can occur (i.e., a repetition of the same experiment, perhaps by different persons), interpretation is the usual end point in the study of social developments. The interpretations are acceptable in varying degrees. To be most acceptable they ought to be internally consistent and consistent with factual knowledge; further, they ought to bring a maximum number of facts and concepts into meaningful relationship. Interpretations that lose out in competition with others are to be abandoned. Others are to be entertained on a purely tentative basis, it being recognized that still more acceptable interpretations may be developed.

As Popper himself points out, when he defines theory as a point of view or an interpretation, he is saying that it is equivalent to a working hypothesis.[18]

Robert K. Merton refers to a similar conception of theory when he says:

Much of what is described in textbooks as sociological theory consists of general orientations toward substantive materials. Such orientations involve broad postulates which indicate *types* of variables which are somehow to be taken into account rather than specifying determinate relationships between particular variables.[19]

Theory in this sense is probably the approximate equivalent of what is sometimes called a "frame of reference."[20]

THEORY DEFINED AS THE CONSUMMATION OF EXPLANATION

We have been dealing mainly with descriptive theory. When we were discussing description in Part I we noted that it serves quite a range of purposes. Sometimes what is called description simply provides us with isolated statements of true information; sometimes it provides a background story or a significant narrative; sometimes, we said, it gives information concerning the organization, structure, and mechanics of a system; and sometimes it provides explanation. The fuller a description is, the more likely it is to include explanation; that is, the more likely it is to include statements describing connections and interrelationships among phenomena so as to give knowledge of reasons for, or causes of, actions or conditions. In other words, the fuller a description the more likely it is to tell us not only "what," but also "how" and "why."[21]

Obviously, this means that descriptive theory is explanatory. A review of the uses and meanings of theory which we have just surveyed shows quickly that the idea of explanation—usually in terms of reasons or causes—is very prominent. The first theory we mentioned—that disarmament might be a good thing—reflects an assumption that armaments may cause (or help to cause) an undesirable state of affairs and that disarmament might be a means of bringing a more desirable state of affairs into existence. In other words, the assumption is that each state of affairs is explained, in whole or in part, by the level of armaments. Similarly, most of the other conjectures, thoughts, or ideas we mentioned above have something to do with explanation. Implicitly the conceptual schemes cited, relating to the motivations of statesmen and the causes of war, are also explanatory: Popper explicitly identified what he called a "crystallization of a point of view" with explanation.

This suggests that theory might be defined in terms of explanation; and, in fact, many do conceive of theory in this sense. Thus Melvin Marx says that "all theories aim at explanation, which means the establishment of functional relationships between variables."[22] Without offering an explicit definition, Eckstein simply assumes that in one of its meanings theory consists of explanation in the sense of ordering experience; under his conception, theories vary from the partial to the comprehensive, depending on the range of political experience that they order.[23] James W. Prothro comments that "every political scientist who earns his pay is a theorist in the sense that he is attempting to arrive at generalizations to explain at least some range of political behavior."[24] Beer and Ulam express the view that the political scientist should "look for uniformities of behavior and recurrent relationships and . . . try to generalize from this empirical basis." And, having stated empirical generalizations or laws, they should go on to introduce theories that explain. The formulation of Beer and Ulam is that "the law or empirical generalization states *what* happens; the theory explains *why*."[25] Bergmann takes the same view: "Statements of individual fact are explained by laws; laws are explained by theories."[26]

. . . A theory is a group of laws deductively connected. More accurately, a theory is a group of laws, usually rather few, from which others, usually a larger number, have actually been deduced and from which one expects to deduce still further ones.[27]

We might recall Bergmann's statement that knowledge of causes and knowledge of laws and theories are virtually the same thing. To Ernest Nagel the word *theory* designates "an explicit formulation of determinate relations between a set of variables, in terms of which a fairly extensive class of empirically ascertainable regularities (or laws) can be explained."[28] And Nagel says: "In science the answer to the question 'why' is . . . always a theory. . . . No matter how far the question 'why' is pressed—and it may be pressed indefinitely—it must terminate in a theory."[29]

It may as well be acknowledged that none of these formulations provides a crystal-clear set of criteria for identifying a theory. Whichever definition is adopted, doubt is likely to be associated with the assertion that a given statement or combination of statements constitutes a theory. The problem is made all the more difficult by the similarities between theories, hypotheses, and laws. In truth, in most contexts, if not in all, the words hypothesis and theory are interchangeable, and laws and theories have so much in common that an effort to establish a clear distinction would not be worth while. As indicated above, Bergmann takes the view that theories incorporate laws. Given the vagueness of the distinctions, there is something to be said for the not uncommon practice of avoiding or minimizing the use of the words and speaking instead of generalizations, propositions, conceptions, or notions.

THE LEVELS OF GENERALITY OF THEORIES

We have noted before that facts can range from the very specific to the very general and that propositions can be made at different levels of generality. If a proposition explains only one or a few events, it is said to be at a low level of generality, whereas if it explains a very large number of events it is said to be at a high level of generality. Now it is obvious that facts and propositions combine to make theories, and that the theories may be expressed at various levels. We can have low-level or "narrow gauge" theories, or we can have high-level or general theories (or "theory in a grand manner"), or we can have intermediate theories.[30] Perhaps it will be helpful to compare a theoretical system to a tree. The outermost small branches would represent the data—the facts and concepts—with which we begin. As we proceed inward from these outermost branches, we find that they merge into somewhat larger branches. Each larger branch becomes a low-level theory explaining relationships between our bits of data. The larger branches in turn merge into others that are still larger; i.e., intermediate theory is developed. And finally we come to the trunk of the tree, representing high-level, general theory. Whether any student of politics has actually arrived at the trunk, i.e., whether anyone has produced a comprehensive or general theory, is perhaps debatable. And those who doubt whether such a theory has been developed must also suspend judgment on the question whether it can be done. If what we now have is a considerable number of partial theories stated at various levels of generality and reflecting various approaches to politics, then we simply cannot yet be sure whether a comprehensive, general theory of political action is achievable. Obviously, it is easier to explain a little than to explain a great deal. In other words, narrow-gauge theories are easier to develop than general theories, and they are more likely to be sound. Difficult as it may be, we at least have a fair chance to develop a theory that explains why a given Congressman voted for the resolution authorizing the American President to use the armed forces in the Middle East in certain circumstances. It is quite a different matter to develop a general theory that explains all international friction or conflict, to say nothing of a still more general theory that would explain all political friction both within and among countries. "Political theory in the grand manner can rarely, if ever, meet rigorous criteria of truth."[31]

A theory that goes against evidence or reason must, of course, be rejected. But, especially at the higher levels of generality, it is often as difficult to prove a theory false as to prove it true. When this is the case, we may have two or more "grand" political theories with approximately equal (but still dubious) claims to validity. Various theories explaining political behavior are in point, e.g., those stressing, respectively, the desire for wealth, power, and deference as motivating factors. Where high-level theories all seem more or less plausible but where it is impossible to confirm one and disconfirm the others with assurance, one possible response is to discard the dubious theories entirely and to concentrate on theories at lower levels of generality. Alternatively, one or another of the high-level theories may be adopted, despite doubts about it.

It is noteworthy that in the natural sciences high-level theories are not uncommonly chosen from among two or more possible alternatives.[32] Observable data and logic regularly preclude the adoption of some theories, but in many cases supplementary considerations come into play in the choices that are made. There is ordinarily a preference for simplicity or economy, and among the reasons for this preference is the probability that simple theories will be more heuristic. Closely related is the preference for those theories that provide the most trustworthy basis for prediction, whether because this permits the theory to be tested or because it contributes to the expansion of knowledge. Social considerations sometimes also influence choices, for there is commonly a preference for theories that are supportive of a philosophic outlook and way of life that is deemed desirable.

Students of politics differ in their inclination to follow the natural scientists in consciously formulating and adopting high-level theories. European scholars seem so far to have been bolder than those of the United States, for a very high proportion of high-level theories, whether normative or descriptive, have come from Europe.[33] The reasons for this are not entirely clear. Perhaps there has been greater stress in the United States on finding "the facts," and less on reflective inquiry. Perhaps there has been a greater tendency in this country to insist that the statements of scholars be correct, whether or not they are thoughful and significant. Perhaps there has simply been a lack of a full understanding of the nature of explanation and of the role of theory in explanation.[84]

Along a different line, the reluctance of American scholars to attempt to develop high-level descriptive theory may reflect complacency both about the present and about the future. Those who believe that the major problems have been solved, and who are therefore pretty well satisfied with things as they are and as they seem likely to be, may perhaps not feel driven to inquire into fundamentals in an effort to learn how the future might be shaped more to their liking. In truth, when things are thought to be going well, there may be a more or less deliberate and conscious refusal to probe into fundamentals for fear that what is learned might be disquieting and disturbing. But with the many and profound changes that are occurring in other realms—in the natural sciences, in military technology and strategy, in the scope of governmental activity, and even in the area of studying and shaping public opinion—it may well be asked whether the future is so sure and whether it is not urgently imperative to find out whether and how it can be shaped in a desirable way. If this is the objective, then it becomes important to develop descriptive theory, and to push it to the highest feasible levels of generality—accepting the risk that high-level theory may be wrong and always attempting to test and to improve it.

MODELS

The word _model_ has come to be widely used, generally without a clear indication of the meaning intended. Again it will be best to seek its meaning(s) through an examination of usage. But note might be made at the outset of the fact that imitation, explanation, and prescription are all associated with the notion of a model and that some confusion results.

Often there are references to physical models of physical things. Thus an architect may prepare a model of a structure that is to be built. An aircraft designer may prepare a model of a projected airplane. An engineer developing a flood control project may construct a physical model of the terrain and rivers involved. A real estate operator may open a model home for inspection. Imitation or duplication, perhaps on a different scale, seems to be the essential feature of a model in this sense. It must be like the real thing in any respects that are important to the purpose at hand. The model and what it represents must be in some degree isomorphic; that is, they must be similar in structure or form or in other significant characteristics. If there is a one-to-one correspondence in every respect between the model and the thing modeled, the isomorphism is said to be complete, and either of the items can be regarded as a perfect model of the other.

These models may also have a good deal to do with explanation and prescription. Unless the models are completely isomorphic—unless the imitation is perfect—some kind of selection occurs. Thus the engineer who makes a model for flood control purposes will include in his replica only the features of the terrain that seem to him to be relevant to floods. He builds his model on the basis of a theory about the cause of floods, and he can check his theory through tests. Similarly, he formulates a theory about the probable effect of placing a dam at a given point, and then checks it in an experiment. Thus he builds explanation into his model, and it represents a theory. In short, if imitation or isomorphism is all that is involved, a model is simply a model. If explanation or prescription is added, the model becomes the reflection or expression of a theory.

Sometimes there are references to physical models in descriptions of social phenomena. Thus a pyramid provides a model of a class structure in society, and scales provide a model used to depict the impartial administration of justice. This usage is obviously figurative and suggestive; no clear meaning is indicated.[35]

Sometimes a mental image is called a model, whether of an actual or a fictitious phenomenon. The process of abstraction, described in Chapter Six, can be said to involve the development of models of this sort. "Abstraction consists in replacing the part of the universe under consideration by a model of similar but simpler structure."[36] To use the same illustration employed in Chapter Six, to become aware of the form cow as opposed to the form bull or the form sheep is to develop models, i.e., images that are simplified and composite versions of a number of individual cows, bulls, and sheep. Under this usage, a model is an abstract image—a simplified and composite version—of a class of phenomena. Such a model is essentially imitative or isomorphic, though the isomorphism is incomplete.

When the notion of an "economic man" is advanced and called a model, it is presumably an abstract mental image that is involved; and the same can be said with regard to the notion of a "political man" or "political type." (An "economic man" always chooses the opportunities for profit in each situation, and the "political man" always chooses the opportunities for power, in preference to other opportunities.)[37] But in this case it is doubtful whether the imitative element is dominant. The thought is not that the model is isomorphic with any one person or even with a composite version of a number of different people. Rather, models of this sort are advanced in connection with searches for explanation. A complete departure from reality is accepted in the hope that it will shed light on reality. Here the notion of a model seems to coincide closely with the notion of "pure theory," described above. That is, it seems to provide a basis for propositions of the "if . . . then" variety. In other words, it permits the statement that if a given person acts as a political man would, he will make such and such a choice in a designated situation. Such statements may be fruitful in suggesting empirical inquiry, but do not themselves add to empirical knowledge.

Obviously, the physical models, the mental images, and the abstract conceptions or fictions to which we have referred can be described. In other words, the models can be made verbal. Verbal models that are explanatory become indistinguishable from theories.

Further, we may start with a verbal model. One legal code or one book or one sentence can provide a model for another. A rule or a descriptive law or a theory may serve as a model for another rule, descriptive law, or theory. Thus, "if the laws of one theory have the same form as the laws of another theory, then one may be said to be a model for the other."[38] Here isomorphism appears again. A correspondence is specified between attributes of the model and what is modeled. Neither explanation nor prescription enters in.

The above references are all to models that are simply imitative or descriptive (explanatory). But we should note that models sometimes represent a conception of the desirable, constituting patterns or ideal types, and so take on a normative or prescriptive quality. Thus one of the characters in the *Pirates of Penzance* claimed, "I am the very model of a modern Major-General." In this sense, there are also model professors, model wives, and model students. And there are models who display dresses in fashion shops and models who pose for artists. To name them as models is to prescribe. Imitation is recommended. Those who want to excel as Major-Generals, professors, wives, or students, and those who want to achieve the beauty of the fashion model or the artist's model should seek an isomorphic correspondence of a one-to-one sort with the model. Now a prescriptive model is obviously a prescriptive theory.

In sum, differing definitions of *model* are advanced, depending on whether the focus is on the imitative aspects of the model or on the explanatory or prescriptive aspects. May Brodbeck advances the one definition, stressing isomorphism and considering it "unnecessary" to give the term such a broad meaning that it becomes a synonym for *theory*.[39] Herbert A. Simon finds that *model* is in fact a synonym for *theory*, and seems to prefer the latter term. Asked to present a paper on "Models: Their Uses and Limitations," he defined his subject in his opening two sentences. "In contemporary usage the term 'model' is, I think, simply a synonym for 'theory.' I am to speak, then, on 'Theories: Their Uses and Limitations.' "[40] In effect, he found the word *model* unnecessary.

THEORY, ACTION, AND DOCTRINE

In the main we have been treating theory (like fact, concept, and so on) as an expression of knowledge. Whatever the level of generality, a theory is a summary statement of what we think we know about the explanation of phenomena.

From the preceding pages, however, it is already apparent that theory is not merely an expression of knowledge.[41] It may also point the way to the acquisition of new knowledge. Suppose, for example, that our efforts to explain the rules of international law lead us to the theory that, by and large, the influence of a state over the development of law on any issue rests on two factors: (1) its reputed or actual ability to impose its desires through coercive measures, and (2) its reputed or actual willingness to employ such measures. In other words, international law is a function of the relative power and interest of the states concerned. The very enunciation of the theory leads to questions concerning circumstances in which it does or does not hold true, and the questions may lead to an enhancement of knowledge. Even more, such a theory concerning international law suggests questions and hypotheses concerning the factors shaping the development of law within countries. If international law reflects a combination of power and interest, what of assumptions that domestic law reflects the common good, or the public interest, or justice? And what of the assumption that government and the state constitute a sort of impartial arbiter, serving to "adjust" conflicting claims? Obviously, the theory points the way to inquiries outside the field in which it was developed. Conant puts special emphasis on this quality. Though he seems to be defining *science* rather than *theory* in the following passage, both here and elsewhere he treats the two words as virtually synonymous.

I venture to define science as a series of interconnected concepts and conceptual schemes arising from experiment and observation and fruitful of further experiments and observations. The test of a scientific theory is, I suggest, its fruitfulness—. . . [its ability] to suggest, stimulate, and direct experiment. . . . A scientific theory is . . . a policy—an economical and fruitful guide to action by scientific investigators.[42]

In another respect, too, theory is more than a simple expression of knowledge. Recall that in Chapter Four we noted that explanation is closely related to prediction: that if we can explain an event after it has happened, then, given knowledge of the elements in the explanation, we should have been able to predict it, at least in terms of the probability of its occurrence. If this is true, and if theory is the consummation of explanation, it follows that theory should be helpful in prediction. Given a theory, we should be able to make deductions from it concerning future events, or concerning the probable consequences of this or that action. We might predict, for example, that an increase in China's relative power will lead to insistent demands for change in some aspects of the legal status quo. Or, given the theory that people who are satisfied and secure tend to want peace and to avoid risk, we might predict that the promotion of economic development in the Soviet Union and a marked reduction in Western activities which seem threatening from Moscow's point of view would enhance the prospects of peace. Conversely, if we accept the theory that the Soviet leaders are relentless in their determination to extend communism wherever they can, then we might predict that the economic development of the Soviet Union would simply provide a basis for a more effective struggle against the West and also that any seeming reduction in the power or determination of the West would encourage bolder and more aggressive Soviet policies. Or, given the theory that in elections people vote according to their economic self-interest, we might predict the reactions of different income groups to the various positions a candidate might take on an economic issue; and we might go further and predict that a substantially egalitarian society is the probable result of democracy and universal suffrage.

In Chapter Four we said that we predict, in part, in order to contribute to the rationality of decision making. Now we can say that we advance theories, in part, for this reason. The scholarly purpose of theorizing may simply be to express knowledge and to help in enhancing it. The social purpose is to provide a basis for more reliable predictions, on the basis of which rational choices can be made.

In this context it may be worth while to note the relationship between what is called theory and what is called doctrine. To the extent that a distinction between them is reflected in usage, it does not seem to rest on differences in substantive content. Rather, it seems to rest on attitudes toward the propositions and on the role assigned to them. Where the propositions are regarded simply as the fruit and the tools of scholarship—where they are related solely to intellectual activity—they may be said to constitute a theory. Where they become a guide to action, they are more likely to be called a doctrine. This distinction has a corollary. Propositions that guide action are, for this purpose, accepted as true; and they may really be believed, perhaps as an act of faith and perhaps fanatically. Where faith and fervor are involved, a theory that guides action is all the more likely to be called a doctrine.[43]

Part III

APPROACHES IN THE STUDY OF POLITICS

Introduction

Parts I and II concerned purposes in the study of politics and the forms in which knowledge is expressed. Now the object is to identify, clarify, and appraise various approaches used in the study of politics and to give briefer attention to the notions of method and technique.

Like so many of the terms that we have examined, *approach, method,* and *technique* are assigned various meanings—or are employed with only the remotest suggestion of the meaning intended. Even such an admirable book as *Approaches to the Study of Politics* contains nothing—at least nothing explicit—to indicate what characteristics of the contents led to the use of the word *approaches* in the title.[1] Five of the seven chapter headings in another book focus on *approaches,* identified as deductive, descriptive, quantitative, sociological and psychological, and practical; but again there is no definition of the word *approach,* no apparent reason why there should not also have been discussions of inductive, normative, qualitative, historical and economic, and other approaches, and no comment on the question whether and in what way the so-called approaches have enough in common to justify the common label.[2] Frequently *approach* and *method* are treated as synonyms, and so are *method* and *technique.* There are references to *methodological approaches*—but with no attempt to distinguish such approaches from others that are presumably nonmethodological.

The word *approach* is used both in relation to politics (or the study of politics) in a global sense and in relation to this or that aspect of politics. For example, one might speak either of a Marxist approach to politics or of a Marxist approach to the problem of war. The meaning assigned to the word in Chapter

Three applies in either case. An approach consists of criteria of selection—criteria employed in selecting the problems or questions to consider and in selecting the data to bring to bear; it consists of standards governing the inclusion and exclusion of questions and data.

The word *method* is commonly assigned either of two meanings. It may denote (1) epistemological assumptions on which the search for knowledge is based, e.g., positivist and rationalist methods, or, much more commonly, (2) the operations or activities that occur in the acquisition and treatment of data. Method in the first sense was discussed in the Introduction to Part I. Here the focus will be on method in the second sense. So conceived, a method may also be called a *technique*; the difference, if any, seems to be that techniques may be more susceptible to routine or mechanical application and more highly specialized, depending less (once they are mastered) on imaginative intelligence.

In brief, approaches consist of criteria for selecting problems and relevant data, whereas methods are procedures for getting and utilizing data.[3]

In Part III the focus will be primarily on approaches and secondarily on methods and techniques. The distribution of emphasis reflects, in the main, an assumption that knowledge of approaches is more important than knowledge of methods. In part, also, it reflects a desire to compensate for past tendencies in political science; for, while questions of method have been widely neglected, questions of approach have been largely ignored.

The number of possible approaches under our definition is very large. It is as if politics were like the center of a circle, approachable from any point on the circle—with one approach, say, for each of the circle's 360 degrees. It would be impractical to attempt to identify each possible line of approach separately. But we can classify them, and then compare and evaluate them by types. The categories employed here have already been listed in Chapter Three. The hope is that explicit attention to the range of approaches open will facilitate conscious and deliberate, and thus presumably rational, choice concerning them—whether the choice be to adopt just one approach or to employ two or more of them in attacking the same problem. Some eclecticism is usually desirable and necessary.

Part III contains five chapters. The first, Chapter Ten, reflects the fact that approaches are sometimes identified with academic disciplines. For example, there are references to historical or economic or psychological approaches. Chapter Eleven examines those approaches that focus on a salient feature of politics, e.g., on institutions, on law, on power, on decision making, and on the decisions themselves (i.e., on the ends and means selected). Chapter Twelve is concerned with the so-called "behavioral" approach and with general systems theory. Chapter Thirteen deals with approaches identified with explanatory theories, whether environmental (i.e., geographic or economic), psychological, or ideological.

These categories are not mutually exclusive. A historical approach might also be economic; and a Freudian approach, classified here under explanatory theories, might be treated as an approach identified with psychology as a discipline. Thus the categories do not meet the requirements of logic. They are employed nevertheless in the belief that they reflect usage and in the belief that it is more significant to comment on usage than to devise an entirely logical classification scheme.

Finally, Chapter Fourteen discusses methods and techniques, the purpose being to elucidate the meaning of some words rather than to give practical instruction. There is a discussion of analysis as a method, of quantitative and qualitative methods, of induction and deduction, of comparison as a method, and of the notion of scientific method.

CHAPTER TEN

Academic Disciplines as Approaches

Approaches are sometimes identified in terms of academic disciplines or subdivisions thereof. Thus there are references to historical, economic, sociological, psychological, geographic, and philosophic approaches. Those employing these terms apparently assume that certain criteria for selecting questions and data go with each academic discipline. We will see to what extent this is true and to what extent political scientists can advantageously employ the criteria of other disciplines in the study of politics.

HISTORICAL APPROACHES

The word *history* is used in a number of senses. There is history-as-actuality, history-as-record, and history-as-written; and history is the name of an academic discipline.

"History-as-actuality means all that has been felt, thought, imagined, said, and done by human beings as such and in relation to one another and to their environment since the beginning of mankind's operations on this planet." History-as-record consists of documentary and other primary evidences of history-as-actuality. History-as-written is presumably based upon history-as-record and consists of various kinds of narratives or accounts of a portion of history-as-actuality.[1] As an academic discipline, history is what is taught and written by members of departments of history.

Obviously, history-as-actuality encompasses a multitude of different kinds of activities. History-as-written can therefore vary considerably in its subject matter. There can be histories of art, of science, of religion, of political life, and so on; and there can be histories concerned with interrelationships among various kinds of activities. For the most part, history-as-written is the work of members of departments of history; but, still, history is also written by others. The word *historian* may therefore designate either a member of a department of history or anyone who writes history; thus a political scientist may also be a historian—if he writes political history. (Lest this appear to rob members of departments of history of distinction, let it be pointed out that under this formulation they have the opportunity to write in such a way as to be political scientists.)

The above statements imply that, regardless of the academic affiliation of the author, history has distinguishing characteristics. (Note that from this point on, *history* will stand for history-as-written, and the word *historical* will refer to history in this sense.) The question now is what the distinguishing characteristics of history are and how sharp they are. In other words, the question concerns the characteristics of historical approaches.

We might begin by recalling that in Chapter Two we discussed the treatment of questions calling for orientation or background. We likened politics to a drama with the world as the theater, and noted that people inevitably enter the theater after the drama has begun. We observed that their need for orientation or background can be met in various ways, e.g., through a chronicle of preceding events, through stories or significant narratives about the past, or through historical or genetic explanation. This gave some indication of the distinguishing characteristics of history, but calls for elaboration.

Aside from the heterogeneity of its subject matter, the principal distinguishing feature of history is that its focus is on the past. More particularly, the focus is on a selected period of time (which may or may not come up to the present), and on a sequence of selected events within the time period. "One characteristic function that sets the historian off from most other scholars is that he thinks about history as a genetic process—as the study of how man got to be what man once was and now is."[2] We might almost say that one distinction between history and other subjects is found in the tenses of the verbs employed. If we ask what powers were originally assigned to the office of the President of the United States and how the powers of the office have grown, we are asking a question calling for historical inquiry. If the inquiry sheds light on the present powers of the office, as it obviously would, it would do so indirectly—through the examination of the past.

A question about the present or future is not historical. For example, if we ask, "What are the powers of the President?" or "What are the probable consequences of a grant of the item veto to the President?" we are not calling for an exposition of history. Evidence supporting some aspects of the answer would undoubtedly be drawn from history (in any or all of the four senses of the word), but the answer would take the form of a series of general propositions or theses stated in the present or future tense. When the answer takes such a form, the inquiry is cross-sectional rather than developmental and is more properly classified as an inquiry in political science than as an inquiry in history.

Historians not only focus on the past but have a pronounced and general tendency to use chronology as an ordering device. After all, history-as-actuality consists of sequential activities or of sequences of events. It is not surprising, then, that historians should normally describe events in at least the rough order of their occurrence.

Beyond this point the characteristics of historical approaches differ considerably. One of the sources of difference relates to the conception of purpose held by the historian. Those whose focus is on the past, like those whose focus is on the present or future, must choose the level of generality at which they want to work, and the characteristics of their writing vary, depending on the choice made. Many of those who write history have confined themselves to very low levels of generality, asking only those questions for which answers were easily ascertainable. They have filled their writing with statements of particular rather than general facts. Their particular facts, furthermore, have been presented as true information rather than as evidence in support of generalizations. Each bit of true information is presumably to be appreciated in its own right, no hint being given of the purposes that knowledge of it might serve. There are no theses or conclusions—no lessons drawn or meaning suggested. Beyond the assertion of low-level fact, history of this sort is pointless. It is comparable to such compilations as are found in the *World Almanac;* or, especially in view of the tendency of many historians to concentrate on particulars that are somehow related to political crises, revolutions, and wars, it might be said that history of this sort is "a tale . . . full of sound and fury, signifying nothing."

The above statements by no means apply to all history. Many historians have reacted against such limited conceptions of their scholarly purpose, and have urged the importance of taking up general questions requiring an ordering or marshaling of considerable bodies of data. The following statement illustrates the thought:

History in the light of the best modern practice is to be sharply distinguished from antiquarianism or the collection of facts for their own sake, and should be defined rather as the study of problems or causes, the interpretation of phenomena—not just accumulating evidence, but linking it together, giving it shape, meaning, and pattern.[3]

In other words, under the best modern practice, historians ask not simply who did what, when, and where, but why it was done, how any given state of affairs came into existence, and what the consequences of actions and states of affairs were. Moreover, they may well go beyond this, asking about the possible existence of trends or regularities or laws. They may ask about causal relationships, and they may look for theories. Gottschalk expresses a similar thought somewhat more formally, indicating that society demands of the historian "that he attempt contrasts and comparisons of historical episodes, situations, and institutions in order to build stringent categories of man's recurrent experiences, and that he propose generalizations that may have validity for some of the categories of past experiences."[4]

Historians who attempt to engage in "the best modern practice," as just described, naturally differ in the degree of caution or abandon they show in the effort to develop generalizations. Traditionally, of course, there has been considerable emphasis on the notion that history deals with the unique; it is not uncommon to see history contrasted with "the generalizing sciences." Even those who seek to develop historical generalizations are influenced more or less by this tradition. Thus Gottschalk says that the historian "is distinguished from other scholars most markedly by the emphasis he places upon the role of individual motives, actions, accomplishments, failures and contingencies in historical continuity and change."[5] And Aydelotte, though calling for generaliza-

tions, holds that history works against them. It is one of the tasks
of historians (i.e., of members of departments of history), he says,
to check the generalizations developed in the more specialized
social sciences, providing "a touchstone against which these formulations can be tested and their weak points shown up."[6] Some other
historians (e.g., Toynbee) have not insisted upon so much caution.

Historical approaches to political questions differ in many ways
in addition to the level of generality involved. After all, the decision to focus on the past calls for another decision: a choice among
possible approaches to the past. In truth, all of the other approaches that we will be discussing in this chapter could be sub-
joined to a historical approach; that is, once the decision is made
to ask for a genetic explanation, it is quite possible to seek it by
taking economic or psychological data into account, or by adopting
other criteria of selection. So, in a sense, most of the remainder
of the chapter should be as applicable to historical as to other
studies of politics.

It may be worth while to stress a point already made: that
members of departments of political science frequently write history. A considerable portion of the work done by political scientists in the field of international relations consists of the exposition
of the recent diplomatic history of various countries—usually at a
rather low level of generality. The subdivision of political science
called political theory is commonly approached historically. A
distinguished figure in the field of public administration, the late
Leonard White, won a Bancroft prize in history for a study of *The
Jacksonians* and a Pulitzer prize in history for *The Republican
Era, 1869–1901*. And history frequently crops up in the work of
political scientists in other subdivisions of the discipline.[7] Thus,
what is said above about the distinguishing characteristics of history has direct relevance to the work of many who think of themselves primarily as political scientists.

Two addenda might be attached to the above discussion of his-
torical approaches, one concerning the tendency, especially among
Marxists, to personify or reify history and the other concerning
Michael Oakeshott's conception of the study of politics.

Especially among Marxists it is common to speak of history
as if it were a Being with purposes, or a Being with life processes
that are regulated by laws beyond human control. The practice
is comparable to the practice of reifying the state, mentioned in

Chapter Six. Under this conception, men are pictured as relatively helpless creatures who can do little more than slow down or speed up a predestined course of development. If history is personified in a strictly figurative sense, perhaps no harm is done. But sometimes statements of the type indicated seem intended to be taken literally, and sometimes they come to be so taken regardless of original intentions. History then becomes a kind of deity, and those who appreciate the nature and purpose of the deity become its agents in promoting progress, while infidels and heretics become evil persons clinging to an outmoded past. The absurdity (and the danger) of the view is rather obvious.[8]

Michael Oakeshott associates a historical approach with a distinctive (and distinctively conservative) view of the function of students of politics. He defines politics as "the activity of attending to the general arrangements of a collection of people who, in respect of their common recognition of a manner of attending to its arrangements, compose a single community."[9] With this definition he couples great emphasis on practice and tradition and great distrust of what he calls Rationalism—the term being given a different meaning from the one encountered before. He describes the inhabitants of states as "hereditary cooperative groups," whose political activity is to a great extent a reflection of an ancestral past. The activity springs in the main, he says, "neither from instant desires, nor from general principles, but from the existing traditions of behavior themselves." Political activity takes the form of "the amendment of existing arrangements by exploring and pursuing what is intimated in them."

In any generation, even the most revolutionary, the arrangements which are enjoyed always far exceed those which are recognized to stand in need of attention, and those which are being prepared for enjoyment are few in comparison with those which receive amendment: the new is an insignificant proportion of the whole.

In studying politics, Oakeshott holds, "what we are learning to understand is a political tradition, a concrete manner of behaviour. And for this reason it is proper that, at the academic level, the study of politics should be an historical study."[10]

In describing Rationalism and evincing his distrust of it, Oakeshott speaks of two types of knowledge, the one called technical and the other called practical or traditional. The distinguishing feature of technical knowledge is that it is "susceptible of precise formulation." It can be developed by deliberate action, by rational inquiry; and it can be set forth in rules or propositions that can be taught and learned. In contrast, practical or traditional knowledge "is not reflective and . . . cannot be formulated in rules."

Practical knowledge can neither be taught nor learned, but only imparted and acquired. It exists only in practice, and the only way to acquire it is by apprenticeship to a master—not because the master can teach it (he cannot), but because it can be acquired only by continuous contact with one who is perpetually practising it.[11]

At another point Oakeshott says that in the most favorable circumstances it takes two or three generations to acquire knowledge of the political traditions of a society.[12]

A central assertion of the Rationalist, as Oakeshott uses the term, is that "practical knowledge is not knowledge at all, . . . that there is no knowledge which is not technical knowledge."[13] The Rationalist thus wants to operate on the basis of precisely formulated, certain knowledge, which Oakeshott considers mischievous and preposterous. It leads to social engineering, to efforts to *make* rather than *attend to* the arrangements of society. Oakeshott would prefer "the unselfconscious following of a tradition." He regards tradition as "pre-eminently fluid" in contrast to Rationalist ideologies, which are characterized by "rigidity and fixity."[14]

Oakeshott's approach is obviously identified with something more than history as an academic discipline. It is associated with a distinctive view of the types and sources of knowledge, of the proper role of the political scientist, and of the kinds of ends and means that it is desirable to pursue or employ in political life.

APPROACHES IDENTIFIED WITH OTHER ACADEMIC DISCIPLINES

Now the problem is to identify the general perspectives associated with other disciplines—the vantage points from which events are viewed. Our concern is with the kinds of data that are considered and the kinds of concepts that are employed. The assumption is that the approaches of the other disciplines might in some cases be useful in handling political questions.

The principal disciplines in question are economics, sociology, psychology, geography, and philosophy.

That approaches employed in these disciplines may be helpful in handling political questions is obvious, if for no other reason than that, as in the case of history, each of these disciplines overlaps some with political science. Many of the same social realities are examined. Questions raised in political science are frequently also raised in at least one of these other disciplines, and the questions are sometimes answered in the same way, in terms of both method and substance. Both political scientists and economists take up questions about governmental fiscal affairs and about relationships between government and the economy. Sociologists have joined—and have come to overshadow—political scientists in the study of voting behavior. Psychologists as well as political scientists are interested in the drives or motivations that affect political behavior. Political scientists and geographers are concerned with the influence of resources and other features of the environment on the power and policy of states. This attempt to make a philosophical analysis of the study of politics is only one of many instances of a close relationship between political science and philosophy. In connection with several of these other disciplines, explanatory hypotheses (causal theories) have been developed which have been widely used in the study of politics—e.g., Marxist and Freudian theories; these will be discussed below. Within these other disciplines, of course, there are differing interests and differing schools of thought; we need pay attention to such differences only where they rather directly concern the study of politics.

Economic Approaches

The focus in economics, to speak tautologically, is on arrangements under which economic activities occur and economic systems operate. This means that it is on the arrangements under which the production and distribution of goods and services occur. A considerable portion of these arrangements are fixed or somehow supervised or regulated by governments, and thus become involved in the political process. The public issues in connection with which political actors pursue conflicting desires are frequently economic issues; in other words, the desires that give rise to political activity frequently concern arrangements relating to the production and distribution of goods and services.

Those taking an economic approach to politics will thus be especially inclined to raise questions about interrelationships between economic and political life. Out of all the varied activities of government they will be inclined to examine particularly those pertaining to economic relationships; e.g., to monetary and tax policies, to legislation concerning relationships between management and labor, to the relative roles of governmental personnel and private persons in making crucial decisions. Further, out of the various factors that motivate the behavior of persons and groups and that provide a basis for explaining and predicting that behavior, those taking an economic approach will be inclined to examine the desire for wealth—for control over the production and distribution of the comforts and luxuries of life.

The word *interests* figures prominently in connection with an economic approach to the study of politics. Though all would agree that some interests are noneconomic, there is a pronounced tendency to attach an economic connotation to the word. Thus, those who treat political developments as the outcome of conflicting class interests are likely to define class in terms of economic status and to define interests in terms of economic advantage. Virtually the same can be said of those who speak of conflicting sectional interests. Discussions of the question whether there is a harmony of interests, either within or among countries, are likely to assume that the reference is to a mutuality of economic advantage. Similarly, the interest or interest-group conception of politics is closely associated with an economic approach, and voting behavior—whether in general elections or in legislative bodies—is frequently explained or predicted in part in economic terms. Those who take an economic approach are likely to seek to relate economic interests to all major public policies and events, wondering, for example, whether the American armament program may not be designed as much to keep the economy operating at a high level as to promote security and peace. And they are likely to take the view that coherence within political parties and struggle among them reflect common and conflicting economic concerns. An economic approach frequently takes on a psychological color, for it is frequently based on an assumption about human motivation: that people commonly act in such a way as to promote their own economic gain.

Sociological Approaches

Sociologists study human behavior, including political behavior, in the context of the social environment. They make the important and obviously sound assumption that the individual, through the very fact of his membership in the family and other groups, becomes involved inevitably in a learning and conditioning process which does much to shape his behavior patterns. The general object of the sociologist, then, is to find regularities in behavior stemming from interaction among individuals, i.e., stemming from social interaction.[15]

A grasp of some of the central concepts that sociologists employ will give an appreciation of the kind of data they regard as significant.

Culture is one of these concepts. It denotes learned behavior patterns shared by numbers of individuals. "Culture refers to the totality of what is learned by individuals as members of society; it is a way of life, a mode of thinking, acting, and feeling."[16]

Society is another central concept in sociology. In the broadest sense it denotes any kind of association among human beings. More specifically, society can be viewed in any of three closely related ways: (1) as a set of social relationships, i.e., as a set of reciprocal expectations which individuals or groups have concerning each other's behavior; (2) as "a large inclusive group in which relationships occur"; and (3) as "a set of institutions which provide a framework for social life." These institutions may be political, economic, religious, familial, educational, recreational, etc. When sociologists view society in the third sense, they analyze these institutions and the relationships among them. Obviously, the word society applies to human associations of many sorts. In some sense there is a world society; there are national societies; and there are, for example, ladies'-aid societies.

Within a society individuals have *status* and play *roles;* figuratively groups or subsocieties are also thought of in terms of status and role. *Status* designates position and at the same time connotes the idea of relationship between one position and another; status relationships have to do with such attributes of different positions as authority, rank, prestige, and power. *Role* designates the pattern of behavior normally associated with a given status.

To sociologists a *social group* is "a number of persons linked together in a network or system of social relationships." Individuals in a society may divide into various *associations* (e.g., the American Political Science Association); and they fall into various *categories* (e.g., professors, factory workers, church members).

When societies are considered as more or less integrated, operating systems, the concept *function* comes into play. We discussed it briefly in Chapter Three in connection with functional explanation. *Function* denotes the "observable objective consequences" of social phenomena. An activity is said to be functional when it contributes to the survival, persistence, integration, or stability of the society in question. As we saw in Chapter Three, functions may be either manifest ("intended and recognized") or latent ("neither intended nor recognized").

Necessarily, sociologists make the fundamental proposition that "individuals who have a similar social background will behave in approximately the same way in similar situations." The very notions of culture and society imply the existence of some common behavior patterns. The effort of sociologists is to identify relationships between behavior patterns and social conditions—between behavior patterns, on the one hand, and status and expectations regarding role, on the other. The effort is to identify groups, associations, and categories of people about whom, or about whose interrelationships, significant generalizations can be made. Obviously, once it is known that certain types of social conditions give rise to certain types of behavior, the possibility arises of influencing or shaping behavior by manipulating social conditions.

Political behavior, political relationships, and political institutions are within the realm of sociology along with other kinds of behavior, relationships, and institutions. Political science thus overlaps with sociology, just as it overlaps with history and economics. Those who take a sociological approach to the study of politics give attention to the kinds of questions and the kinds of data suggested by the concepts mentioned above. They are inclined to ask, for example, about relationships between social status or the social environment, on the one hand, and political attitudes and voting behavior, on the other; and this constitutes a very broad and significant field of inquiry. Political movements of all sorts can be studied on the basis of a sociological approach. Whether or not it is a sociological approach to politics that is involved, many sociological inquiries have provided findings significant to legislative action: for example, inquiries into such subjects as marriage and divorce, crime, juvenile delinquency, slums and urban renewal, etc. And sociological and anthropological inquiries into foreign cultures have provided knowledge significant to the effective conduct of foreign relations.

Psychological Approaches

Psychologists also study human behavior, including political behavior. In contrast to the sociologist, who stresses the influence of the social environment in his explanations, the psychologist looks primarily at the individual himself. Chinoy illustrates the difference by citing the case of the woman in a mink coat; the sociologist would view the coat as a source of status for its wearer, whereas the psychologist would view it as a source of ego gratification. Actually the distinction between sociology and psychology is not in all respects sharp. Scholars in each field stray some toward the focus of the other field. When the straying goes far enough, the label social psychologist is likely to be adopted.

Though psychologists are agreed that their focus is on the individual, they are not agreed on what it is about the individual that deserves emphasis. Some focus on the way man perceives his environment, some on the learning process, some on emotions and motivations, some on motor activity, and some on still other aspects of the individual or his experience. In connection with each focus there are further differences—for example, differences in the amount of emphasis given to physiological phenomena and laws.[17]

Probably all of the foci employed by psychologists have implications for political activity. Perception is clearly significant politically. How a voter or a statesman perceives his environment obviously influences his reaction to it. An individual's image of political reality, like his image of other aspects of reality, has consequences for his behavior; and the problem of developing and imparting an accurate image is at least as great in the political as in other fields. Emotion and motivation are obviously of prime importance in political life, for political activity is always purposive. The study of motor activity—of stimulus and response—is presumably as relevant to political as to other spheres of action.[18]

So far, the psychological assumptions made by those who study politics have generally related to reasons for action—to emotion and motivation. Machiavelli and Hobbes both stressed security of life and property as a motive and held that the desire for it was inseparable from the desire for power. Hobbes' statement was: "I put for a general inclination of all mankind, a perpetual and restless desire of power after power, that ceaseth only in death." Bentham assumed that all men seek happiness. Some such assumptions concerning human desires or purposes underlie all general interpretations of political behavior. Sometimes politics is viewed as simply another manifestation of class struggle, the principal motivation being regarded as the desire for wealth. Those influenced by Sigmund Freud in taking a psychoanalytic approach to the study of human behavior deal largely in motivations. It is also possible to define politics as struggle among actors pursuing conflicting desires on public issues. The definition calls attention to desires, and therefore to reasons and motives for action, without specifying any one kind of desire as dominant.

Given the purposive character of political behavior, it is quite understandable that psychological approaches would be predominantly motivational. But other kinds of psychological data deserve at least to be explored. It seems especially probable that studies in perception—or in degrees of sensitivity to different classes of events—might be very enlightening. Students of political history have shown considerable sensitivity to the Terror that accompanied the French Revolution, but little to the mass executions that accompanied the suppression of the Paris commune. Why? How many such contrasts exist? Are members of the elite in any society as sensitive to immoral or illegal acts by others of their own kind as to the immoral or illegal acts of subversive elements? Americans are sensitive to lies expressed by the Soviet government and to its violations of obligations. Are we equally sensitive to the lies and violations of allied governments? Of our own government? Why? And what difference does it make?

Geographic Approaches

A geographic approach to politics involves an effort to correlate political events and trends with almost anything that can be depicted on a map. The location of mountains, rivers, and seas has clearly had a bearing on political developments over the world. The same can be said of the distribution of natural resources of all varieties, of the distribution of rainfall, of differences in temperature, of the availability and nature of routes and means of transportation and communication, and so on. The distribution of ethnic or racial groups has had and is continuing to have a profound influence on the political organization of the world. Some of those who have taken a geographic approach to the study of politics have gone to extremes, claiming that certain facts of geography have constituted the sole cause of far-reaching developments and even making breath-taking predictions on as limited a basis. Sir Halford Mackinder, for example, once declared:

> Who rules East Europe commands the Heartland:
> Who rules the Heartland commands the World-Island:
> Who rules the World-Island commands the World.[19]

(Mackinder's "Heartland" consisted of the present Soviet Union along with certain additional territories west and south of it. His "World-Island" consisted of Europe, Asia, and Africa.) The naïveté of such dicta as this should not be allowed to discredit geographic approaches to politics. The facts of geography are clearly among those that influence many kinds of political decisions; frequently, too, they do much to determine the operational results of those decisions. Given knowledge of various other types about a political actor (e.g., knowledge of the purposes of statesmen in international relations), knowledge of geography may help provide a basis for predicting decisions that will be made and the probable results of the decisions.

Philosophical Approaches

Especially in view of the title of this book, a word concerning philosophy and philosophical approaches to the study of politics is in order. As the word *philosophical* is used in the title, it refers to thought about thought; a philosophical analysis is an effort to clarify thought about the nature of the subject and about ends and means in studying it. Put more generally, a person who takes a philosophical approach to a subject aims to enhance linguistic clarity and to reduce linguistic confusion; he assumes that the language used in descriptions reflects conceptions of reality, and he wants to make conceptions of reality as clear, consistent, coherent, and helpful as possible. He seeks to influence and guide thinking and the expression of thought so as to maximize the prospect that the selected aspect of reality (for us, the selected aspect is politics) will be made intelligible.[20]

In Chapter Nine when we discussed political theory as a subdivision of political science we noted that the word *philosophy* is also used in other senses. It may denote efforts to arrive at truth through the use of reason. The truth sought may be normative, descriptive, or prescriptive. The object of philosophic inquiry in this sense is to establish standards of the good, the right, and the just, and to appraise or prescribe political institutions and practices in the light of these standards. This conception is reflected in Stephen K. Bailey's description of the philosophic approach. He says that its object is to determine what is in the interest of the public; and he identifies interests more with ends than with means.[21]

The name of an academic discipline obviously leaves much to be desired in terms of the clarity of the criteria it provides for selecting questions and data. A political scientist who employs a historical approach still has as many choices to make as do historians themselves; actually, the term "historical approach" is probably misleading, for there are many historical approaches. If a political scientist were to set out taking a historical approach, he would get about as much guidance from the label as would a historian who adopted a political approach to history. A general type of inquiry is vaguely suggested, to be sure, but that is all. No very specific criteria of selection are indicated. The really tough problems remain unsolved.

The same can be said of economic, sociological, psychological, geographic, and philosophic approaches. Each term vaguely suggests a type of inquiry, but gives little guidance in the formulation of the questions to take up and the data to select.

If those who take an approach identified with an academic discipline do not do something more to identify their criteria of selection, the likelihood is that they will end up presenting compilations of miscellaneous information in their teaching and writing. They will have only the very dullest and most ineffective of tools in attacking the intellectual problems that confront the world. They may not even develop an awareness of the problems; and, if they do, one fact may seem as relevant as another, provided it is historical or economic or sociological or whatever. If political inquiry is to be desirable, significant, and contributory to rationality in decision making, approaches to it must be more sharply delineated than they are simply by naming an academic discipline.

CHAPTER ELEVEN

Approaches Identified with Salient Features of Political Life

Students of politics sometimes adopt approaches that are identified with central or salient features of political life. This often amounts to identifying an approach with a definition, for definitions commonly focus on the salient and provide criteria for selecting questions and data. Thus, in this chapter, some of the approaches to be examined are also definitions.

The first section of the chapter is devoted to a series of definitions depicting politics as a struggle among actors pursuing conflicting desires on public issues. If definitions are to be employed as approaches, these are more to be recommended than some others in terms of the guidance they give in the selection of questions and data. Subsequent sections of the chapter will deal with the institutional approach (identified with definitions under which the study of politics is the study of the state or of government), the legal approach, the power approach, the interest-group approach, approaches focusing on decision making, and the approach that focuses on the decisions themselves, i.e., on the ends and means selected.

THE STRUGGLE AMONG ACTORS
PURSUING CONFLICTING DESIRES ON PUBLIC ISSUES

Probably the most helpful of the definitional approaches are those that call for a focus on human beings who think and act and who engage in cooperation and conflict on issues concerning group policy or intergroup relationships. One such definition, or brief description, is offered by C. J. Friedrich.

Modern political science is largely a critical examination of common-sense notions concerning the working of political institutions and procedures. Three axiomatic truths regarding the nature of power lie at its foundation: namely, that power ordinarily presupposes a group of human beings who can share objectives, interests, values, in other words, a community; second, therefore power presupposes objectives, interests, values, ends, which these human beings can share, fight over, or exchange; third, that all power situations contain both consent (shared objectives) and constraint (contested objectives). . . . Modern political science . . . is concerned with the instruments or techniques of political action in terms of the objectives they are supposed to serve.[1]

Similarly, Harold Lasswell, urging a focus on the decision process, has advanced a conception of politics of the same general type.

Whether we are thinking of a body politic as a whole or face-to-face situations we are considering "arenas" in which "participants" are striving to accomplish their purposes by influencing "outcomes." The purposes are directed toward "preferred events" ("values" and "interpretations" of values in terms of "institutional practices"). Participants are seeking to maximize power and other values by influencing outcomes. They use the values at their disposal as "base values" according to "strategies."

And Lasswell summarizes this conception by saying that in the decision process:

Participants (with various value perspectives) employing base values by various strategies interact in an arena to influence outcomes and effects.[2]

A historian suggests that

in one way or another, directly or indirectly, political research has to deal with the determinants of *public policy*. It has to show how and why the activities, institutions and structure of a society give rise to one kind of policy rather than another. Each field of research in political science seeks to discover the important determinants in the formulation and execution of public policy.[3]

David Easton, speaking of a political system rather than simply of politics, says

The boundary of a political system is defined by all those actions more or less directly related to the making of binding decisions for a society; every social action that does not partake of this characteristic will be excluded from the system and thereby will automatically be viewed as an external variable in the environment.[4]

According to an older definition:

No matter how the question may be obfuscated, whenever it tends to involve a utilization of the machinery of government then it becomes a "political issue"; those concerned with it are involved in "political activity," and the phenomenon becomes one of those which it is the function of the political scientists to observe.[5]

Finally, a succinct definition by Quincy Wright deserves special note. Wright defines politics as "the art of influencing, manipulating, or controlling [groups] so as to advance the purposes of some against the opposition of others."[6]

Though the words in these definitions differ considerably, the meanings conveyed have much in common. If we elaborate on them and modify them somewhat, a conception of politics emerges about as follows.

Politics stems from human needs and wants, or from associated desires and purposes. Shared desires provide the basis for the existence of groups, and of groups within groups; conflicting desires give rise to struggle among individuals and groups. Those groups are political that are so organized that decisions can be made and actions taken on their behalf. The population of a state is a group, government acting on behalf of the group.

Desires and purposes lead to activity, some of which is political. Activity is political when it relates to a public issue, and it relates to a public issue when two conditions are met. In the first place, it must relate to the decision making of a group, i.e., it must concern group policy, group organization, or group leadership, or it must concern the regulation of intergroup relationships. In the second place, it must come within the realm of the controversial. "Politics exists only when ends or means are controversial."[7] Most commonly the activity must confront opposition if it is to be classified as political. This is suggested by the notion that politics should stop at the water's edge, which means that disagreement should stop there and that a united front should be presented to the foreign adversary. It is also suggested by the desire that sometimes exists to keep an issue out of politics; this is a desire to keep it out of the realm of contention where factions committed to contradictory positions struggle to secure acceptance of their views and, instead, to keep it in a realm where reasoned inquiry occurs by uncommitted people who seek an agreed solution. Even governmental activity is regarded as nonpolitical where all participants accept it as routine. Thus, the editing of most governmental publications is nonpolitical—unless someone chooses to raise a question about it and throw it into the realm of controversy.

Speaking literally, only individuals can have desires or purposes and engage in political activity. But when they act on behalf of a group it is often convenient to speak figuratively and to refer to the desires and the purposes of the group. Thus individuals and, figuratively, groups may be political actors. Those who seek to influence or control governments, and those who act in the name of government, may all be political actors.

To sum up, politics can be defined as: (1) activity occurring within and among groups (2) which operate on the basis of desires that are to some extent shared, (3) an essential feature of the activity being a struggle of actors (4) to achieve their desires (5) on questions of group policy, group organization, group leadership, or the regulation of intergroup relationships (6) against the opposition of others with conflicting desires. More briefly, politics may be defined as a struggle among actors pursuing conflicting desires on public issues.

This definition comes close to being lexical, i.e., to reflecting usage. It applies to political struggles within and among all kinds of groups. Political scientists, of course, generally choose a more restricted terrain, and so adopt a narrower stipulative definition which specifies that their prime concern is with actors and issues related somehow to civic or governmental or intergovernmental affairs. Thus they study individuals and groups whose actions are designed to affect government; and they study actions of governments, at least where public issues are actually or potentially involved.[8]

Especially in the briefer version of the definition, there is more emphasis on struggle than is found in some of the other definitions quoted. The emphasis is deliberate, but should not be interpreted to suggest that cooperation is not an important feature of politics. Those on the same side in any struggle presumably cooperate with each other—usually after a struggle among themselves over the terms on which cooperation will occur.

Obviously, these various definitions reflect and provide criteria for the selection of questions and data about political life. In so far as a definition can provide such criteria, the one given above—derived from the others quoted—seems to be most accurate as a brief description and therefore most trustworthy in the guidance it gives to teaching and research. Such advantages as it possesses can be made clear through comparisons with other definitions. We might note, however, that the heuristic quality of any definition is bound to be limited. In identifying salient features of politics, it suggests a focus; it suggests what to look at; but it does not indicate what to do about what is seen. A compilation of low-level facts —dead-end information—is a possible result of any purely definitional approach.

AN INSTITUTIONAL APPROACH: POLITICS DEFINED AS THE STUDY OF THE STATE OR OF GOVERNMENT

An institutional approach is common in the study of politics. Choice of the approach follows quite understandably from the widely accepted view that the study of politics is the study of the state or of governmental and related institutions. Those who define politics in this way are likely to ask questions calling for an examination of one or another aspect of institutional activity, and regardless of the nature of the questions they are likely to bring data relating to institutions into their answers.

Those taking an institutional approach have little difficulty in identifying the institutions with which they are concerned. A government as a whole is an institution, and no doubt the name can also be properly applied to many of the agencies and subdivisions of government—to Congress, for example. Political parties are institutions. But though it is easy to name institutions, it is rather difficult to define the term. What are the attributes of a government, or of an agency or a subdivision of a government, that justify the use of the label? The question is not an idle one. Those who study institutions are bound to operate on a definition of the term, and the phenomena at which they look are bound to vary along with the definition.

Sometimes the visible evidence of an institution is the building that houses it, but a conception that identifies an institution with its housing arrangement is obviously absurd. Institutions are sometimes conceived as offices and agencies arranged in a hierarchy, each office or agency having certain functions and powers. Obviously, more of the significant features of an institution are identified by this conception than by considering housing arrangements, but there is something unrealistic and incomplete even about this.

For an institution to exist there must be people, and not simply offices and agencies. The people must act and react. They man the offices and comprise the agencies, and they make demands on the offices and agencies. Some are charged with the performance of certain functions, and others expect them to perform these functions. Those involved have status and play roles. Thus an institution may be said to consist of the activities of people in an integrated structure (i.e., an integrated system of behavior), these activities being somehow patterned or regularized or expected or authorized and being more or less persistent; some of those participating in the institutional activities may be officeholders, but not all of them need be. Voters who are not officeholders are, for example, participants in governmental institutional activities.[9] Even this definition, broad as it is, does not reflect the meaning intended when war or the family is called an institution, or when there is a reference to a mental institution. It is likely that no definition will reflect all the uses of the term. If a broad and brief definition is desired, perhaps the following is as good as any: an institution is any persistent system of activities and expectations, or any stable pattern of group behavior.

As suggested above, the meaning of an institutional approach varies with the definition of institution. Those who have conceived governmental institutions as offices and agencies have been inclined to teach and write about government accordingly, organization charts being suggestive of much of what they have done. Under this conception the study of politics becomes, at the extreme, the study of one narrow, specific fact after another. One simply identifies the level of government with which to be concerned (federal, state, local) and the branch (executive, legislative, judicial). On the basis of these choices, one proceeds to identify offices and agencies with which to deal, and then tells of the composition and the duties or functions of each one, perhaps along with statements about interrelationships among them. Constitutional and other legal arrangements are likely to figure rather heavily in such descriptions. Analogously, students of international politics who conceive of institutions as consisting of offices and agencies have been inclined to stress those aspects of international politics in which organization charts can be used and law cited. Thus emphasis is given to the organization of the United Nations and the various agencies associated with it, perhaps along with detailed studies of provisions of the Charter.

This narrow conception of an institution has been associated, probably in a causal way, with several tendencies in political science that seem unfortunate. One is a tendency, at least until recent years, for political scientists to neglect the individual. After all, they were studying institutions, not individuals! The result is that it has been left largely to others—mainly to sociologists and social psychologists—to develop polling techniques, to study voting behavior, to discover relationships between political and other attitudes, etc.

Political scientists taking a narrow institutional approach have also tended to neglect international politics. Since for long there were no world institutions analogous to the state or government, there seemed to be nothing in this area for political scientists to talk about. The subject could be left to the historians or, perhaps, the lawyers! Books that presumed to give introductions to political science or to survey the principles or elements of politics therefore concentrated on domestic politics. And, when they made forays into the international field, it was mainly to take up questions concerning law and organization. Somehow the term international *relations* gained currency rather than international *politics*, possibly because of an inability to think in terms of politics in the absence of governmental institutions.

At the same time, the institutional approach, narrowly conceived, has been associated with a tendency to neglect the role of violence in politics. Obviously, violence and the threat of it play a vitally important role. A very high proportion of the states of the world have come into existence and have had their boundaries determined by violence. Within countries, governments come and go—sometimes with considerable frequency—through civil wars and *coups d'état*; and even where such events do not occur they are sometimes threatened. Fear of war or hope of successful war, and plans and preparations for defense or aggression, have long been major preoccupations of governments. But when institutions are conceived in terms of offices and agencies that can be depicted on organization charts, there is no place for revolution and war. Civil and international war are thus assumed to be extraneous to politics—rude interruptions of political life.[10] And the work of political scientists thus fails to account for major political events.

An institutional approach, or an approach based on a definition under which the study of politics is the study of government and the state, is not always so narrowly conceived, and need not be. As suggested above, broader definitions are employed under which an institution is regarded as a stable pattern of group behavior. So conceived, institutions consist of stylized behavior, and help to create it. They reflect conformity and regularity in behavior, and their existence helps to induce individuals to accept conformity and regularity. They minimize the chaotic and the erratic. A high proportion of the decisions that individuals make are made not as a result of conscious and deliberate thought but more or less automatically and unthinkingly on the basis of institutional conditioning. Commonly, though not always, the behavior patterns that comprise institutions are rational; in any event, institutions are means of serving ends, which gives basis for question concerning their rationality.[11]

More realistic criteria of selection are provided by a broad conception of institutions than by a narrow one. Even so, it is doubtful whether they are as helpful as is desirable. An injunction to study stable behavior patterns of a political sort is rather vague. No very clear criteria for the inclusion and exclusion of questions and data are indicated. The statement that politics is a struggle among actors pursuing conflicting desires on public issues is probably clearer in the guidance that it gives. At any rate, those who choose an institutional approach are likely to supplement it with another, even if they adopt a broad definition of the term institution.

A LEGAL APPROACH

Institutional and legal approaches are sometimes interrelated. Obviously, governmental institutions (usually conceived in this context as offices and agencies) have much to do with law. They exist in accordance with constitutional law, and their activities have to do with the enactment, amendment, interpretation, and execution of law. Thus those who adopt or discuss an institutional approach may virtually equate it with a legal approach.[12]

Whatever the relationship between the two, a legal approach has been widespread.[13] In connection with almost any general question that may be posed, many are inclined to assume that some or all of the subquestions and some or all of the relevant data will be of a legal sort. Thus, the question who will be the next President of the United States may be answered in part by a reference to the constitutional requirement that he be native-born and at least thirty-five years of age; and the question of the probable action of the United States in case Laos should invade Cambodia may be answered in part in terms of a careful exegesis of the Charter.

Nor is a legal approach to be disparaged. After all, both the procedures and the substance of political action at every level are often controlled by law. In the field of both domestic and international politics, law frequently prescribes the action to be taken in given contingencies; it also forbids action or fixes the limits of permissible action. Where political actors are law-abiding—as they very commonly are—knowledge of the law provides a very important basis for prediction. It provides a basis for persistent patterns of activity and expectation—for stable patterns of group behavior.

To say that a legal approach is very important is not to say that it is always the most appropriate. Obviously, many political questions relate to law only in a remote way, if at all. Even where the law is relevant, it may be misleading to rely upon it entirely for the answer to the question asked. For example, questions concerning the location of control over the official actions of government cannot always be answered with confidence solely on the basis of an examination of legal arrangements. The power of decision that is formally lodged in a given office may be exercised, as a practical matter, by persons having no legal status whatsoever. Further, it should be remembered that the law is not always clear. Questions concerning its meaning and its application to specific issues are forever arising. Sometimes such questions are submitted to judges, who presumably try earnestly to arrive at answers on a detached and disinterested basis. Even in such circumstances, however, the process by which ambiguities and vaguenesses are cleared up is one in which the social background and personal predispositions of the interpreter of the law are likely to play a significant role. In other words, in the case of many kinds of questions that are apparently legal, nonlegal data are likely to be relevant. Finally, it should be remembered that a legal approach is limited in another way: it has little relevance, if any at all, to questions about what the law should be. Determination of the content of the law through legislative power is a political act, ordinarily to be explained on the basis of something other than a legal approach.

There has been a tendency on the part of some of those utilizing a legal approach to reify the law, or at least to treat it as something that exists naturally, beyond the control of men. In connection with many questions, such a perspective is scarcely compatible with realistic political inquiry. It is more realistic to regard law as a reflection of the desires of those who win out in the political struggle; it is an instrument through which they express and give effect to their will. It thus registers the score in the game.[14]

THE POWER APPROACH

Power is obviously a salient feature of political life, and the term is sometimes made to designate an approach. The suggestion is that those working in the field of political science should select questions and data pertaining to power and the struggle for power, perhaps defining the field in these terms. For example, Frederick Watkins some years ago came to the conclusion that

The proper scope of political science is not the study of the state or of any other specific institutional complex, but the investigation of all associations insofar as they can be shown to exemplify the problem of power.[15]

More recently William A. Robson has declared,

It is with power in society that political science is primarily concerned—its nature, basis, processes, scope and results. . . . The "focus of interest" of the political scientist is clear and unambiguous; it centres on the struggle to gain or retain power, to exercise power or influence over others, or to resist that exercise.[16]

Various definitions of power have been advanced. Hans Morgenthau employs the term to designate "man's control over the minds and actions of other men." Then he proceeds to distinguish between political power and military power. The essence of political power, he says, is a "psychological relationship between two minds," whereas military power is associated with violence—with "the physical relation between two bodies, one of which is strong enough to dominate the other's movements." According to Morgenthau, the armed strength of a nation may be classified as either political or military power, depending on whether or not it is actually being employed in violence. "When violence becomes an actuality, it signifies the abdication of political power in favor of military or pseudo-military power."[17]

The above definition of power has more to commend it than the subsequent distinction between political and military power. The distinction can be tested by imagining a man with a sword, brandishing it in a threatening fashion at another man who stands there with his back to a wall, bare chest exposed. As long as the sword simply cuts the air, the relationship between the two men is presumably psychological. Suppose, however, that the wielder of the sword begins to flick the tip of it into the skin of his opponent. At what point does the "psychological" relationship become "military"? As soon as the skin is broken? If life and strength remain unimpaired, why is the relationship less "psychological" than before? Actually, the slashes of the sword are likely to influence the thoughts and the will of the victim (and thus have a "psychological" effect) as long as consciousness remains. And slashes that produce unconsciousness may have a psychological effect if consciousness is regained. Perhaps armed power ceases to be political and becomes military only in death.

The above distinction between political and military power is open to question also on a very different count. Though it surely was not so intended, it tends to reinforce the view, cited above, that violence is extraneous to politics—a rude interruption of the political process. Further, it reinforces the thoughtless assumption sometimes encountered that when war occurs the diplomats (and perhaps the whole political leadership) should abdicate in favor of the generals. Clausewitz had a sounder view, that war is "a continuation of political commerce, a carrying out of the same by other means." The struggle that is the essence of politics remains political whether pursued verbally or violently. Military power can be regarded as a subdivision of political power better than as a substitute.

There are variations on the definition, quoted above, under which power denotes "man's control over the minds and actions of other men." Some prefer to make power denote the existence of an ability or a capacity to control rather than the existence of actual control. If we define politics as a struggle among actors pursuing conflicting desires on public issues, we can say that in relation to any given set of issues an actor has power in proportion to his ability to achieve his desires. A slightly different view is that "power is the capacity to affect others without being as much affected."[18]

The above discussion suggests that political power can be subdivided, military power being named as one of the subdivisions. Precisely what the other subdivisions would be in a logical and articulate classification scheme is difficult to say. There are references to economic power and to power resting on education and propaganda. People speak of persuasive and coercive power, perhaps recognizing that the power to coerce frequently enhances an ability to persuade. Discussions of international politics not infrequently include rather long lists of the "elements of power," the elements sometimes being grouped in a strained fashion into categories called tangible and intangible.

Little would be gained by pursuing classification schemes of the above sort here. We might, however, attack the problem from a somewhat different angle. We will assume a situation in which there are two political actors, one a wielder and the other a victim of political power. Note that this situation is simplified in that only one of the actors is wielding power, whereas in most practical situations each actor would be wielding it—and simultaneously each would be the victim of the other's power. The point is that the elements of power that the one actor is wielding fall into two categories.

The first category includes elements identified primarily with the wielder himself. He has desires. The achievement or implementation of these desires somehow involves the victim. The extent of the power of the wielder depends in part on the intensity of his desires; i.e., on his willingness to accept costs and risks to get what he wants. Beyond that, the extent of the power of the wielder also depends in part on his ability, at an acceptable cost or risk, to do either or both of two things: on the one hand, to shape or influence the desires of the victim, and/or, on the other hand, to provide or withhold or take away something the victim desires (in other words, to grant indulgences to the victim or to inflict deprivations on him). The possible indulgences and deprivations are of many different sorts, both material and immaterial. Goods, services, and various kinds of opportunities (e.g., economic opportunities) can be provided or withheld. Knowledge and skills can be imparted or denied. Psychological satisfactions can be granted or refused. Life itself may be saved or taken away; or, in the case of groups, existence may be provided for, safeguarded, or destroyed. The ways of influencing desires, of granting indulgences, and of inflicting deprivations cover a wide range from the subtlest of suggestions to the greatest extremes of violence.

The second category includes elements of power identified with the victim. His habits, propensities, rules, and principles—most generally, his desires—often help to determine the extent of the power of the wielder. The power of a government over its subjects varies with the extensity and intensity of the habit of obedience to law. The power of a party boss to extract commitments from a candidate varies with the integrity and ambition of the victim. Committee chairmen in the U.S. Senate have power because the immediate victims of the power maintain the seniority rule. When Britain and France made it a rule in the Ethiopian affair not to impose any sanctions that might lead to war with Italy, and when they let this be known, their rule gave power to Mussolini; he could determine the limits within which they had to confine their action. When Gandhi led India in civil disobedience, his power resided to a considerable extent in the rules or principles to which Britain was committed; had Britain adhered to Nazi or Communist principles, Gandhi's power would surely have suffered, if he had survived at all. The commitment of the United States to observe international law sometimes gives the smallest and weakest state the power of defiance. Fortunate is the political actor who derives the power to achieve what he wants entirely from the habits, propensities, rules, or principles of the other actor.

The principal merit of a power approach is implicit rather than explicit. It rests implicitly on the assumption that in political life actors of some kind (whether individual human beings or organized groups) are struggling to achieve purposes. It shares this advantage with other approaches, including the one mentioned above under which politics is regarded as a struggle among actors pursuing conflicting desires on public issues.

The principal weakness of the power approach is its lack of precision. As indicated above, the word *power* covers a considerable range of meaning. Power is said to derive from sources ranging from tacitly accepted rules of politeness to the possession of spaceships; and it is said to manifest itself in situations ranging from a request that the salt be passed at the dining table to a situation in which states are exchanging all-out thermonuclear blows. The question concerns not the truth of such statements but their implications. A concept with so broad a meaning cannot be very clear. When it covers so many kinds of events and relationships, a handicap is imposed both on the individual who is attempting to formulate and express a thought and on the individual who is attempting to understand what another has said.[19]

Sometimes those advocating a power approach think of it not so much in terms of the problem of power as in terms of a theory or definition that politics is a struggle for power. The difficulty with the statement is that it adds to the vagueness of the word *power* itself. Political actors rarely, if ever, struggle for power alone. They pursue other purposes, too. The theory that politics is a struggle for power does not say how much power is desired or what price political actors are willing to pay for it in terms of other values. The thoughtless assumption that all political actors constantly seek a maximization of power at any price is obviously false.

Those adopting the power struggle conception of politics should, and sometimes do, add statements indicating the sphere of activity they have in mind. Perhaps the sphere is that of governmental affairs and intergovernmental relations. Perhaps it is wider, embracing all types of groups within and among which a power struggle can be said to occur. The sphere of activity may or may not include, for example, a struggle for power in a corporation, manifesting itself in competitive efforts to buy up stock and win proxies; and it may or may not include competition among cigarette producers to control consumer choices.

APPROACHES FOCUSING ON INFLUENCE
AND VALUES

Definitions of politics advanced by Harold D. Lasswell and David Easton have been quoted favorably above. Some earlier definitions by each of them also deserve to be noted, for they offer guidance to the scholar in selecting the questions and the data to be considered in the study of politics.

Lasswell, in his early work on *Politics,* uses the subtitle, "Who gets what, when, how?" and says that "the study of politics is the study of influence and the influential." At another place he describes political analysis as "the study of changes in the shape and composition of the value patterns of society."[20] Similarly, Easton has defined political science as "the study of the authoritative allocation of values as it is influenced by the distribution and use of power."[21] The authoritative allocation is to occur within a society.

The principal weakness of these conceptions is that they are enigmatic or vague, or both. The key words are difficult to define, or are so broad in their application that they are of dubious help in identifying the political. What is influence? How are the influential to be identified? Does the question "Who gets what, when, how?" necessarily guide one to a study of politics? What is meant by the term *value?* What is meant by a value *pattern?* What is intended by the *shape* and *composition* of a value pattern?

Influence is presumably exerted by a Sunday school teacher on her pupils, by an attorney on his client, by a doctor on his patient, and by an advertiser on a prospective buyer; the teacher, the attorney, the doctor, and the advertiser are thus presumably among the influential. But surely a study of "influence and the influential," when thought of in such terms as these, would not necessarily be a political study. Nor does the question "Who gets what, when, how?" really help much to identify the field of politics or the kind of studies to undertake within the field; it might serve with almost equal effectiveness to guide studies of robbery or of sex.

The term *values* does not provide much guidance, either. Among the values that Lasswell lists are well-being (i.e., "the health and safety of the organism"), skill, enlightenment, rectitude, and affection. Surely a study of the "shape" and "composi-

tion" of a "pattern" of these values would not necessarily be a
political study. Similarly there are other values that are in no
sense exclusive to the political realm. Something must be added
to the key word *values* to permit an identification and study of
the political.

Easton's addition, referring to the "authoritative" allocation of
values within a society "as influenced by the distribution and use
of power," is an improvement. It focuses attention not so much
on all values as on those that are authoritatively allocated. The
authoritative allocation must be for and within a society, and not
for a casual and transitory group; it must be a matter of social
policy. Further, if there is an allocation of values that is not somehow influenced by the distribution and use of power, the process
would presumably fall outside the field of politics. These thoughts
are all potentially helpful, but the words *allocation, values,* and
authoritative all provide room for some doubt about the meaning
intended. There are vexing problems in formulating a satisfactory definition of the definition.

THE INTEREST OR INTEREST-GROUP APPROACH

Sometimes students of politics, influenced more or less by Arthur F. Bentley, call attention to interests or groups or interest
groups. Thus, David B. Truman, saying that groups lie "at the
heart of the process of government," undertakes to develop "a
conception of the political process in the United States that will
account adequately for the role of groups, particularly interest
groups." He defines an interest group as "a shared-attitude group
that makes certain claims upon other groups in the society." It
becomes political "if and when it makes its claims through or upon
any of the institutions of government." Truman denies that a
focus on groups means a neglect of individuals. His point is that
"when men act and interact in consistent patterns, it is reasonable
to study these patterns and to designate them by collective terms"
like group or party or nation. The study of groups and the study
of individuals are held to be "two approaches to the same thing."[22]

Truman's conception of the interest-group approach makes it
quite compatible with others that either have been or remain to
be described. In particular, it is compatible with the definitional
approach under which politics is viewed as a struggle among actors

pursuing conflicting desires on public issues, and it can appropriately supplement approaches focusing on government, on law, and on power. Similarly, an interest-group approach can be "behavioral," and, quite apart from identifying a salient feature of politics, it can be joined with any of several possible theories to provide explanations of political developments. These types of approaches are to be discussed below. Truman has demonstrated that an interest-group approach, conceived in his terms, can contribute very effectively to the explanation and prediction of political events.

Formulated in a strictly Bentleyan fashion, the interest-group approach is less satisfactory—perhaps because it is less clear. Bentley urged that the student of politics focus on activity. In his view, an individual person was really not an appropriate unit of study; the appropriate unit was the act of the individual. "The individual is his activity."[23]

Similarly, a group consists of "mass activity." Moreover, an interest is "the equivalent of a group." "The group and the interest are not separate. There exists only one thing, that is, so many men bound together in or along the path of a certain activity."[24] In connection with the stress on activity, Bentley made a major issue of the role to be assigned to "motives, feelings, desires, emotions, instincts, impulses, or similar mental states, elements or qualities." He thought it common to regard such phenomena as "independent or semiindependent factors in explaining social life." As independent or semiindependent factors, he derogatorily called them "stuff"—e.g., "soul-stuff." He thought they were commonly reified. And he objected to the practice of citing reified soul-stuff in efforts to explain behavior and events. "The use of specific forms of soul-stuff gives us absolutely no help in interpreting the doings of social men."[25]

What Bentley really meant is in some doubt. The political activity of men obviously includes speaking, writing, developing and identifying rules of behavior, enacting constitutions and laws, etc. Surely it is not simply the act that is important in each case; the results of the action must also count. What is said may be more important than the act of saying it. Knowledge of the rule or law may be more important to the explanation and prediction of behavior than knowledge of the activity that produced or that reflects the rule or law. Knowledge of institutional patterns of behavior and knowledge of the persistent motivations of men are obviously important.

After disparaging efforts to explain in terms of desires, motives, ideas, feelings, etc., Bentley himself seemed to reintroduce them into his scheme. For example, he said that

"ideas" and "feelings," as set apart concretely, serve to indicate the values of the activities which are our raw materials. . . . There is not a shred of all the activity which does not present itself as an affair of feeling and intelligence. . . . It can only be stated as purposive activity (in a very broad sense of the word purposive), as the doings of wanting-knowing men in masses. . . . We must get our raw material before us in the form of purposive action, valued in terms of other purposive action.[26]

It is not clear where this leads us. On the one hand, feelings, faculties, ideas, and ideals give us "no help," and, on the other hand, they "serve to indicate the values of the activities which are our raw materials."

To add to the confusion, we might note that Bentley's definition of *interest* is at least unusual. In this kind of context, it is not ordinarily considered enough to identify the word with activity. The word is more commonly associated with a judgment or belief about the desirability of pursuing a given end or the advantage of employing a given means. Thus, it may be in a man's interest (as a goal or end) to seek election to the Senate, in which case it may also be in his interest (as a means) to take a popular stand on a pending issue; and it will be against his interest (i.e., it will jeopardize the achievement of the declared goal) if he takes a stand that is unpopular. Given this notion of *interest,* a man's means-interest might be determined more reliably through scholarly inquiry into causal relationships than by observing his activity.

Some of the confusion associated with Bentley's approach may stem from his conception of explanation. To him explanation meant an identification of causes. And since feelings, faculties, ideas, and ideals did not seem to be causes, he tried to drive them from the field of inquiry—only to find that he could not get along without them. It seems much more sensible to grant that feelings, faculties, ideas, and ideals may help to explain behavior. The suggestion is made above that they can well be classified as *reasons* rather than *causes*. Of course, as is also suggested above, an explanation that appeals only to factors such as these is bound to be incomplete. Once reasons for action are cited, one may wish to go on to cite reasons and causes for the reasons, and causes of causes.[27]

In sum, there is justification for Peter H. Odegard's conclusion on Bentley's conception of the group or interest-group approach to politics: "A theory of politics which excludes where it does not frankly reject a concern for values, which denies that reason has a significant role to play in the process of government, and which devalues the individual by its exaltation of the group, is, I suggest, inadequate."[28]

APPROACHES FOCUSING ON DECISION MAKING

Decision making is prominent among the various central or salient features of politics, though at least until recently it received relatively less attention than institutions, laws, and power as a basis for a distinctive approach. After all, every act reflects a decision; and so, tacitly, does inaction. Every actor is a decision maker. Those acting for political parties decide which candidate to nominate. Voters decide whether to vote and for whom. Legislators decide which proposals to advance or support. Executives decide what legislation to seek, whether to sign or veto acts of the legislative body, precisely which steps to take in executing or administering the law, and what policies to pursue where action is left to their discretion.

Decision making refers, of course, to the process by which actors choose among ends and means.

We will consider four types of studies concerning this process: (1) those that focus on characteristics of decision makers, the assumption being that these characteristics explain or help to explain the choices made; (2) those that focus on "partisans of issues," i.e., on persons or groups who lack official decision-making authority but who do or might exercise influence or power over those who possess such authority; (3) those that focus on specific decisions, asking about the process involved in reaching them; and (4) those exploring or employing game theory. There is some overlapping among these types. The discussion of the first two types is based upon Peter H. Rossi's study of "Community Decision-Making."[29]

The Characteristics of Decision Makers

Studies in this category vary in scope and nature. Biographical studies are made—intensive examinations of the background, attitudes, and activities of specific individuals.[30] Instead of a complete biography, there may be an inquiry into one aspect of a person's record, e.g., a psychiatric study designed to lay bare his motivations.[31] Some studies focus on a relatively large number of individuals; e.g., on the members of a state legislature, or on the justices who have served on the Supreme Court through American history, or on various kinds of elites.[32] In cases of this sort, the questions asked are likely to concern such characteristics as class and ethnic origin, education, religious affiliation, occupational or professional record, level of income, ideological predilections, and age. Sometimes so many individuals are involved (e.g., in inquiries into decision making by voters) that sample survey methods must be employed.

Studies of these kinds may serve either or both of two purposes. In the first place, they may provide information showing what types of persons most commonly participate in elections or what types most commonly obtain leading political or governmental positions; in other words, they may identify the political activists. In the second place, these kinds of studies may contribute to the explanation and prediction of behavior. This is a quite obvious possibility where the focus is on one person and where a high proportion of the relevant data is available. Through intense study, the purposes of one person and the rules by which he acts may become fairly plain. Where larger numbers are involved, practical considerations usually compel greater selectivity in the data sought. It may or may not be possible to inquire into purposes and rules that are peculiar to each of a multitude of individuals; quite commonly, as suggested in the preceding paragraph, only the most easily obtainable empirical data can be considered. Such data may or may not be equally relevant to all kinds of decisions. If they provide basis for any prediction at all, it is likely to be in terms of relative probability. Thus it may be possible to predict that out of a thousand people six hundred will make a certain decision, even though it is impossible to predict the decision of a single one of these people, considered alone. The unreliability of predictions of the behavior of a single individual is likely to be all the greater when a change in his status and role is involved which is not reflected in the data. A man who becomes a legislator or a judge may or may not be influenced in his new position by precisely the same factors that influenced him before, or by the same factors that influence people who are substantially like him except for the position held; the position may expose the occupant to new pressures, new expectations, and new perspectives, and thus produce behavior that is more typical of the status and role involved than of decision makers having a certain set of personal characteristics. Where mass voting behavior is concerned, these caveats are not quite so applicable. The change in status and role, if any, is minimal; and the usual object is not to predict how a given individual will vote but how a mass of voters are likely to divide. Here considerable success may be achieved.

The "Partisans of Issues"

The label is Rossi's. Decision-making studies in this category focus on the wielding of unofficial power and influence. (According to Rossi, if sanctions are involved in the effort of one actor to affect the behavior of another, he is exerting power; otherwise he is exerting influence.) Rossi divides such studies into three subcategories: (1) those that focus on "potentials" for power and influence; (2) those that focus on "reputations" for power and influence; and (3) those that focus on "actual" power and influence, perhaps in case studies.

In the first of these subcategories are studies that locate people who presumably have a potential for power and influence through the resources they control or through the positions they hold. For example, those who control corporate wealth or communication media may be identified, as well as those who hold positions of leadership in organizations of various kinds, e.g., a chamber of commerce or a trade union. They are assumed to be in a position to engage in persuasion or coercion, or both. There is no effort to demonstrate that they actually exercise power or influence; rather, the actuality is inferred from the potentiality. The decision of a government official may then be attributed by inference to a private agency that is in a position to exert power or influence over him.[33]

Studies in the second subcategory inquire into opinions about the location of power and influence. Selected persons—usually those who are thought to be in a position to know—are asked to identify those whom they regard as powerful or influential in a given community. People then are identified as powerful and influential in terms of their reputations.[34] And again it may be assumed rather than proved that they actually exercise power and influence when political decisions are to be made.

Studies in the third subcategory focus on the actual power and influence of "partisans of issues." There may be a study of a pressure group which indicates how or how much it influenced a decision or a series of different decisions.[35] Or there may be a study of the history of a particular piece of legislation which includes an effort to determine the extent and methods of the exertion of unofficial power and influence.[36] This approach to decision making obviously has much in common with the interest-group conception of politics.

The Process of Making Specific Decisions

Rather than focusing on the characteristics of decision makers or on the "partisans of issues," a third approach focuses on actors in the process of making specific decisions. There have been various applications of this approach, whether relating to real-life situations or to laboratory experiments. In a sense, a high proportion of the writing on politics and government, both historical and contemporary, has regularly dealt with the process of decision making. Some studies of voting behavior are studies of the making of specific decisions.[37]

The most elaborate description and analysis of this approach is that of Richard C. Snyder.[38] Though concerned primarily with international politics, his work is applicable to domestic politics as well. The barest summary of his conception of the decision-making approach is all that can be presented here. Utilization of the approach calls first of all, of course, for the selection of the decision on which to focus; we will assume it is a decision that has been made rather than one that is impending, and that the purpose is to explain rather than to predict. Along with the selection of the decision to examine goes a selection of the decisional unit—whether an individual official, an agency or branch of government, or the government as a whole. To explain the decision, account must be taken of the organizational context and the situation or setting in which it was made. Relevant features of the setting are likely to be rather complex and extensive; for example, important foreign policy decisions frequently call for consideration of a mass of political, economic, and military data concerning a number of states. Assuming that the decision-making process officially involves a number of persons, questions need to be raised about their spheres of competence, about the communication network and the information available, and about motivations. In truth, data called for by almost any other approach is also likely to be called for by an approach that focuses on actors in the process of decision making. Obviously, they may be influenced by the activities of "partisans of issues," and their own characteristics are bound to condition the outcome; so the other decision-making approaches already discussed can be subsumed under this one. The desire for power is likely to be among the motivations involved, and the legal and institutional framework within which the process occurs may be of crucial importance. Psychological, sociological, economic, and historical data may be relevant. Further, one or more of the approaches consisting of an explanatory theory (to be discussed below) could also be subsumed under a decision-making approach.

The very breadth or comprehensiveness of the focus on the process of making specific decisions is its principal weakness. If decisions are to be studied with the thoroughness that Snyder's analysis suggests, relatively few of them can in practice be examined. His framework seems to do more to extend than to simplify and facilitate the tasks involved. It indicates that a vast mass of data is potentially relevant without providing criteria of selection. In Chapter Three we expressed the view that as a practical matter explanation must be selective. Snyder's framework suggests a contrary view; that the aim should be to make explanation exhaustive. Herbert Simon's view might be noted: the decision "is too gross a unit of analysis" and it "must be dissected into its component premises."[39] This seems to be similar to the view that the focus could well be on the rules by which people act.

Game Theory

The hope of students of game theory is that they can develop a scheme that will be helpful to decision makers who must choose a plan of action—a strategy—in a situation involving some kind of competition or conflict. Simplification is employed in the hope that it will lead to insights that are otherwise less likely to be gained. The simplification is reflected in such assumptions as the following: that there are only a very few parties involved in the conflict—usually only two or three; that each party has only a very few alternatives among which to choose; that the criteria of judgment of all parties (i.e., the ends that each party pursues) are known to all; and that each party is thoroughly rational. Since certain games — e.g., poker — involve simplified decision-making situations, study of the problems has tended to focus on games and the subject has come to be called game theory.

Very few political scientists have so far worked with game theory, whether to develop it or to apply it. It is perhaps too soon to say how fruitful the approach may be.[40]

ENDS-MEANS ANALYSIS

The pursuit of ends and the employment of means are obviously central or salient features of politics, just as decision making is. An approach to politics through the analysis of ends and means is thus quite possible. The approach relates to the desires and purposes of political actors, to reasons for action, and to the methods employed. Decision-making and ends-means approaches might be defined so as to overlap, for ideas concerning ends and means influence decision making. But it is possible to think of motivations and methods, of ends and means, apart from the process by which choices are reached. Instead of thinking of them as elements influencing the process of choice, they can be regarded as the results of the process—the choices themselves. They can be thought of in terms of policy rather than in terms of policy making.

We discussed ends and means briefly in Chapter Two. We noted that precisely the same event or state of affairs can be regarded as either an end or a means, or as both simultaneously. An end is desirable for its own sake; it is self-justifying; it is postulated as good or right. A means is desirable for its effectiveness in contributing to the achievement of an end; it is not self-justifying. To say that an event or state of affairs should be an end is to express a value judgment. To say that a specified means is an effective way of pursuing a given end is to assert a fact. Statements expressing value judgments are normative. Statements of fact are

descriptive. Statements are prescriptive, containing both normative and descriptive elements, when they recommend means to be
employed in the pursuit of an asserted or an assumed end.

The principal requirement in ends-means analysis is a clear
answer to the question whether it is an end or a means that is
being discussed; in other words, the principal requirement is clarity on the question whether the statements being made are normative or descriptive, or prescriptive. The field of the normative,
as indicated in Chapter Two, can range from the very narrow to
the very broad, depending on how much is postulated as good or
right, but there cannot be much purely normative discussion. The
person who starts to discuss his normative judgments in the sense
of supporting or justifying them shifts over into the realm of
either the descriptive or the prescriptive. Most ends-means statements fall into one or another of these categories. Studies of
human motivation and of the ends that people pursue, though
dealing with the value judgments of others, are bound to be descriptive in the main. And, of course, studies of the effectiveness
of given means, or of the consequences of this or that, are also
descriptive. Arguments in behalf of a certain course of action
are prescriptive.

These distinctions are important in terms of the reasoning and
evidence required to support the various kinds of statements.
From a positivist point of view, normative statements, being postulated and volitional, cannot be proved to be sound or correct;
neither can they be refuted. They reflect emotion, will, taste. Descriptive statements, however, are subject to test or check; they
call for supporting reason and evidence, and, in principle, can
be proved or disproved. Prescriptive statements can be divided
into their normative and descriptive components, and each component can be treated accordingly.

There is risk of confusion in an alternative formulation, which
is not uncommon—a formulation under which ends are divided
into such categories as immediate, intermediate, and ultimate.
The practice permits at least two interpretations.

In the first place, those engaging in it may not be thinking in
terms of the distinctions suggested above, and they may be quite
ready to grant that any of the ends they describe as immediate or
intermediate might be regarded alternatively as a means; for that

matter, if they are using the word *ultimate* loosely, they might grant that even what they call ultimate ends might alternatively be classified as means. If this is the case, and if everyone is aware of the loose usage involved, confusion can be avoided.

In the second place, those engaging in the practice may be taking the deliberate view that there is no real basis for the distinction between ends and means—that the two are hopelessly intertwined. As suggested above, there is something to be said for this view, for most events and states of affairs are in truth ends and means simultaneously. We want them for their own sake and at the same time we also want them for their contribution toward the achievement of something else. Under this outlook, nothing is simply a means, and so there is no basis for distinguishing between ends and means. Instead, everything tends to be treated as an end or as a value, and ends or values are then classified into instrumental values, on the one hand, and goal values, on the other.[41]

Whatever may be said for this view, it deprives the scholar of a basis for sound inquiry; it frustrates efforts to develop reliable propositions; it blocks scientific study. If the object is to develop verified or verifiable generalizations, then it is imperative to distinguish between ends and means, between value and fact. And this is clearly permissible. To grant that the same event or state of affairs may be regarded as either an end or as a means does not imply that the two categories are inseparable. On the contrary, they are separable for analytical purposes; one can choose the aspect at which to look.

Perhaps the principal value of an ends-means approach is that it inherently involves emphasis on the purposive character of human behavior. Though other approaches permit this emphasis, none of them calls for it so explicitly. There have been many demonstrations of the ease with which human purposes can fade into the background and perhaps be lost from sight when the focus is on institutions or laws or even power. Institutions tend to be treated as mechanical structures, or as organic beings with purposes of their own. Law tends to be regarded as something to which man is subjected through the will of God or Nature or Justice. Power tends to be treated as the only end or means. Reification and mental side-slipping of these sorts are rendered less likely by an approach that focuses attention on human beings who employ means that they choose in pursuing the ends that they also choose.

Though the limits of the applicability of an ends-means approach have not been determined, it seems likely that it will apply wherever the question permits a focus on people acting. For when they act they necessarily pursue ends and employ means. The student employing an ends-means approach may then choose, for example, to identify the people whose actions are relevant to the question posed, to identify the ends that they pursue, and to identify the means that they do or might employ. In other words, he can describe the ends pursued and the interrelationships among these ends, accepting as ends those that are so regarded by the actors under study; and he can go on to describe the methods by which, and the limiting conditions under which, the ends are or might be pursued. The approach is applicable to every level of political activity in every realm.[42]

CHAPTER TWELVE

Behavioral and Analogical Approaches

References are sometimes made to a "behavioral approach" to the study of politics, and a few political scientists recommend an approach that goes under the label "general systems theory." Since the rule in Part III of this book is to follow usage in identifying possible approaches, these two call for brief comment.

BEHAVIORAL APPROACHES

The terms the *behavioral sciences, political behavior,* and *behavioral approach* have become prominent in recent years. The term *behavioral sciences* applies to all those sciences that pay special attention to the behavior of animals, especially man. In this sense all of the social sciences, including history and psychology, are behavioral sciences. The term political behavior, in its lexical meaning, denotes all human political activity. In this sense, the study of political behavior is the study of politics, and not the study of a subdivision or aspect of politics. Though stipulative definitions of *political behavior* are sometimes advanced, as when a course or a book is given this title, none of them has gained general currency.

If lexical definitions were relied upon, the term *behavioral approach* might be dismissed as virtually meaningless. Or it might be taken to denote an approach focusing on all political activity, which makes it denote so much that no very specific meaning is conveyed. But the term has a stipulative meaning, however imprecise it may be; and, in contrast to the situation with regard to the term *political behavior,* this general meaning is widely accepted.

A behavioral approach is distinguished predominantly by the nature of the purpose it is designed to serve. The purpose is scientific—a term that we will discuss in Chapter Fifteen. In this context the notion of scientific purpose has several connotations. It calls for an effort to develop generalizations about political behavior, i.e., to advance hypotheses about relationships, to discover uniformities or regularities or laws, and to suggest theories; the higher the level of generalization, the better. At the same time it denotes an insistence that the generalizations be verified or verifiable. Normative propositions are avoided; the object is description, including explanation and descriptive statements about normative attitudes. If prescriptive statements are made, their normative component falls outside the realm of science. The requirement that the generalizations be verified or verifiable calls for empiricism—for reliance on observation and refusal to rely on alleged a priori truths. It also calls for precision in the definition of concepts, clarity in the formulation of hypotheses, and, in effect, restraint about calling a generalization anything other than a hypothesis until it has been demonstrated to be true. In addition to generality and verifiability, the notion of a scientific purpose connotes system; that is, the object is to develop a set of verified generalizations that fit together in a coherent system—a coherent, interlocking network—giving a comprehensive description and explanation of the realm of behavior in question.

A behavioral approach is also distinguished by the methods employed. They must be such as to produce results that are reliable. They should permit replication—repetition of the study by another person, with the same result.

Given the above connotations for purpose and method, a behavioral approach has also come to be identified with the type of question asked or the type of inquiry attempted. As indicated above, the questions call for description, and not for normative or prescriptive statements. And within the realm of description, the questions are limited to those that can be answered reliably on the basis of the methods available. When a contradiction develops between the desire for a high level of generality and the desire for a high degree of reliability, the latter prevails. The student who takes a behavioral approach is not likely to ask broad and vague questions like what caused the decline and fall of the

Roman Empire or whether the military power available to the Soviet bloc is greater than the power available to the West or whether liberalism is likely to triumph in Africa. Nor is he likely to focus on ideologies or constitutions or laws or upon the organizational structure of institutions. Rather, he is likely to stick to questions that call for a relatively narrow range of evidence and logic; further, he may well focus on the behavior of individual persons or of relatively small groups. Studies of the characteristics of decision makers and of factors influencing decision making—whether by voters, officials, or others—are likely to be behavioral; so are studies of the distribution of opinions and attitudes. Some associate game theory and systems theory (to be discussed below) with a behavioral approach to politics.

As the above illustrations suggest, the behavioral approach is not necessarily distinct from some of the other approaches. A study may involve both a behavioral and a decision-making approach, for example. To state this in the language employed in Chapter Seven, our scheme for classifying approaches is not entirely logical in that the categories are not mutually exclusive.[1]

ANALOGICAL APPROACHES: GENERAL SYSTEMS THEORY

Like game theory, general systems theory ranks among the more esoteric of the possible approaches to politics.

As the label suggests, the focus is on *systems*. "Systems are bounded regions in space-time, involving energy interchange among their parts, which are associated in functional relationships, and with their environments."[2] There are thus a very large number of types of systems. The atom is a system, and so are molecules, crystals, viruses, clocks, engines, ocean fleets, animals (including humans), small groups, societies (including political societies), planets, solar systems, galaxies, etc.

When the reference is to *general* systems theory, the intention is that the theory should be relevant to many or all kinds of systems, from the smallest subsystem of an atom to the systems composed of galaxies. Those systems theorists who wish to narrow down their field of inquiry may speak of general *behavior* systems theory, which covers "living systems, extending roughly from viruses through societies."[3]

To describe the common or comparable features of systems,

the systems theorists have developed a number of new concepts, or have given new meanings to old concepts. Thus there are systems with functions having variables and parameters. For each system there are inputs and outputs, implying throughputs, which are coded or uncoded. Living systems are said to suffer strain, which is reducible, and to tend to maintain steady states or homeostasis through various means, including feedback mechanisms. The operation of a number of different kinds of systems can be described in terms such as these.

Proponents of systems theory entertain several hopes. One is that various systems will be found to have enough in common to permit some kind of transfer of knowledge; thus, knowledge of the operation of an organism might also apply to the operation of an organization, and vice versa. Knowledge of each system would thus be enhanced by increases in knowledge of other systems. A second hope is simply a limited version of the first one. It is that the study of one system may have heuristic value for the study of other systems, suggesting the kinds of questions to ask, the kinds of experiments to conduct, and the kinds of knowledge that it may be possible to acquire. A third hope is that if systems are viewed in all their complexity as operating wholes rather than being subdivided into components and examined part by part, knowledge can be gained that might otherwise be missed.

It remains to be seen whether efforts to develop systems theory will lead to much of a payoff. Skepticism has been expressed. Confronted with the analogies of systems theory and with the fact that one set of concepts is applicable to many types of systems, one critic suggests that the most appropriate reaction is, "So what?"[4] Another, though granting that scattered analogies have heuristic value, remains "unconvinced that the common content of the several systems theories is sufficiently great to justify the investment of much effort in the construction of an elaborate formal structure."[5] Still another appraises systems theory as "a huge misstep in the right direction—the direction of systematic empirical analysis."[6]

It is quite possible to apply the concepts associated with general systems theory to political systems alone. There is an international political system, comprised of the political systems of states, which in turn consist of a series of subsystems; and the study of these systems and subsystems provides bases for comparisons and analogies which may be very helpful to those seeking an understanding of any one of them. At least, in making comparative studies, political scientists have long acted on this assumption. One can study political systems without also studying molecular and galactic systems. But if the focus is so restricted, then the contribution of general systems theory to the study of politics is reduced to the distinctive concepts employed. Moreover, though it is obviously possible that knowledge can be gained by studying political systems as operating wholes, it is not clear that one needs to adopt the vocabulary of systems theorists for this purpose.

When those taking a systems theory approach confine their attention to political systems, it is in point to ask to what extent they are really concerned with *systems* and to what extent their concern is with *theory*. The impression is sometimes given that they are motivated mainly by a desire to get away from the tendency to describe politics at very low levels of generality. Systems theorists aim at very high levels of generality, but so can other theorists.[7]

CHAPTER THIRTEEN

Approaches Identified with Explanatory Hypotheses or Causal Theories

So far in the chapters of Part III we have examined approaches that are identified with (1) an academic discipline, (2) a salient feature of politics, (3) a behavioral outlook, and (4) analogies among systems. All of these approaches provide general criteria that students of politics can employ in deciding on the questions or problems to take up and in selecting the data to consider in relation to them. Thus all of them reflect or suggest a conception of what is important to an effort to understand or predict or control the course of political events. They point in a general way to ideas and data that are presumed to be significant.

Now we turn to approaches that are identified with explanatory hypotheses or causal theories. The difference is more one of degree than of kind, for all kinds of approaches reflect or suggest conceptions of the significant. But the explanatory hypotheses do it more explicitly. Whereas an approach identified with an academic discipline, for example, simply points to a field of inquiry and to the varied data associated with it, an approach that is expressed in a hypothesis or theory points to a more specific type of data and to a way of ordering it. If we say, on the one hand, that the causes of war are economic or psychological, we are pointing generally to data identified with academic disciplines. If we say, on the other hand, that capitalism causes war or that the human craving for

deference is the cause, then we have more explicit guidance in selecting the data to consider; the general hypothesis or causal theory
needs simply to be applied to specific cases that arise. Thus,
though some of the considerations advanced in this section are
related to others advanced earlier, when we were identifying approaches with such academic disciplines as geography, economics,
and psychology, it is hoped that a distinction will be apparent.

Considered as approaches to the study of politics, explanatory
hypotheses or causal theories can be grouped into three broad
categories, depending on the relative emphasis on (1) environmental influences, (2) psychological data and considerations, and
(3) ideological data and considerations.

APPROACHES EMPHASIZING ENVIRONMENTAL INFLUENCES

Approaches that are rather distinct from each other fall within
this category. In one subdivision fall those that emphasize geographic influences—or that stem from an initial tendency to do so.
In the second subdivision fall those that specifically emphasize
certain economic aspects of the environment.

Geographic and Related Approaches

Harold and Margaret Sprout have made the most extensive and
the most recent study of explanatory hypotheses which stem from
a focus on geographic influences and which are relevant to the
study of politics. What follows on this subject is patterned after
their work.[1]

Geographers have sometimes used language suggesting an endorsement of rather extreme causal theories. Sir Halford Mackinder's theory concerning the importance of the Heartland, cited
above, illustrates the point. Others suggest the broad view that
the distribution of things over the face of the earth (e.g., climate
and the various kinds of natural resources) has been—and presumably will continue to be—determining; in other words, that all
human decisions and the results thereof have been dictated by an
inanimate nature, and, presumably, that if history could be started
over again it would turn out the same way, given the same geographic conditions. There have been other statements picturing
Nature as a Being with purposes of its own, possessing and exer-
cising the power to control man's fate. Probably no geographer—
or anyone else—would endorse either of these positions when they

are stated so explicitly. Language suggestive of the position is presumably to be dismissed as rather loose rhetoric.

The fact seems to be that few, if any, questions about human behavior can be answered solely on the basis of geographic data and considerations. Always, or almost always, other factors enter in—e.g., the desires or purposes or values of those involved. Statements to the effect that geography determines foreign policy—or any other kind of behavior—are almost certain to be false. Perhaps it is because of this that there has been a tendency to shift away from purely geographic data and to consider the much broader realm of the environment.

Though no one definition of the concept *environment* is everywhere accepted, we can properly make it denote all factors outside the environed person that relate to his behavior or condition or status. It includes both natural and man-made phenomena. It is geographic, economic, political, and so on. The environment of one person includes the attitudes, expectations, and practices of all other persons whose behavior in any way relates to his own. It is equivalent to what Snyder, in his study of decision making, calls the setting.

Note that the reference here is only to the environment as it really exists. Phrases like "environment as it is imagined to be" and "environment as apperceived" and "psychological environment" are acceptable if handled with care, but they are a potential source of two sorts of confusion. On the one hand, they may create the impression that two different environments exist—the real one and the one that is apperceived; but, obviously, an incorrect apperception of the environment is simply that, and not a different environment. On the other hand, these phrases may suggest that the images one has of his environment are part of the environment; and then the distinction between the environed person and the environment is lost.

Note, too, that the reference here is to the environment of individuals. It is also possible to treat a group or a political entity as a unit having an environment, but there are hazards in the practice. Groups and political entities are not indivisible wholes surrounded externally by an environment. Rather, they are composed of individuals; and group action is really the action of some or all of the individual members. Thus, it is their individual environments that ordinarily count, and their individual environments include features that are internal to the group. The setting in which the individual decision maker operates is both external and internal.

Emphasis on the role of the environment has led to several kinds of hypotheses. The Sprouts label one of them "environmental possibilism." The essence of it is the simple proposition that the environment imposes limits on what it is possible to do. The more accurate is one's apperception of the environment, then, the more capable he is of (1) selecting courses of action that are feasible and (2) explaining or predicting the operational results of courses of action that others undertake. The man whose apperception is realistic will not try to walk across a lake, and he will be able to predict the operational result if someone else attempts it.

The Sprouts label another kind of hypothesis "environmental probabilism." As the name suggests, hypotheses falling in this category concern various kinds of probabilities: that a given decision will be made, that a given event will occur, that a given operational result will be achieved, and so on. Obviously, hypotheses of this sort call for consideration of many kinds of environmental data in addition to the geographic; psychological, ideological, economic, and other data are likely to be involved. This suggests what is perhaps the major weakness of the approach: that, like the decision-making approach, it gives minimal help in selecting the questions to ask and the data relevant thereto. Not only is the whole of the environment made the realm of inquiry, but images of the environment no doubt need to be studied as well. The approach is so broad and inclusive that those who take it will be virtually compelled to supplement it with another approach that is clearer in providing criteria of selection.

The Sprouts label another category of environmentalist hypotheses "cognitive behaviorism." These hypotheses reflect the principle that it is one's knowledge of the environment rather than the environment itself that influences behavior; i.e., it is the image of the environment that influences decision making. The principal point is that the wisdom of decision making is bound to be affected by the accuracy and comprehensiveness of the image.

Economic Approaches

Explanatory hypotheses or causal theories that stress economic aspects of the environment might be incorporated in one or another of the categories described above, but it is probably best to follow the more usual practice and treat them separately. They rest on a broader base than the strictly geographic approaches, and on a narrower base than the very general environmentalist approaches; and they appear to be more precise.

The name of Karl Marx towers so definitely over all others associated with economic approaches that our focus may as well be on him, though we should note that a great many others—before Marx as well as after—have expressed views that are in some respects the same.

There is danger of confusion of purpose in discussing Marx and his theories. When we were examining the meanings of the word *theory* in Chapter Seven we said that it sometimes designates the consummation of explanation. In this chapter we are discussing approaches, and we are saying that a theory can be an approach to explanation as well as the consummation of explanation; it can be a starting point as well as an end point. Like any other type of approach, a theory can give guidance in the formulation of questions to ask and in the selection of relevant data; it can provide criteria of relevance or criteria of significance. Once a theory has been developed, it can give guidance in the search for new facts and explanations. Our present purpose in discussing Marxist theories is to show how, and how well, they serve as guides—as criteria for determining what is significant.

The following statements by Marx convey, in rather stark form, some basic elements in his thought.

The mode of production of the material means of existence conditions the whole process of social, political, and intellectual life. It is not the consciousness of men which determines their existence, but on the contrary it is their social existence that determines their consciousness. . . .

Men, developing their material production and their material intercourse, alter along with this their real existence, their thinking and the products of their thinking. Life is not determined by consciousness, but consciousness by life.

Marx's collaborator, Friedrich Engels, expressed approximately the same thought:

The ultimate causes of all social changes and political revolutions are to be sought, not in the minds of men, . . . but in changes in the mode of production and exchange; they are to be sought not in the philosophy but in the economics of the period concerned.[2]

In short, Marx advanced a materialist theory—sometimes called historical or dialectical materialism. In his eyes, men struggled within and against a difficult environment to meet their needs and wants. "Forces of production" were brought to bear in the struggle, reflecting the technology and other circumstances of the time. Marx held that the "forces of production" were basic and that, as they changed, the relationships of men with them and with each other necessarily changed as well. The forces of production constituted the foundation on which a superstructure arose. The superstructure consisted of the thoughts and practices of men, manifested in part in their economic, political, religious, and other institutions or patterns of activity. All aspects of human behavior, according to Marx, were somehow conditioned or affected by the material base. Changes in the base would make changes in the superstructure inevitable. In sum, Marx held that "in trying to explain the history of man and his institutions, the essential thing to look for is the manner in which men have gone about the task of mastering their environment."[3]

All history, said Marx and Engels, has been the history of class struggles. In existing and previous societies, relationships to the productive forces included a division of labor, which meant that there was also a division of interests. Since men were "conscious and purposive animals," able to recognize their interests and motivated to fight for them, they aligned themselves into classes as their interests dictated, each class struggling for its own advantage.[4] The dominant or ruling class controlled both economic and political life. Government and the state, then, were class instruments, employed to protect and promote the interests of those in control—under capitalism, the bourgeoisie. Through law and police action at home, and through diplomacy and war abroad, the bourgeoisie pursued its advantage—exploiting others economically and oppressing them politically. It developed and championed political ideologies and religious and moral principles as rationalizations and justifications of its class interests. But productive forces change; technological and other developments occur. Automatically, then, need arises for change in productive relationships; the

superstructure must be altered in conformity with the requirements of the base. The changes that create the need also create the
prerequisites for meeting the need, for oppressed and exploited
classes develop consciousness not simply of their interests but of
effective means of pursuing them, while at the same time the power
of the ruling class is undermined. The ruling class, of course, attempts to defend its privileged position by all possible means,
including violence; but the laws of historical development are
against them. Sooner or later a readjustment of the superstructure
must and does occur.

The above is simply a sketch of a portion of Marxist theory.
We would have to qualify the sketch and elaborate on it if the
object were to appraise the theory as an end point—as the consummation of explanation. But even a very brief and incomplete
sketch of the theory is enough to suggest how it can serve as a
starting point—a guide to inquiry. It suggests questions to ask,
e.g., what is the class affiliation of the political actor in question,
or what is the role of, say, the democratic socialist in the class
struggle? It suggests the kind of data to take into account—data
centering around the pursuit and protection of economic interests
by rational persons. It is applicable to many kinds of problems
at many times and places. Far-reaching and comprehensive, it provides guidance in asking and answering questions concerning virtually every phase of political life. It is an all-embracing and all-
pervasive system of thought. Those who accept it find not only
that it guides but that it is likely to dominate such inquiry as they
make into every variety of social phenomenon.

Marx obviously contributed much to the development of
knowledge, and he developed an approach that others have employed to great advantage. At the same time, his theory has been
demonstrated to be unsound in a number of respects. Who can
say whether the guidance it has provided has been predominantly
helpful and true or predominantly misleading and false? Assuming for present purposes that the development of knowledge of
politics is the prime object, it is unfortunate that Marxism became
less a system of hypotheses guiding political inquiry than a theory
guiding political action. As a theory guiding action it became a
doctrine, if not a dogma, supported by true believers. And true
believers who employ it as a guide to inquiry naturally tend to

shape their inquiries so that the results support their faith. This
has undoubtedly led to the perpetuation and extension of error.
At the same time, those who are detached scholars rather than true
believers have in many cases found a Marxist approach to political
questions to be very fruitful.

APPROACHES EMPHASIZING PSYCHOLOGICAL OR PSYCHOANALYTIC THEORIES

We noted earlier, when we were defining *approach* in terms of
academic disciplines, that psychological approaches to politics are
generally motivational. It follows that those who delve into psychology or psychoanalysis for explanatory hypotheses or causal
theories that are relevant to political behavior generally come up
with hypotheses or theories about motivation.

Freudian theories are in point. In seeking to explain human
behavior—or, more strictly, neurotic human behavior—Freud emphasized certain implications of the socialization of the individual,
i.e., of the process by which individuals are restrained and trained
so as to become acceptable members of society. His view was that
desires that had to be restrained were frequently repressed so thoroughly that the individual ceased to be conscious of them, but that
they could nevertheless continue to influence behavior from the
realm of the unconscious. In truth, as conceived by Freud, psychoanalysis was largely a study of the role of the unconscious in bringing about departures from the usual rules of behavior.[5] He was
so impressed with the prevalence of intense drives of love and
hate, of which the individual was freqently unaware, that he came
to postulate the existence of what he called Eros, the impulse of
love and life, and the existence of Thanatos, the impulse toward
death and destruction. In his view, men went through life driven
in these opposite ways. In all realms of behavior, including the
political, they were driven by Eros and Thanatos.

To Freud, rationalization, displacement, and projection were
significant psychological mechanisms through which the unconscious affected conscious behavior. In this context rationalization
designates the process by which the individual finds socially acceptable reasons for doing what he is actually prompted to do
by socially unacceptable, unsconscious desires. Displacement designates a process that occurs when the individual finds it impru-

dent or socially unacceptable to release impulses along the "natural" channel or at the "natural" target; unconsciously, and perhaps after a period of time during which the impulse is repressed, he deflects or redirects the activity along another channel or at another target. Projection designates a process by which the individual attributes his own shameful characteristics or designs to others and so rids himself of guilt for evil thought and deed.

Freud's theories, and the processes just defined, have an obvious bearing on political activity. The concepts Eros and Thanatos are too vague to be more than suggestive of explanations of behavior, but their suggestiveness applies as much to political as to other kinds of behavior. If anything, rationalization, displacement, and projection are probably more common in the realm of political behavior than in other realms. The fact that selfish purposes are so rarely admitted in politics establishes a presumption that a good deal of rationalization occurs. The frequency with which scapegoats are created suggests that displacement is common. And the regularity with which a monopoly of shameful conduct is assigned to the other side gives basis for the suspicion that projection takes place. In short, those seeking to explain and predict political behavior are often guided to significant data by taking a Freudian approach.

In addition to Freud, other psychoanalysts and psychiatrists also offer guidance that is helpful to students of politics. Whenever they advance a hypothesis or theory about any sizable range of behavior, an application to political behavior is to be expected. Alfred Adler, Karen Horney, and Erich Fromm are among those whose work is especially relevant.[6] They give considerable stress to the view that men are possessed by feelings of inferiority, humiliation, and insignificance, and that they are driven to seek superiority, glory, and significance. Obviously, the political arena is among those in which these ends can be pursued.

Non-Freudian psychologists, especially those seeking to be meticulously scientific, are less notable than those influenced by Freud for hypotheses and theories of direct relevance to political behavior. Nevertheless, some of their inquiries provide helpful guidance. This is especially true of studies of frustration and aggression, which have produced theories that are obviously relevant to political behavior.[7]

Harold D. Lasswell is especially prominent among the political scientists who have taken up a psychological approach to politics.[8] In this connection he concerns himself especially with the values that people pursue and, more particularly, with the sources and implications of the desire for power. He demonstrates in case studies that the reasons for political action are sometimes definitely psychological in origin: that purely personal insecurities and anxieties—and purely personal aspirations—are influential in guiding political behavior. He regards the deference values, including power, as especially notable. He constructs a model of what he calls the political type, the essential feature of the political type being that he makes it a rule to choose whatever course of action will maximize power—all other values being sacrificed to this one. Lasswell obviously thinks that persons who approach the extreme of his model are not uncommon in politics, but he rejects the view that all men, or even all political leaders, belong in this category. In so far as Lasswell endorses a hypothesis or theory that men strive for power, he makes it a theory of limited rather than universal applicability.

Clearly, all of these hypotheses or theories may serve as approaches to the study of politics. If we want to know why a given person acted as he did, or if we want to predict his probable action in the future, psychological data may well be relevant; and these hypotheses or theories are likely to be helpful in guiding the student to the type of data that will have explanatory or predictive value.

APPROACHES EMPHASIZING IDEOLOGIES

What Is an Ideology?

Various meanings are assigned to the word *ideology*. We can get at them best by recalling that people hold beliefs about matters of both fact and value. They believe that certain statements or propositions are true descriptions of reality, and they believe that certain other propositions indicate what is good or right. They entertain beliefs about what is and about what ought to be.

Beliefs that are exclusively matters of fact are not called ideological, which means that an ideology is never purely descriptive. Beliefs about questions of value must be involved before an ideology is said to exist. This means that ideologies are always normative, at least in part; they reflect or suggest conceptions of what ought to be.

The word ideology is sometimes applied to almost any set of beliefs about what ought to be, provided they are reasonably coherent and consistent. In other words, the term applies to almost any normative scheme. Ordinarily, however, belief in the set of values is associated with the acceptance of certain descriptive propositions of an explanatory or causal sort. Thus, those who accept the ideology of liberalism assert, as a value, that the human personality has worth; they say that human dignity ought to be promoted and respected. At the same time, they believe that as a matter of fact human beings are capable of governing themselves democratically and that democratic government is most likely to respect the worth of the individual and the dignity of man. In other words, the existence of democracy is accepted as a condition or cause of the achievement of a value. Similarly, Marxists accept certain values and offer both an explanation of failure to achieve these values and a prescription for bringing their achievement about.

Karl Mannheim modified and added to the above conception of an ideology. His basic point was that beliefs are "relational," i.e., related to the situation of the observer. What people think, he held, is socially determined. Their conception of their interests is shaped by their experience in society, and, in turn, they view social issues in terms of their interests. Their beliefs, i.e., their ideologies, are thus reflections of their interests, and are not to be treated as true.

According to Mannheim, there are both "particular" and "total" conceptions of ideology. Persons gain a "particular" conception when they become aware of the "relational" nature of the ideology of their political opponents. The ideas comprising the opponent's ideology are seen "as more or less conscious disguises of the real nature of a situation, the true recognition of which would not be in accord with [the opponent's] interests. These distortions range all the way from conscious lies to half-conscious and unwitting disguises; from calculated attempts to dupe others to self-deception." The "particular" conception, however, is a step toward a "total" conception. Under the latter, all ideologies, including one's own, are recognized to be reflections of interests in terms of a given situation.

To begin with, a given social group discovers the "situational determination" of its opponents' ideas. Subsequently the recognition of this fact is elaborated into an all-inclusive principle according to which the thought of every group is seen as arising out of its life conditions.

. . . All historical knowledge is relational knowledge, and can only be formulated with reference to the position of the observer.

Once a "total" conception of ideology has been grasped, according to Mannheim, it "develops into the sociology of knowledge." That is, all beliefs are held to be conditioned or colored by the interests and social situation of the believers. The view taken is like that of Karl Marx, cited above, under which thoughts are regarded as the creatures of changing material conditions of life. Mannheim granted that "the ultimate criterion of truth or falsity is to be found in the investigation of the object." But he held that "the examination of the object is not an isolated act; it takes place in a context which is colored by values and collective-unconscious, volitional impulses."[9] Thus all beliefs, all knowledge, are ideological and relational, with universal agreement unobtainable.

Gustav Bergmann offers a definition that reflects a different point of view. He distinguishes between fact and value, and suggests that the propositions in which people believe comprise a *rationale* as long as the distinction is understood and maintained. An individual proposition or statement is to be labeled "ideological," however, when "a value judgment [is] disguised as, or mistaken for, a statement of fact." And a *rationale* becomes an *ideology* when it "contains ideological statements in logically crucial places." To illustrate his conception of an "ideological statement" Bergmann cites Thomas Jefferson, who asserted that "these truths" (not these value judgments) were self-evident. And he cites the various claims based on appeal to alleged natural law.[10] This amounts to an assertion of the view that when a rationalist thinks that right reason has provided him with truth about a question of value, he is really (and perhaps unwittingly) disguising his value preferences as matters of fact.

The value judgments that figure in a rationale or an ideology are sometimes called ideals or rules of conduct or a moral code or a philosophy of life. As reasons or motives for action, they influence and guide behavior. One of Bergmann's significant points is that the motive power of a value judgment is often increased when the actor considers it to be a statement of fact. Those who are hesitant about endorsing a faith explicitly, feeling that this kind of thing is not quite in accord with the rule of reason and science, sometimes find it possible to accept a faith, and to support it fervently, when it is disguised as a fact or set of facts.

No matter which definition of ideology is employed, ideological explanation has much in common with explanation in terms of reasons, discussed in Chapter Three. Ideological beliefs provide reasons for action, with accompanying rules, reasons, and doctrines. When they comprise an ideology, they are not haphazard, scattered, and inchoate but fit together in a system—a coherent whole.

Problems in Approaches Focusing on Ideologies

The assumption on which an ideological approach to the study of politics rests is that belief systems guide behavior and, therefore, that if explanation and prediction are desired questions should be asked and data sought concerning these belief systems.

One can accept the assumption and still see many problems. The beliefs of which an ideology consists are not always precise; on the contrary, they are frequently rather vague, susceptible to formulation in different ways by different actors or at different times. Thus, one question concerns the conception of the ideology that a specific political actor has; moreover, it may be in point to ask whether his conception seems to be in process of change and, if so, in what direction. This suggests that different persons who ostensibly subscribe to the same ideology may interpret it differently, or that their interpretations may be either diverging or converging; if the ideology provides basis for a political movement, then, knowledge of the similarities and differences in various interpretations of the ideology may sometimes be significant. The history of communism, for example, is full of bitter factionalism in which doctrinal issues have figured very prominently, each feuding person or party generally claiming to have a monopoly of truth. Knowledge of these ideological differences frequently provides a basis for explaining or predicting the course of events.

Not only are ideologies commonly vague, and thus susceptible to different interpretations, but the situations in which they are applied are also likely to be more or less confused. For example, communists take the view that there is a revolutionary tide in history and that the tide ebbs and flows. One kind of strategy is called for when the tide is ebbing, and another kind when it is flowing. But measuring devices for determining whether there is an ebb or a flow are not always reliable. Different communists may themselves render different judgments on the issue. Thus, noncommunists who are trying to employ the ideology as a basis for explanation or prediction must concern themselves not only with the way in which different communists interpret the doctrine but also with the way in which they define the situation in which the doctrine is applied.

As if to complicate the problem even more, the same political actor sometimes subscribes to two or more differing ideologies— e.g., liberalism (or communism) and nationalism. Though these ideologies may be quite compatible in many respects, contradictions are almost certain to arise; and in these cases a choice has to be made. Explanations or predictions of behavior must then include explanations or predictions of choices between the competing ideologies.

Finally, it is probably best to avoid the assumption that all acts are influenced or governed by ideological considerations. Personal lusts and ambitions, for example, are nonideological, yet they obviously supersede ideology at times in influencing individual behavior. In the case of persons who are in positions of considerable political power, such personal motivations may come to be of great importance in shaping the course of events.

In sum, though it is obviously true that knowledge of the ideology or ideologies to which a political actor subscribes is often helpful in explaining or predicting his behavior, it is not always an easy guide to apply.

The difficulties should not be exaggerated. In a great many respects it has obviously made a difference, for example, that communists have ruled in Moscow, that Fascists once ruled in Rome and Nazis in Berlin, and that believers in liberalism and democracy have ruled in London and Washington. Similarly, the development of nationalism in Europe and its spread over much of the earth has had profound effects on the course of political events. It would be very surprising if anyone could satisfactorily describe and explain the major political developments of recent decades without reference to one or more of these ideologies.

Quite apart from the great affairs of state, the behavior of persons is sure to vary some, depending on whether they are communists, Fascists, liberal-democrats, or nationalists. Moreover, explanations and predictions of the behavior of a person in, for example, Britain or the United States are likely to be facilitated if it is known whether he is reactionary, conservative, progressive, or radical.

If we were allocating space in proportion to the usefulness of the various approaches, we would have to assign much more space to explanatory hypotheses that focus on ideology. We would also have to devote more space to the merits of the approach and less to its difficulties. However, on the assumption that the usefulness and merits of the approach will be recognized without being stressed, we will not pursue the matter further.[11]

E. H. CARR'S TWO "METHODS OF APPROACH"

In *The Twenty Years' Crisis* E. H. Carr describes what he calls two "methods of approach" to politics, one utopian and the other realist.[12] Though his implicit definition of "approach" is in some elusive way different from the one being employed here, his characterization of these "methods of approach" deserves to be noted briefly.

According to Carr, the utopian is inclined "to ignore what was and what is in contemplation of what should be," and the realist is inclined "to deduce what should be from what was and what is." The antithesis between the two shows up in five respects. (1) The utopian believes in the possibility of giving effect to his will, changing the course that events would have taken in the absence of his effort; in contrast, the realist "analyses a predetermined course of events which he is powerless to change." The one is creative, and perhaps naïve. The other reconciles himself to uncontrollable causality, and so submits. (2) The utopian gives paramount emphasis to his wishes or normative standards; he may treat values as facts, as in alleging that all men are created equal. In contrast, the realist gives paramount emphasis to practice, and is inclined to regard normative standards as codifications of practice or reflections of conceptions of advantage. (3) The utopian is intellectual, emphasizing reason and right principles, whereas the realist is the bureaucrat who eschews principle and who handles each problem "on its merits," guided by tradition and intuition. (4) The utopian is generally on the Left politically, whereas the realist is on the Right. And (5) the utopian subordinates political activity to ethical principles, whereas the realist is a relativist who derives ethical principles from reality.

What Carr seems to be doing is to create models of two types of political actors. At the same time, the models help to provide a basis for classifying the viewpoints, if not the approaches, of students of politics. They obviously bear, too, on the definition of politics with which one begins. The views that Carr attributes to the realist, for example, are suggestive of the conception of politics advanced by Michael Oakeshott, described in Chapter Ten.

Two final comments on the above taxonomy of approaches to the study of politics may be in order. The first is that, if the classification scheme is sound, all or nearly all approaches actually employed should fit into one or another of the categories; the qualifier on this is that many students of politics are eclectic in their approach, mixing quite different types of data. In many cases, such eclecticism is highly desirable. The second general comment is that no one of the approaches should be regarded as being necessarily and always the best. Students of politics do and should feel free to choose among them, basing their choice on any of a number of considerations: their own personal training and skills, the nature of the general problem that they confront, the audience at which they are aiming, and so on. At the same time, the object should be to develop causal theories that are applicable to all questions concerning the explanation and prediction of events.

CHAPTER FOURTEEN

Methods

In the Introduction to Part III we noted that when the word *methods* is given clear meaning it ordinarily is made to denote either (1) epistemological assumptions on which the search for knowledge is based or, much more commonly, (2) the operations or activities that occur in the acquisition and treatment of data. We noted, too, that in the latter of these meanings a method may also be called a technique.

We have discussed methods in the first of the above meanings at various points through this book, especially in the Introduction to Part I and in Chapter One. Here, therefore, the focus is on method in the second sense.

When methods are identified and defined in terms of the types of operations or activities that occur in the acquisition and treatment of data, they are described in various ways: as analytical, quantitative, qualitative, inductive, deductive, comparative, scientific, etc. The focus here will be on these labels and on the categories they identify, even though this involves some overlapping. There will be no attempt to present a logical and articulate classification scheme.

ANALYSIS AS A METHOD

We have defined analysis above as a process by which the parts of a whole are identified. The object of an analytical method is thus, presumably, to identify the components of whatever is being examined. Commonly, too, analysis is accompanied by an effort to find out how the parts are related—how they fit together to make the whole. This may be extended to cover the study of the functional relationship of the parts. Strictly speaking, analysis should be contrasted with synthesis, as suggested above, but such purity of usage is not always maintained.[1]

Aside from designating a method distinct from synthesis, the term *analysis* may be used to help describe other methods. For example, qualitative and quantitative methods are described as qualitative and quantitative analysis; comparative methods are said to call for comparative analysis; and so on.

We might note, incidentally, that the word *analytical* is used in still other ways. In the field of international politics, at least, those who grope for appropriate labels sometimes seize upon the word simply for lack of a better one—perhaps making it describe an approach rather than a method. There has been discontent, for example, with the chronological-historical approach to the subject, in which the eye is on the past, and a shift toward another approach in which the eye is on current or prospective situations and problems. But what label can be attached intelligibly to the latter kind of approach? Sometimes it is called *topical*, but topics are also taken up in chronological-historical surveys. It might be called cross-sectional—any selected state of affairs in a sequence being considered a cross-section of a developmental process. Sometimes the difference lies—at least in part—in the level of generality employed, but at best this is an unreliable basis for distinguishing between the approaches at issue. Treatments of a given kind of subject might be ranged on a scale from those that are simply informational to those that are fully thetical, but the chronological-historical treatments would not all fall at the same end of such a scale. Actually, what is said in the chapters of Part III should already have demonstrated that there are many alternatives to a chronological-historical approach rather than just one; and this implies that the quest for a single label for the alternatives is doomed to failure. Nevertheless, the word *analytical* is sometimes employed. The practice is unfortunate, for all kinds of approaches, including the chronological-historical, may involve analysis. Similarly, there is risk of confusion if approaches are classified as ideological, on the one hand, or analytical, on the other.[2] There is also risk of confusion when theories are divided into two categories labeled analytic and normative.[3]

QUANTITATIVE AND QUALITATIVE METHODS

Qualitative methods predominate in the study of politics and have been used over a much longer period of time. This might suggest that we give them precedence in the discussion. But it will be easier to distinguish between the two if we deal with quantitative methods first.

Methods are most obviously quantitative when they involve counting or measuring. More broadly, references to numbers or to numerical relationships are quantitative, even if the reference is simply to a date, which reflects the counting of units of time since the birth of Christ. Many items other than units of time are also counted or measured: words, themes, topics, column inches, people, votes, dollars, units of production, etc. Those who stress the importance of quantitative methods obviously want them to be applied in a rather meticulous way, insisting that what is counted be precisely defined and objectively identifiable, and that the counting itself be done with care. Procedures are to be such as to permit successful replication. The knowledge gained is to be demonstrably true.[4]

Subjective choices must be made even in connection with the use of quantitative methods. The selection of the question to ask or the hypothesis to test is subjective; and the intuition or insight or imagination of the scholar plays an important role in this connection. Similarly, the judgment or other qualities of the scholar come into play if the items to be counted must be defined, or if items that differ somewhat are nevertheless to be grouped for purposes of simplified quantification, or if questionnaires are to be constructed or interviews held, or if sampling is to occur. Subjective elements are thus bound to affect the usefulness, and perhaps they will affect the reliability or the validity, of the results of the application of quantitative methods. Nevertheless, the method is classified as quantitative if, after a certain point, it calls for counting or measuring according to clear, fixed rules.

Qualitative methods are most easily defined as those that are not quantitative—those that do not involve more or less meticulous counting or measuring. Or, they may be defined as those that rely throughout on personal qualities of the scholar: his logic or judgment or insight or imagination or intuition, or his ability to form accurate impressions and to see relationships.

For example, when a method is impressionistic or when it involves only very rough estimates rather than precise counting, it is classified as qualitative, even though it leads to statements that are quasi-quantitative. If we say that something happens *usually, frequently, more often than not, commonly, generally, rarely, etc.*, we are making statements of a quasi-quantitative sort; and the same can be said of other kinds of statements, e.g., that more emphasis is given to one consideration than to another. Similarly, if we say that there has been an increasingly widespread tendency to regard deterrence rather than war as the function of armed establishments, or if we say that the idea of the welfare state gained in prominence in the 1930's and came to be generally accepted by the 1950's, we are making quasi-quantitative statements. But such statements commonly reflect impressions or very rough estimates rather than actual counting or measuring—as this statement itself does; and this means that the method is qualitative.

Similarly, methods are qualitative when they rest on the application of the intelligence of the scholar to the presence or absence of evidence, relative frequency not being involved. The intelligent examination of a single statement by the President of the United States may provide a basis for explaining or predicting governmental action; in some situations the absence of a statement has similar significance. Knowledge of an action, or of a series of quite different actions, of the Soviet government may likewise give basis for answering a question that otherwise would be unanswerable. Similarly, if inferences or conclusions are drawn from an examination of only one case, or if there is no assurance that the few cases that are examined constitute a fair sample of the total number, the method is called qualitative. For there is heavy reliance on the judgment of the scholar.

Given such differences, it follows that the two types of methods differ in their applicability whether to different types of questions or in different kinds of situations. The tendency is to treat complex questions qualitatively; many of them must be so treated for the simple reason that it is impossible or impractical to subdivide or reformulate them in such a way as to permit quantification.

Statistical techniques are not appropriate to realms of organized complexity where some statements can be made only of two or more things

considered in their interrelationship, where the pertinent fact is not the
presence or absence of something in such and such quantity but rather
the nature of the arrangement of the observable entities.[5]

Questions pertaining to events or conditions or practices or institutions that are either unique or highly distinctive are ordinarily
treated by qualitative methods, for the opportunity to do counting
of a helpful sort is then limited. Questions concerning the meaning or significance of words or events generally are treated by
qualitative methods. As already indicated, this means that qualitative methods are employed in the treatment of most of the
questions that political scientists examine. Quantitative methods
have been employed mainly in connection with questions pertaining to large numbers of units of the same type, e.g., voters,
and in connection with content analysis.[6]

Harold D. Lasswell comments that between the wars and during World War II "the disciplines which possessed quantitative
methods were the ones that rose most rapidly in influence."[7] There
is no doubt that results achieved by quantitative methods are
widely regarded as more reliable—and may, in truth, be more reliable—than those achieved by qualitative methods. As political scientists come to employ quantitative methods more fully (and they
are doing it in increasing numbers), political science will do doubt
gain in influence, too. At the same time, there is no magic in
method. The best of methods will hardly be fruitful unless its use
is guided by imagination and the right sort of purpose. It seems
plausible that the questions that are asked do more than the methods that are employed to determine the influence of individual
scholars and disciplines. Those who confine themselves to the
pursuit of facts at a low level of generality or whose output consists simply of miscellaneous information can scarcely expect to
achieve much influence. But those with an imagination and a
sense of purpose which lead to the asking of significant questions
can hope for more. It may even be that they will use or develop
methods—perhaps quantitative methods—that theretofore seemed
irrelevant or unnecessary.

INDUCTIVE AND DEDUCTIVE METHODS

Thomas P. Jenkin classifies the methods employed by political
theorists as (1) logical-deductive, (2) historical-descriptive, and (3)

empirical-hypothetical.[8] Though employing somewhat different
terminology, we have already discussed methods (and approaches)
coming within his second and third categories. Now there must
be a brief mention of the first category, broadened so that induction and deduction can be compared.

Induction and deduction both denote reasoning processes, in
which "supposed truths [are employed] as evidence in support of
other supposed truths."[9] The old view was that the two are antithetical and that in induction reasoning proceeds from the particular to the general whereas in deduction it goes the other way.
This conception is open to serious criticism. It is better to differ-
entiate between the two by saying that we employ inductive methods when we seek to establish truth by observing reality, and that
we employ deductive methods when our concern is primarily with
the implications of given premises. Inductive methods are empirical and logical, whereas deductive methods are purely logical. In
induction, a basic question is whether the data employed check
with experience; only if they do are we justified in believing that
the inferences drawn from the data are true or warranted. In deduction, the premises (whether descriptive or normative) are
simply taken as given, and the basic question concerns the inferences that can validly be drawn from them. Induction offers the
possibility of developing net additions to knowledge of reality,
whereas deduction is tautological, permitting us to do no more
than to spell out implications already contained in the premises.
Deductive inferences that are logically derived and therefore valid
may nevertheless be false if one or more of the premises are false.[10]

Obviously, political scientists employ—and must employ—both
inductive and deductive methods. And, just as obviously, these
methods are not employed apart from, but rather are ancillary to,
the other methods that we have already discussed: the analytical,
quantitative, and qualitative methods.

THE COMPARATIVE METHOD

The comparative method consists of identifying similarities
and differences. The process is pervasive in political inquiry, as
in all inquiry. Finding that various phenomena are similar
enough, we may group them together and give them a label,
which means that the comparative method enters into the process

of concept formation. By the same token, the identification of comparisons and contrasts is basic to classification. Via conceptualization and classification the comparative method is basic to thought and expression. Whenever we make distinctions, whether between events or practices or functions or institutions, we are making comparisons. Similarly, when we make a prediction—perhaps on the basis of a law or a theory—and when we check the prediction against reality, we are comparing the expectation and the event. Through identifying similarities and differences—by making comparisons and drawing contrasts—we get a clearer image of things observed and a sharper understanding of the meaning of the symbols we employ.[11]

Like inductive and deductive methods, the comparative method is ancillary to other methods. As noted above, analysis is frequently comparative analysis. Quantitative and qualitative methods commonly involve comparisons, and the use of inductive and deductive methods may do so.

Assuming that an appreciation of the benefits to be derived from comparisons is desired, it is probably unfortunate that a branch of political science has been called *comparative* government. It is odd, in the first place, that the term should designate the study of foreign governments only. A connotation of the term is also odd: that when two or more governments are treated in the same course or text, the treatment is automatically comparative. Actually, the juxtaposition of the treatment of governments gives no assurance that the treatment will be more comparative than when the focus in the book or course is on only one government. Further, texts—and presumably courses—on comparative government have all too often consisted of institutional description, with institutions conceived in terms of structural organization or constitutional arrangements and with description consisting of facts at a low level of generality. Such "comparative" treatments are likely to lead to boredom and to a despairing "So what?"

A point made above deserves to be stressed again: there is no magic in method, whether the method be comparative or other. The rule, to which exceptions sometimes occur by accident, is that a method will produce interesting and fruitful results only if it is applied intelligently, i.e., purposefully. The best of methods is unlikely to compensate for a failure to ask the right questions. Once the right questions have been asked, and once the right hypotheses have been advanced in answer to these questions, then method becomes important. But the scholar who simply starts out to compare two governments—or other items—is likely to end up with comparisons that are pointless.[12]

SCIENTIFIC METHODS

The fact that *methods* is plural is significant here. Descriptions of "the" scientific method are patently misleading, for the implication is that there is only one. In fact, there are many. The processes by which important scientific advances have been made are scarcely reducible either to method or to rule. Those who strive to master one or another method that is ostensibly scientific in the hope that it will guide them to scientific achievement are likely to be disappointed. The most sophisticated and scientific method is not a substitute for whatever it is—the intelligence, the insight, the intuition, the flash of genius—that leads the inquiring person to ask the right question or to grasp the significance of a relationship that hitherto went unobserved or unappreciated. With the question once posed or with the relationship noticed, any of a variety of methods may come into play.[13]

The above is on the assumption that methods are procedures. If they relate more to attitudes than to procedures, a different statement can be made. As an attitude, scientific method

consists in the persistent search for truth, constantly asking: Is it so? To what extent is it so? Why is it so?—that is, What general conditions or considerations determine it to be so? And this can be seen on reflection to be the demand for the best available evidence, the determination of which we call logic. . . . In essence scientific method is simply the pursuit of truth as determined by logical considerations.[14]

In the end, methods are to be judged scientific or not depending upon the reliability of their results. If successful replication is possible, or if the findings are clearly based on evidence that is convincing to those in a position to judge, the method employed is ordinarily regarded as scientific. Though addressed to the nature of scientific study rather than scientific method, the following statement by Charles S. Hyneman is in point.

A political scientist pursues scientific study (1) if he has as his object of inquiry a matter that can be illuminated by empirical evidence, (2) if he accords to empirical evidence highest probative force, (3) if in search for, analysis, and evaluation of evidence he approaches the highest standards other social scientists have proved to be attainable, and (4) if he reports his procedures and his findings in a way that affords other students ample opportunity to judge whether his evidence supports his findings.[15]

These statements about scientific methods and scientific study relate, of course, to the nature of science itself. Perhaps it would have been better to delay discussion of scientific methods until the concept science had itself been examined. It is to the substantive concept that we now turn.

Part IV
SCIENCE?

CHAPTER FIFTEEN

The Study of Politics: A Science?

Although there have been frequent references in this book to political *science* and political *scientists*, little attention has been paid to the meaning of the italicized words and to the question of the justifiability of their use in this connection. Minor exceptions occurred when we noted that the purpose of those taking a behavioral approach is scientific, meaning that they pursue knowledge characterized by verifiability, system, and generality, and when we discussed scientific methods at the end of the preceding chapter. Now the time has come to discuss these words more fully in an effort to see what relationship they reasonably have to the study of politics.

DEFINITIONS OF SCIENCE AND SCIENTIFIC

Common Elements in Various Definitions

The requirements of verifiability, system, and generality appear in most definitions of science.

The meaning of verifiability. The question whether a proposition is verified is essentially a subjective question or, better, an intersubjective one. A proposition is said to be verified when it has been checked or tested by many specialists in the relevant field of knowledge and when they all take the view that belief in it is warranted. They may become convinced that it is warranted by the weight of evidence or testimony; they are likely to become convinced more surely if the proposition gives basis for predictions that are regularly confirmed by experience. It sometimes happens that knowledge that is thought to be verified (i.e., a belief that is thought to be warranted) turns out to be false, for people can be united in error as well as in truth.

Scientific knowledge is sometimes said to be certain or exact rather than verifiable, but these words are misleading. General, inductive propositions cannot be certain. Until all possible instances of an inductive generalization have been examined, certainty is a logical impossibility. Scientists deal in probabilities rather than in certainties.[1] The probability that some propositions will hold true is so great that, for practical purposes, they can be treated as certainties, but this does not gainsay the principle. The principle is especially important for the social sciences, where the probability that propositions will hold true is frequently not so overwhelming as in the natural sciences. As to the word *exact*, it is true that even probability statements can be made with exactness; that is, they can be stated so that the meaning is precise. But if the proposition is that something can be relied upon to happen in one case out of ten, it seems a bit incongruous, and it may be confusing, to describe this as exact knowledge.

The requirement of verifiability leads to two subsidiary requirements.

In the first place, if scientific knowledge is to be verifiable, science must be empirical; that is, scientific statements must be descriptive of the empirical world. *Science* and *scientific*, then, are words that relate to only one kind of knowledge, i.e., to knowledge of what is observable, and not to any other kinds of knowledge that may exist. They do not relate to alleged knowledge of the normative—knowledge of what ought to be. Science concerns what has been, is, or will be, regardless of the "oughts" of the situation. Neither do *science* and *scientific* relate to alleged knowledge of the metaphysical. Scientists and others hold many different beliefs about the normative and the metaphysical; but the work of the scientist as such neither establishes nor refutes such beliefs. The basis for them, if there is one, is provided by something other than science. "Science is a way of describing reality; it is therefore limited by the limits of observation; and it asserts nothing which is outside observation. Anything else is not science."[2] Essentially the same thought is conveyed by the statement that "science is the study of those judgments concerning which universal agreement can be obtained."[3] The assumption is that universal agreement is obtainable in principle only on propositions that are susceptible to the tests of logic and observation.

In the second place, if scientific knowledge is to be verifiable, the methods employed in obtaining it must be reliable. That is, specialists in the field in question must accept the view that the methods can be depended upon to produce trustworthy results. If the method produces different results when applied by different qualified persons, it will presumably be judged unreliable.[4] The desire for reliability and, ultimately, verifiability has been the chief factor leading to the adoption of quantitative methods.

The meaning of system. Knowledge is said to be systematic when it is organized into an intelligible pattern or structure, with significant relationships made clear.

To achieve system, scientists seek out similarities and differences, putting like things together. An untidy fact—one that does not fit anywhere in the classification scheme—is likely to be a source of acute discomfort until a place is found for it, perhaps by reconstructing the classification scheme. While looking for similarities and differences, scientists also look for relationships, whether correlations or causal relations. They want to know what is related to what, both within and among the categories of their classification scheme. Concern for system means that scientists want to proceed from particular toward general facts, from knowledge of isolated facts toward knowledge of connections between facts. It is not enough to say that they want knowledge; the knowledge sought is knowledge of relationships. "The ideal of science is to achieve a systematic interconnection of facts."[5]

The meaning of generality. The knowledge provided by a telephone directory is verifiable, and it is presented in an orderly and systematic way. There are no untidy facts. Alphabetical interrelationships are perfectly clear, and so is the significance of the relationship between names and telephone numbers. If these criteria were the only ones involved, a telephone directory would be a scientific monograph. But something is obviously wrong with this formulation.

One quality that is lacking is generality. We noted in Chapters Two and Six that we go to higher and higher levels of generality as we are able to employ concepts and make statements that apply to more and more objects, instances, or events in any one class. The number of possible levels of generality is indefinite. Concepts themselves imply generalization; i.e., they imply that the things named have enough in common to justify being classified together and given the same label. Thus, statements about Iowa

City or the United States are automatically generalizations, for these concepts are general. Higher and higher levels of generality are achieved in statements about all municipalities in Iowa, in the United States, or in the world. True statements at every level of generality may well have significance, but the number of contexts in which they are significant is likely to increase with the level of generality.

Reasons for the stress on generality were given in Chapters Two and Three. There we said that explanation and prediction are major purposes of scientific work, and that explanation and prediction require the implicit or explicit use of generalizations (e.g., reference to rules, laws, or theories). An itemization of individual, unique facts—as in a telephone directory—does not alone provide either explanation or prediction; such an itemization must be somehow associated with one or more generalizations if it is to have explanatory or predictive value. For the telephone directory the relevant low-order generalization is that the telephones of persons will ring when their numbers are called. To shift the illustration, Pearl Harbor provides a basis for explaining (or, on December 7, 1941, predicting) the American declaration of war against Japan by being associated with the generalization that when such attacks occur such responses are to be expected with a high degree of probability. The object in science is to develop generalizations so that explanation and prediction can occur to the maximum possible extent.

Scientific knowledge on any subject, designed to facilitate explanation and prediction, can be thought of as a pyramid rising from a base of specific bits of data up through more general facts to propositions, laws, and theories. Stress on the higher levels of generality leads some to specify that "science is a definite species of theoretical knowledge," and it leads others to insist on the notion of integrating knowledge, i.e., on the notion of the unity of science.[6] The ideal is sometimes said to be the development of theory at such a high level of generality that all laws, propositions, and facts can be deduced from it.[7]

Special Aspects of Definitions

Does science consist simply of knowledge that is verified, systematic, and general? Or does the word denote not only this but also something more?

James B. Conant speaks of static and dynamic conceptions of science.

To say that science consists of knowledge is to take the static view. Under this definition, science would persist even if scientific inquiry were to cease and the further growth of scientific knowledge were to stop.[8]

Conant objects to this conception. Existing knowledge, he says, is "part of the fabric of science, but it is not its essence."[9] The essence is to be found, rather, in the contribution that each scientific development makes to further development; it is to be found in attitudes, in searching activity, in the excitement of inquiry. Under this dynamic conception, science is a speculative enterprise, involving continuous probing into the unknown; and if the search for more knowledge were stopped, the essence of science would be gone. Collingwood takes a similar view: "Science . . . does not consist in collecting what we already know and arranging it in this or that kind of pattern. It consists in fastening upon something we do not know, and trying to discover it. . . . Science is finding things out."[10]

What, then, does it mean to ask whether political science is a science? At the minimum the question is whether political science comprises knowledge characterized by verifiability, system, and generality. Dynamically considered, the question also asks whether political scientists are simply husbanding, and perhaps rearranging, such knowledge, or whether they seek continuously to add to it.

We should note once again that the questions apply only to descriptive, and not to normative, knowledge.

OBSTACLES IN THE SCIENTIFIC STUDY OF POLITICS

Formidable difficulties stand in the way of scientific political inquiry. Some relate primarily to the political scientist and others to his subject matter.

The Search for "Facts" vs. the Development of Science

Ignorance on the part of political scientists of the nature and purpose of scientific work is surely among the obstacles to the development of a science of politics. At least, there is considerable basis for the impression that a high proportion of those calling themselves political scientists think of themselves as scientists only

in a very loose and figurative sense, if at all. The strong tendency
has been simply to gather facts—and to write and teach facts—for
the sake of the facts. We have noted this tendency before, especially in connection with the discussion of institutional description. Moreover, stress on "the facts" has frequently been accompanied by an apparently deliberate effort to avoid generalization,
or at least to keep it at the lowest possible level. Not uncommonly,
this has been done in the name of objectivity. Much of this book
has been a commentary on this conception of the purpose and
role of the political scientist.

In relation to the natural sciences the point is sometimes made
that a considerable portion of those who have made striking dis-
coveries have had only the most meager knowledge, if any, of the
philosophy of science. And the point is also made that those who
have deliberately schooled themselves in the philosophy of science,
though sometimes achieving fame as philosophers, have rarely, if
ever, become notable as scientists. In the main, famous scientists
seem simply to ask questions and to go after the answers. Thoughts
along this line may have led Lindsay Rogers to his view that "the
fundamental defect of the most social science [is that] it has had
no Newton to give it a great vision, and until such a man appears,
there are no real tasks for the second- and third-rate minds."[11]
Still, awareness of the fact that imaginative question-asking is
essential to the development of a science may alone be of some
help. It is open even to second-rate minds to improve political
science somewhat. After all, others paved the way for Newton,
and he built on their work.

Obstacles to the Verification of General Propositions

Other difficulties relate more to the subject matter of politics
than to the sophistication of the political scientist.[12]

Verifiability vs. generality. Probably the greatest obstacle to
the scientific study of politics stems from the fact of frequent in-
compatibility between the requirement of verifiability and the
requirement of generality. In many cases, if political scientists
confine themselves to propositions that are verifiable they must
also confine themselves to low levels of generality; and if they go
to high levels of generality, their propositions are likely to be
unverifiable.

Simple and specific questions, whether calling for explanation or prediction, are often rather easy to answer. In other words, answers at a low level of generality can often be verified in the sense that all specialists in the field agree that belief in them is warranted. If the question is why a particular Congressman voted as he did after admittedly accepting a $10,000 bribe, we are not likely to have to look long for an explanation; for that matter, given knowledge of the bribe, it will be easy to predict the vote in advance. And the explanatory or predictive proposition will no doubt be verifiable.

More general questions are commonly more difficult to answer. In other words, answers at a high level of generality may not be verifiable. If the question is why all the members of the House of Representatives vote as they do on an issue, and especially if the answer is to consist of one or more generalizations based on the classification of data, the answer is likely to be extremely difficult to develop; and prediction of the outcome is likely to be even more difficult than explanation after the event.

The multitude of variables and the necessity of selection. As we noted in Chapter Three, explanation must ordinarily be selective. We must choose a type of explanation, a level of discourse, and an approach (i.e., criteria of relevance), and even after doing this we may not be able to consider all the data falling within the limits of the choices made. The possibilities that are open are so numerous and the number of potentially relevant factors is so large that exhaustive explanation is ordinarily impracticable. We explain in terms of factors that we judge to be most significant, and we say little or nothing about other factors. In other words, we explain complex events by selecting what we consider to be the most significant of the relevant variables, and we neglect or ignore other variables as well as the constants. The probability is that different specialists will select differing bodies of data, and thus their explanations will differ. One specialist may explain in terms of one set of factors while another chooses a somewhat different set, and there may or may not be basis for deciding whose judgment has been better. In truth, assuming that each explanation is incomplete, they might in principle be equally sound.

The same sorts of considerations apply in connection with efforts to predict, for, as we saw in Chapter Four, explanation and prediction have much in common. If we can explain an event after it has occurred by identifying its causes, then knowledge of the causes should have enabled us to predict it. But if, as a practical matter, our explanations of complex events must be selective, this also means that our efforts to predict must be based on only some rather than all of the relevant factors. And if the factors that we neglect or ignore turn out to be more significant than we anticipated, the prediction is likely to go awry. When the United States ratified the North Atlantic Treaty, it was obviously on the basis of the prediction that this action would have more desirable consequences than any available alternative. But the soundness of the prediction necessarily depended upon the prescience with which relevant factors were selected; and it is inconceivable that some contingencies that still lay in the future could have been foreseen. Though there was a considerable measure of agreement among specialists on the desirability of ratifying the treaty, it would be too much to say that their predictive propositions met the test of verifiability. Further, experience itself is not always a sure test, for it may be impossible to know what would have happened in the absence of the decision being tested.

The inconstancy and variety of human purposes. Predictive propositions may be unverifiable not only because the supporting evidence is selected rather than complete but also because of the inconstancy and variety of human desires and rules of action. Even at a low level of generality—even if only one individual is considered—there is a likelihood of change; what was true of him ten years ago may or may not be true today, and what is true of him today may or may not be true ten years hence. His conception of the ends that are worth pursuing and of the means that are effective is not likely to remain constant. Sometimes the very fact that conceptions of ends and means are made explicit and scrutinized induces change. Further, not only does one individual develop different attitudes as time passes, but there is variety among individuals. What is true of one, temporarily or permanently, may or may not be true of another. Significant differences exist even among individuals whose social experience seems quite similar, and the differences may well become extreme where contrasting cultures are involved. This means that predictive propositions at the higher levels of generality are especially hazardous— especially likely to be unverifiable.[13]

This picture should not be overdrawn. Though an individual cannot be counted on to hold his desires and his rules of action constant, he can be counted upon to adhere persistently to a considerable portion of them. Moreover, the nature and direction of changes are themselves sometimes predictable, as when they are associated with age or status or economic circumstance. Further, though individuals differ from each other, they also share common characteristics which permit them to be classified. In very many ways the behavior of an individual through time and the behavior of classes of individuals are regularly reduced to law and explained by theory on a common-sense basis; e.g., every driver of an automobile accepts it as a descriptive law that drivers of oncoming cars will try to avoid head-on collisions, and the theoretical explanation is that drivers want to remain alive. Students of human behavior—psychologists, sociologists, political scientists, and others —have sought other laws and theories on a scientific basis, and many have done it successfully. The very fact that it has been done indicates that the question is not whether but to what extent verifiable propositions can be developed about political behavior. Obviously, no one can know how far it is possible to go in identifying the characteristics of individuals that are significant to their behavior and in identifying relationships that give a basis for prediction. Nor can any one know how far it is possible to go in classifying people and making generalizations about them by classes. Of course, for present purposes, it is a significant fact that reliable generalizations about individual and mass political behavior are not very numerous.

Environmental change. Quite aside from the inconstancy and variety of human desires and rules of action, note might also be made of the fact that change in other realms also constitutes an obstacle to the development of a science of politics. Many aspects of both the human and nonhuman environment are always changing, and beliefs that are warranted in one environmental situation may be made obsolete. Technological, economic, social, and other changes occur, rendering previously warranted beliefs untenable—or simply inapplicable in the new situation. Many of the findings of political scientists thus apply only as long as conditions on which they are based persist; in this sense they are impermanent and "writ on water." The cumulative development of knowledge is thus made difficult. It is often imperative to study

pending and impending problems, but the effort may contribute
little or no knowledge that has enduring value.[14]

The problem of verbiage. Finally, the very necessity of using
words makes it difficult to develop explanatory and predictive
propositions that are at a high level of generality and that are
verifiable. It is one thing to convey meaning in a simple form,
using mathematical and other symbols that are precise and succinct. And it is something else again to convey it in sentences,
paragraphs, chapters, and books. The symbolic, shorthand language of mathematics permits the making of brief, clear-cut statements which specialists can easily grasp and check. Errors can
be corrected. Succinct rules and formulas can be added cumu-
latively to those already known so that a precise and coherent
structure of knowledge develops. But in connection with most
of the questions asked in political science, symbolic, shorthand
language has not so far been used. Instead, words are made to
flow, sometimes in considerable volume. Particularly when an
author strains to be "objective" and to confine himself to "the
facts," it is likely to be a major task to get at the meaning he is
presumably trying to convey; and considerable effort may be re-
warded by no more than a rather vague or ambiguous impression.
Testing or checking such impressions may well be an even more
formidable task, and using them as building stones in a structure
of knowledge is likely to be a highly questionable procedure.[15]

In principle, of course, it is possible to reduce difficulties trace-
able to the quantity of verbiage. The most radical and obvious
reduction occurs when quantitative methods are employed, for
then the results can be presented, in large part at least, through
the use of numbers and other mathematical symbols. A less radical
but still significant reduction might also occur through a deliberate effort to formulate explanatory and predictive propositions
explicitly. In other words, the problem of verbiage might be
reduced somewhat by an explicit effort to advance theses.[16] Most
theses can be stated fairly succinctly. And then they can be employed to provide criteria for the inclusion and exclusion of data.
Data is included only when it is considered significant to efforts
to confirm or disconfirm the thesis that has been advanced. It
must be acknowledged, however, that even with the maximum
use of quantitative methods and even with fully thetical writing

a significant handicap to the development of political *science* is likely to persist in the form of the mass of verbiage that must be employed. And the higher the level of generality attempted, the more likely is this to be true. "Facts" at a very low level of generality can ordinarily be stated very succinctly.

A summary. A summary statement may be in order. It is that at low levels of generality and in relation to rather simple questions it is frequently possible to make explanatory and predictive propositions that are verifiable. As we go to higher levels of generality and to more complex questions, however, the development of propositions that are verifiable is a much more difficult task. In this realm, a very high proportion of the propositions that political scientists now make (perhaps including this one) are unverifiable.

Other Problems

We said earlier that scientific knowledge is not only verifiable and general but also systematic. And we said that knowledge is systematic when it is organized into an intelligible pattern or structure, with significant relationships made clear; connections between facts are likely to cause more concern in achieving system than the facts themselves. To what extent does or can political science achieve system in this sense? The best answer probably is that the requirement of system does not cause as much difficulty as the other requirements. Some sort of system can be achieved at every level of generality. As we noted, the telephone directory can be said to be systematic. Similarly, descriptions of governments and of political processes at low levels of generality can be presented in a systematic fashion, though the connections shown between the facts may be of a rather trivial sort. At higher levels of generality, system is also possible; and, by definition, the relationships that are made clear will be of significance in a wider realm. In short, political science meets the requirement of system without much difficulty or doubt.

Little need be said about difficulties attendant on the attempt to meet the special aspect of Conant's definition of science, i.e., that the essence of science is to be found in its dynamism—its speculative probing into the unknown. The difficulties are obvious. Yet there are many examples of dynamism in the study of politics; and there is no reason why speculative probing into the unknown should not occur on an ever-increasing scale.

REACTIONS TO OBSTACLES TO SCIENTIFIC STUDY

Several sorts of reactions occur to the fact that there are obstacles to the scientific study of politics.

One reaction is either to refuse to grant that there is an issue or to dodge it. Students of politics on the faculties of some universities say that their departments are departments of politics or of government rather than of political science, and some of the professional journals likewise refer, in their titles, to politics; undoubtedly the variation sometimes reflects a desire to avoid claiming scientific quality. This attitude is quite sensible, and might advantageously have been adopted here. After all, the study of politics is likely to go on in about the same way whether or not the label *science* is employed. The label alone is not crucial. The analysis of the study of politics contained in the first three parts of this book will presumably stand unaffected by a decision on the question whether to call the subject a science.

Another reaction is to use the term political science (as well as the term social science) but to assert that in this context *science* means something different from what it means in the context of the natural sciences. The terms *nomothetic* and *idiographic* have been employed to distinguish between the two kinds of science.

Nomothetic sciences, corresponding roughly to the physical sciences, search for abstract, universal laws. Idiographic sciences—exemplified by the more concrete cultural and historical disciplines—deal with unique, more or less extended temporal events, seeking to represent them fully and exhaustively rather than abstractly.[17]

The question of the acceptability of this kind of distinction turns largely on the question whether the difference cited is considered one of degree or of kind. We have already noted that in political science it is usually difficult to achieve both verifiability and generality at the same time; but the natural sciences face a comparable difficulty. The difference must be one of degree. If the adjectives *nomothetic* and *idiographic* are taken to mark this difference in degree, they may be useful concepts. On the contrary, if they are taken to mark sharp and complete differences—differences in kind —they are misleading.

The author of the above statement of the distinction between nomothetic and idiographic sciences goes on to assert:

Political science is not concerned with general laws. The subject-matter of politics is basically the specific problem and particular institution: a constitution for post-war Germany, the present goals of Soviet foreign policy, the legislative process in Congress, or the reform of a city or state government.[18]

Surely this is a misleading and incorrect statement. Political science *is* concerned with general laws, whether or not they are called by this name. It is also concerned with the reasons and rules for action, with theories, and with the necessary and sufficient conditions of events. How else could explanation and prediction occur? How else could decisions be made? (Let it be said once again that decisions and predictions go hand in hand. Provisions in the postwar German constitution are chosen, just as all decisions are made, on the basis of the prediction that the choice will lead more probably than any known alternative choice to the desired consequences.) Specific problems and particular institutions can scarcely be discussed intelligently without asserting or assuming a generalization of some kind; and frequently the generalization is in the form of a general law. Discussing policy toward the Soviet Union, President Truman once declared that if the history of the 1930's teaches us anything, it is that the appeasement of aggressors is the sure road to war. He did not label this a law of international politics, but he treated it as one; and the statement is in the form of a general descriptive law. It is doubtful whether the enactment of a single bill by Congress could be described without reference to a general law (e.g., that enactment by each house requires a majority vote); and surely a discussion of "the legislative process in Congress" could not occur except on the basis of generalizations, many of which would constitute descriptive laws. As to the reform of a city or state government, we might refer to the law of politics advanced by Karl Popper and cited in Chapter Eight that political reform commonly arouses opposition, the intensity of the opposition roughly increasing with the significance of the reform. The corollary might also be recalled: that vested interests commonly develop around the status quo and want to preserve it. In short, though the word *science* might be given a somewhat different shading when applied to political rather than

natural phenomena, the differences should be regarded as differences of degree rather than in kind.

Other reactions to the difficulties in making the study of politics scientific range from acknowledgments of deficiencies to expressions that come close to contempt. Some members of the profession who take note of the word *science* do so only to grant that
the scientific qualities of the discipline are limited or embryonic.[19]
Those outside the field who list or discuss "the sciences" commonly
give no evidence of thinking of political science in this connection,
though they may think of economics, of sociology, and even of
history.[20] Conant thinks that archeology comes closer to being
a science than history, and does not mention political science.[21]
Even a book on *Common Frontiers of the Social Sciences*, edited
by Mirra Komarovsky, almost entirely ignores political science;
the discipline is not even mentioned among those "dealing with
social behavior and institutions," although economics, sociology,
anthropology, social psychology, and history are mentioned.[22]
Some of those who contemplate the alleged science of political
science evince disappointment if not contempt. Walter Lippmann
once remarked, "Nobody takes political science very seriously, for
nobody is convinced that it is a science or that it has any important bearing on politics."[23]

Still another reaction is the adoption of a "behavioral"
approach to the study of politics, emphasizing the importance
of scientific quality. Under the behavioral approach the pronounced tendency is to take up only those questions about politics
that can be handled quantitatively; generality and system are
sought, but only in so far as they are compatible with the supreme
requirement of verifiability. Those taking a behavioral approach
seem to take the view that it is better to aim at a structure of
knowledge that is trustworthy but limited than at a structure that
is comprehensive but untrustworthy. And there is much to be said
for this point of view, especially if there is a substantial prospect
that the structure of trustworthy knowledge can sometime be made
extensive.

The answer to the behavioralists on this point is that those
who must make political decisions, whether they are individual
voters or heads of states, cannot wait for a science of politics to
develop; they must act now. And they need advice and help.

Few would argue that political scientists should proffer advice and help in the absence of some special expertise, but many would question whether the political scientist must wait to speak until his knowledge meets all the tests of science. If his beliefs in the realm of descriptive knowledge are more likely to be warranted than the beliefs of laymen, many would say that they should be expressed, due caution being exercised not to make claims concerning verification that go beyond the limits of reason and evidence.

And to this behavioralists might retort that the more political scientists devote their abilities and energies to rendering advice on kaleidoscopically changing current issues, the longer it will be before they develop a science that is worthy of the name.[24]

NOTES

Notes

INTRODUCTION TO PART I

1. Quoted by A. R. M. Murray, *An Introduction to Political Philosophy* (London: Cohen & West, 1953), p. 93.

2. Quoted by Arnold Brecht, *Political Theory* (Princeton: Princeton University Press, 1959), p. 203.

3. Robert A. Dahl and Charles E. Lindblom, *Politics, Economics, and Welfare* (New York: Harper, 1953), p. 38.

4. Herbert A. Simon, *Administrative Behavior* (2d ed.; New York: Macmillan, 1957), pp. 67, 75–77, 102. Cf. Felix E. Oppenheim, "Rational Choice," *Journal of Philosophy*, 50 (June 4, 1953), 341–50.

CHAPTER ONE

1. Cf. T. D. Weldon, *The Vocabulary of Politics* (Harmondsworth: Penguin Books, 1953), pp. 17–30; Karl R. Popper, *The Open Society and Its Enemies* (Princeton: Princeton University Press, 1950), pp. 21–36 and *passim*. A discussion of the types and purposes of definitions will be found below in Chapter Six.

2. Alfred Jules Ayer, *Language, Truth and Logic* (New York: Dover Publications, n.d.), esp. pp. 35–41; Arnold Brecht, *Political Theory* (Princeton: Princeton University Press, 1959), pp. 174–82.

3. Hans Reichenbach, *The Rise of Scientific Philosophy* (Berkeley and Los Angeles: University of California Press, 1951), pp. 291–302; Ayer, *Language, Truth and Logic*, pp. 102–9.

4. Ayer, *Language, Truth and Logic*, p. 73. Cf. Reichenbach, *The Rise of Scientific Philosophy*, pp. 31–32.

5. Herbert A. Simon, *Administrative Behavior* (2d ed.; New York: Macmillan, 1957), pp. 67, 75–77, 102. Cf. Felix E. Oppenheim, "Rational Choice," *Journal of Philosophy*, 50 (June 4, 1953), 341–50; Robert A. Dahl and Charles E. Lindblom, *Politics, Economics, and Welfare* (New York: Harper, 1953), pp. 25–54.

6. Ernest Nagel, *Sovereign Reason* (Glencoe: Free Press, 1954), p. 34.

7. For discussions of the role of values in connection with political research see Simon, *Administrative Behavior*, Chapter 3; Herbert A. Simon, "Development of Theory of Democratic Administration: Reply," *American Political Science Review*, 46 (June 1952), 494–96; Gunnar Myrdal, *Value in Social Theory* (London: Routledge & Kegan Paul, 1958); Thomas I. Cook, review of Lasswell and Kaplan, *Power and Society*, in *Journal of Philosophy*, 48 (October 25, 1951), 690–701; Thomas

I. Cook, "The Methods of Political Science, Chiefly in the United States," in UNESCO, *Contemporary Political Science* (Paris: UNESCO, 1950), pp. 75–90; Dwight Waldo, " 'Values' in the Political Science Curriculum," in Roland Young, ed., *Approaches to the Study of Politics* (Evanston: Northwestern University Press, 1958), pp. 97–102; Hans Kelsen, "Science and Politics," *American Political Science Review*, 45 (September 1951), esp. 643–44.

8. Brecht, *Political Theory*, esp. Part IV, pp. 367 ff. For critiques of positivism in addition to that of Brecht, see Dwight Waldo, *The Study of Public Administration* (Garden City, N.Y.: Doubleday, 1955), pp. 62–65; Waldo, " 'Values' in the Political Science Curriculum," *loc. cit.*, pp. 105–7; and Leo Strauss, "What Is Political Philosophy?" *Journal of Politics*, 19 (August 1957), 343–68.

CHAPTER TWO

1. William H. Walsh, *An Introduction to Philosophy of History* (London: Hutchinson's University Library, 1951), p. 33.

2. *Ibid.*, p. 62. Cf. Karl Popper, *The Poverty of Historicism* (London: Routledge & Kegan Paul, 1957), pp. 20–21; and J. W. N. Watkins, "Ideal Types and Historical Explanation," in Herbert Feigl and May Brodbeck, eds., *Readings in the Philosophy of Science* (New York: Appleton-Century-Crofts, Inc., 1953), p. 733.

3. W. B. Gallie, "Explanations in History and the Genetic Sciences," *Mind*, 64 (April 1955), 160–80.

4. John Herman Randall and George Haines, "Controlling Assumptions in the Practice of American Historians," in Social Science Research Council, Committee on Historiography, Bulletin 54, *Theory and Practice in Historical Study* (New York: SSRC, 1946), p. 20. Cf. Louis Gottschalk, *Understanding History* (New York: Knopf, 1951), pp. 212 ff.

5. Cf. Benjamin F. Wright, "Research in American Political Theory," *American Political Science Review*, 38 (August 1944), 727; Charles Fairman, "The Estate of Political Science," *Western Political Quarterly*, 1 (March 1948), 8.

6. Morris R. Cohen and Ernest Nagel, *An Introduction to Logic and Scientific Method* (New York: Harcourt, Brace, 1934), p. 312.

CHAPTER THREE

1. Cf. R. S. Peters, *The Concept of Motivation* (New York: Humanities Press, 1958), pp. 1–26; Gustav Bergmann, *Philosophy of Science* (Madison: University of Wisconsin Press, 1957), esp. pp. 75–84; William Dray, *Laws and Explanation in History* (London: Oxford University Press, 1957), esp. pp. 122–25; Arthur Spiethoff, "Pure Theory and Eco-

nomic Gestalt Theory; Ideal Types and Real Types," in Frederic C. Lane, ed., *Enterprise and Secular Change. Readings in Economic History* (Homewood, Illinois: Richard D. Irwin, 1953), p. 449.

2. Karl R. Popper, *The Open Society and Its Enemies* (Princeton: Princeton University Press, 1950), pp. 289–90, 448–49.

3. In addition to Peters, *The Concept of Motivation*, cited above, see Dray, *Laws and Explanation in History*, p. 157; and Peter Winch, *The Idea of a Social Science* (New York: Humanities Press, 1958), pp. 45–52.

4. Peters, *The Concept of Motivation*, pp. 35–36, 46–47. Cf. Winch, *The Idea of a Social Science*, pp. 75 ff.

5. For a discussion of causal and "dispositional" explanation, see Dray, *Laws and Explanation in History*, pp. 152–53. Cf. Peters, *The Concept of Motivation*, pp. 112–13; Winch, *The Idea of a Social Science*, pp. 91–3, 117.

6. Ernest Nagel, *Logic Without Metaphysics* (Glencoe: Free Press, 1956), p. 249.

7. Robert K. Merton, *Social Theory and Social Structure* (Glencoe: Free Press, 1957), p. 22.

8. Marbury B. Ogle, Louis Schneider, and J. W. Wiley, *Power, Order, and the Economy* (New York: Harper, 1954), esp. p. 70.

9. Merton, *Social Theory and Social Structure*, p. 63.

10. Popper, *The Open Society and Its Enemies*, p. 288.

11. Nagel, *Logic Without Metaphysics*, p. 251. Cf. Ernest Nagel, "Symposium: Problems of Concept and Theory Formation in the Social Sciences," in American Philosophical Association, Eastern Division, Volume 1, *Science, Language, and Human Rights* (Philadelphia: University of Pennsylvania Press, 1952).

12. Ernest Nagel, "Teleological Explanation and Teleological Systems," in Sidney Ratner, ed., *Vision and Action* (New Brunswick: Rutgers University Press, 1953), pp. 214–15.

13. Arnold Brecht, *Political Theory* (Princeton: Princeton University Press, 1959), pp. 82–8.

14. Social Science Research Council, Committee on Historiography, Bulletin 64, *The Social Sciences in Historical Study* (New York: SSRC, 1954), pp. 29–30. See also Howard K. Beale, "What Historians Have Said About the Causes of the Civil War," in Social Science Research Council, Committee on Historiography, Bulletin 54, *Theory and Practice in Historical Study* (New York: SSRC, 1946), pp. 53–102.

15. Patrick Gardiner, *The Nature of Historical Explanation* (London: Oxford University Press, 1952), p. 109; Social Science Research Council, Committee on Historiography, Bulletin 64, *The Social Sciences in Historical Study*, p. 101; J. W. N. Watkins, "Ideal Types and Historical Explanation," in Herbert Feigl and May Brodbeck, eds., *Readings in the Philosophy of Science* (New York: Appleton-Century-Crofts, 1953), p. 734; Carl G. Hempel, "The Function of General Laws in History,"

in Herbert Feigl and Wilfrid Sellars, *Readings in Philosophical Analysis* (New York: Appleton-Century-Crofts, 1949), pp. 465–66; C. Wright Mills, "Two Types of Social Analysis," *Philosophy of Science,* 20 (October 1953), 266–75.

16. "The Logic of Historical Analysis," in Feigl and Brodbeck, *Readings in the Philosophy of Science,* pp. 698–99.

17. Ernest Nagel, "The Logic of Historical Analysis," in Feigl and Brodbeck, *Readings in the Philosophy of Science,* p. 697. Cf. William H. Riker, "Causes of Events," *Journal of Philosophy,* 55 (March 27, 1958), 281–91.

18. C. G. Hempel and Paul Oppenheim, "Studies in the Logic of Explanation," in Feigl and Brodbeck, *Readings in the Philosophy of Science,* pp. 327–28.

19. Cf. Harold and Margaret Sprout, *Man-Milieu Relationship Hypotheses in the Context of International Politics* (Princeton: Center of International Studies, 1956), pp. 72–101; W. B. Gallie, "Explanations in History and the Genetic Sciences," *Mind,* 64 (April 1955), 172.

20. Quincy Wright, *A Study of War* (Chicago: University of Chicago Press, 1942), Vol. II, Appendix XXV, "The Application of Scientific Method to Social Problems," p. 1360.

CHAPTER FOUR

1. Herbert A. Simon, *Administrative Behavior* (2d ed.; New York: Macmillan, 1957), p. 77. Cf. Olaf Helmer and Nicholas Rescher, "On the Epistemology of the Inexact Sciences," *Management Science,* 1 (October 1959), 25–52.

2. American Political Science Association, *Goals for Political Science* (New York: William Sloane Associates, 1951), p. 24.

3. James W. Fesler, "Goals for Political Science: A Discussion," *American Political Science Review,* 45 (December 1951), 998.

4. Louis Hartz, "Goals for Political Science: A Discussion," *American Political Science Review,* 45 (December 1951), 1001–2. Cf. William Robson, *The University Teaching of Social Sciences: Political Science* (Paris: UNESCO, 1954), p. 44.

5. Robson, *The University Teaching of Social Sciences,* p. 47.

6. Lindsay Rogers, "Goals for Political Science: A Discussion," *American Political Science Review,* 45 (December 1951), 1022.

7. Robson, *The University Teaching of Social Sciences,* p. 51.

8. Gunnar Myrdal, *Value in Social Theory* (London: Routledge & Kegan Paul, 1958), p. 35.

9. Quincy Wright, "Political Science and World Stabilization," *American Political Science Review,* 44 (May 1950), 3, 7.

10. In Roland Young, ed., *Approaches to the Study of Politics* (Evanston: Northwestern University Press, 1958), p. 84.

11. David Easton, "Harold Lasswell: Policy Scientist for a Democratic Society," *Journal of Politics,* 12 (August 1950), 451, 468.

12. Harold D. Lasswell and Abraham Kaplan, *Power and Society: A Framework for Political Inquiry* (New Haven: Yale University Press, 1950), p. xii.

13. Harold D. Lasswell, "The Immediate Future of Research Policy and Method in Political Science," *American Political Science Review*, 45 (March 1941), 134–35. Cf. Harold D. Lasswell, "The Semantics of Political Science: Discussion," *American Political Science Review*, 44 (June 1950), 425; Harold D. Lasswell, "The Political Science of Science: An Inquiry into the Possible Reconciliation of Mastery and Freedom," *American Political Science Review*, 50 (December 1956), 961, 978; William Anderson, "The Role of Political Science," *American Political Science Review*, 37 (February 1943), 1–17; E. S. Corwin, "Democratic Dogma and the Future of Political Science," *American Political Science Review*, 23 (August 1929), 569–92.

14. Alfred Cobban, "The Decline of Political Theory," *Political Science Quarterly*, 68 (September 1953), 330. Cf. Social Science Research Council, Committee on Historiography, Bulletin 54, *Theory and Practice in Historical Study*, p. 9.

15. Harold D. Lasswell, "Current Studies of the Decision Process: Automation versus Creativity," *Western Political Quarterly*, 7 (September 1955), 382–83.

16. Charles S. Hyneman, *The Study of Politics* (Urbana: University of Illinois Press, 1959), pp. 9–17.

17. Cf. Benjamin F. Wright, "Research in American Political Theory," *American Political Science Review*, 38 (August 1944), 740. Robson, *The University Teaching of Social Sciences*, pp. 112–13.

18. C. Wright Mills, "Two Types of Social Analysis," *Philosophy of Science*, 20 (October 1953), 268–69; Popper, *The Open Society and Its Enemies*, pp. 403–6; John Herman Randall and George Haines, "Controlling Assumptions in the Practice of American Historians," in Social Science Research Council, Committee on Historiography, Bulletin 54, *Theory and Practice in Historical Study* (New York: SSRC, 1946), pp. 22–3; Arnold Brecht, *Political Theory* (Princeton: Princeton University Press, 1959), Chapters II and III.

CHAPTER FIVE

1. Quoted by Harold D. Lasswell and Abraham Kaplan, *Power and Society: A Framework for Political Inquiry* (New Haven: Yale University Press, 1950), p. x.

2. William J. Goode and Paul K. Hatt, *Methods in Social Research* (New York: McGraw–Hill, 1952), p. 8.

3. Francis Graham Wilson, *The Elements of Modern Politics* (New York: McGraw–Hill, 1936), p. 2.

4. David Easton, *The Political System* (New York: Knopf, 1953), p. 53.

5. Meanings of the word *fact* are discussed in Morris R. Cohen and

Ernest Nagel, *An Introduction to Logic and Scientific Method* (New York: Harcourt, Brace, 1934), pp. 217–18. Cf. Sidney Hook, "Problems of Terminology in Historical Writing: Illustrations," in Social Science Research Council, Committee on Historiography, Bulletin 54, *Theory and Practice in Historical Study* (New York: SSRC, 1946), p. 124; Gustav Bergmann, *The Metaphysics of Logical Positivism* (New York: Longmans, Green, 1954), p. 303.

6. Julian Huxley, "Darwin Discovers Nature's Plan," *Life*, 44 (June 30, 1950), 83. Italics added.

7. John H. Hallowell, "Politics and Ethics," *American Political Science Review*, 38 (August 1944), 648–49.

8. Cf. E. H. Carr, *The New Society* (Boston: Beacon Press, 1957), pp. 9–10. Carr quotes Carl Becker as saying, "The facts of history do not exist for any historian until he creates them." See also Easton, *The Political System*, p. 53.

9. Cf. Hallowell, "Politics and Ethics," p. 649.

10. Patrick Gardiner, *The Nature of Historical Explanation* (London: Oxford University Press, 1952), pp. 73–77.

11. *Ibid.*, p. 79.

12. Cohen and Nagel, *An Introduction to Logic and Scientific Method*, pp. 199, 392. Cf. Gunnar Myrdal, *Value in Social Theory* (London: Routledge & Kegan Paul, 1958), pp. 51–52; Karl R. Popper, *The Open Society and Its Enemies* (Princeton: Princeton University Press, 1950), pp. 443–45; Easton, *The Political System*, pp. 66–78.

CHAPTER SIX

1. Richard Robinson, *Definition* (Oxford: Clarendon, 1950), p. 170.

2. Social Science Research Council, Committee on Historiography, Bulletin 64, *The Social Sciences in Historical Study* (New York: SSRC, 1954), pp. 25–26, 91.

3. Louis Gottschalk, "The Historian's Use of Generalization," in Leonard D. White, ed., *The State of the Social Sciences* (Chicago: University of Chicago Press, 1956), p. 436.

4. T. D. Weldon, *The Vocabulary of Politics*, Pelican Books A278 (Harmondsworth: Penguin Books, 1953), pp. 17–30. Karl R. Popper, *The Open Society and Its Enemies* (Princeton: Princeton University Press, 1950), pp. 21–36 and *passim*.

5. Charles B. Hagan, "The Group in a Political Science," in Roland Young, ed., *Approaches to the Study of Politics* (Evanston: Northwestern University Press, 1958), p. 45.

6. James B. Conant, *Science and Common Sense* (New Haven: Yale University Press, 1951), p. 32.

7. Cited above, footnote 1.

8. Robinson, *Definition*, p. 177.

9. *Ibid.*, p. 155.

10. Cf. Weldon, *The Vocabulary of Politics, passim*; and Popper, *The Open Society and Its Enemies*, esp. Part I.

11. Robinson, *Definition*, p. 167.

12. R. H. S. Crossman, as quoted by Robinson, *Definition*, p. 167.

13. Georgi Aleksandrov, *The Pattern of Soviet Democracy* (Washington: Public Affairs Press, 1948), p. 23.

14. Robinson, *Definition*, p. 170.

CHAPTER SEVEN

1. Jacob Bronowski, *The Common Sense of Science* (Cambridge: Harvard University Press, 1953), p. 21.

2. Paul F. Lazarsfeld and Allen H. Barton, "Qualitative Measurement in the Social Sciences: Classification, Typologies, and Indices," in Daniel Lerner and Harold D. Lasswell, eds., *The Policy Sciences, Recent Developments in Scope and Method* (Stanford: Stanford University Press, 1951), p. 157. The discussion of classification that follows is based upon the work of Lazarsfeld and Barton, esp. pp. 156–65. Cf. Talcott Parsons and Edward A. Shils, eds., *Toward a General Theory of Action* (Cambridge: Harvard University Press, 1951), p. 49.

3. Harold D. Lasswell and Abraham Kaplan, *Power and Society: A Framework for Political Inquiry* (New Haven: Yale University Press, 1950), pp. xvi–xvii.

4. Morris R. Cohen and Ernest Nagel, *An Introduction to Logic and Scientific Method* (New York: Harcourt, Brace & Co., 1934), p. 277.

5. James W. Prothro, "The Nonsense Fight Over Scientific Method: A Plea for Peace," *Journal of Politics*, 18 (August 1956), 570.

6. David Easton, *The Political System* (New York: Alfred A. Knopf, 1953), p. 4.

7. Social Science Research Council, Committee on Historiography, Bulletin 64, *The Social Sciences in Historical Study* (New York: SSRC, 1954), p. 93.

8. Cf. Norman R. Campbell, "The Structure of Theories," in Herbert Feigl and May Brodbeck, eds., *Readings in the Philosophy of Science* (New York: Appleton-Century-Crofts, 1953), p. 290.

9. Bronowski, *The Common Sense of Science*, p. 56.

10. "Research in Political Behavior: The Implications of Research in Political Behavior," *American Political Science Review*, 46 (December 1952), p. 1007.

11. Peter Winch, *The Idea of a Social Science* (New York: Humanities Press, 1958), esp. pp. 59–61.

12. Richard C. Snyder, H. W. Bruck, and Burton Sapin, *Decision-Making as an Approach to the Study of International Politics* (Princeton: Princeton University, Organizational Behavior Section, 1954), p. 52.

13. R. S. Peters, *The Concept of Motivation* (New York: Humanities Press, 1958), esp. p. 5.

14. Nathan Leites, *The Operational Code of the Politbureau* (New York: McGraw-Hill, 1951); Nathan Leites, *A Study of Bolshevism* (Glencoe: Free Press, 1953).

15. For discussions of the term *principle*, see Herman Finer, "Principles as a Guide to Management," *Public Management*, 17 (October 1935), 287–89; Dwight Waldo, *The Administrative State* (New York: Ronald, 1948), p. 169; Leonard D. White, "The Meaning of Principles in Public Administration," in John M. Gaus, Leonard D. White, and Marshall E. Dimock, *The Frontiers of Public Administration* (Chicago: University of Chicago Press, 1936), esp. pp. 18–19; and Herbert A. Simon, *Administrative Behavior* (2d ed.; New York: Macmillan, 1957), pp. 20–21, 39.

16. Simon, *Administrative Behavior,* pp. 20–21.

CHAPTER EIGHT

1. Lewis White Beck, *Philosophic Inquiry* (New York: Prentice-Hall, 1952), pp. 120–21.

2. Norman Campbell, *What Is Science?* (New York: Dover Publications, 1952), p. 49.

3. *History of the Communist Party of the Soviet Union (Bolsheviks), Short Course* (New York: International Publishers, 1939), p. 115.

4. C. Northcote Parkinson, *Parkinson's Law* (Boston: Houghton Mifflin, 1957, esp. p. 12.

5. *Research Frontiers in Politics and Government* (Washington: The Brookings Institution, 1955), pp. 213, 217.

6. Cf. *supra,* p. 35.

7. Beck, *Philosophic Inquiry,* pp. 120–21.

8. Gustav Bergmann, *Philosophy of Science* (Madison: The University of Wisconsin Press, 1957), p. 120.

9. Morris R. Cohen, *Reason and Nature: An Essay on the Meaning of Scientific Method* (New York: Harcourt, Brace, 1931), pp. 357–58. Cf. Olaf Helmer and Nicholas Rescher, "On the Epistemology of the Inexact Sciences," *Management Science,* 1 (October 1959), 27–30.

10. "We suggest that the term 'law' should be reserved only for those empirical generalizations such as Pareto's or Gresham's law or the law of diminishing returns, or diminishing marginal utility. It is such laws as these that it is the central object of science to discover." T. W. Hutchison, *The Significance and Basic Postulates of Economic Theory* (London: Macmillan, 1938), p. 63.

11. Karl R. Popper, *The Poverty of Historicism* (London: Routledge & Kegan Paul, 1957), pp. 62–65. Cf. George E. G. Catlin, *A Study of the Principles of Politics* (London: Allen & Unwin, 1930), Chapter III. "The Laws of Politics: Attempts at Formulation," pp. 100–134.

12. *Philosophy of Science,* esp. pp. 91 ff.

13. In Roy C. Macridis, ed., *Foreign Policy in World Politics* (Englewood Cliffs: Prentice-Hall, 1958), pp. 78–94.

14. Cf. Stanley H. Hoffmann, "International Relations, The Long Road to Theory," *World Politics*, 11 (April 1959), 357–58.

15. Campbell, *What Is Science?* p. 79. Cf. C. G. Hempel and Paul Oppenheim, "Studies in the Logic of Explanation," in Herbert Feigl and May Brodbeck, eds., *Readings in the Philosophy of Science* (New York: Appleton-Century-Crofts, 1953), pp. 321–22; Karl R. Popper, *The Open Society and Its Enemies* (Princeton: Princeton University Press, 1950), pp. 445–57.

16. *Philosophy of Science*, p. 9.

CHAPTER NINE

1. Robert G. McCloskey, "American Political Thought and the Study of Politics," *American Political Science Review*, 51 (March 1957), 115–29.

2. Norman R. Campbell, "The Structure of Theories," in Herbert Feigl and May Brodbeck, eds., *Readings in the Philosophy of Science* (New York: Appleton-Century-Crofts, 1953), p. 288. Cf. Gustav Bergmann, *Philosophy of Science* (Madison: University of Wisconsin Press, 1957), p. 34.

3. Cf. Chapter 14, "Democratic Practice and Democratic Theory," in Bernard R. Berelson, Paul F. Lazarsfeld, and William McPhee, *Voting* (Chicago: University of Chicago Press, 1954).

4. Cf. R. Duncan Luce and Arnold A. Rogow, "A Game Theoretic Analysis of Congressional Power Distributions for a Stable Two-Party System," *Behavioral Science*, 1 (April 1956), 83–95.

5. Thomas P. Jenkin, *The Study of Political Theory* (Garden City: Doubleday, 1955), pp. 6–7.

6. T. W. Hutchison, *The Significance and Basic Postulates of Economic Theory* (London: Macmillan, 1938), p. 23.

7. Seymour M. Lipset *et al.,* "The Psychology of Voting: An Analysis of Political Behavior," in Gardner Lindzey, ed., *Handbook of Social Psychology* (Cambridge: Addison-Wesley, 1954), II, 1128.

8. Anatol Rapoport, "Various Meanings of 'Theory,'" *American Political Science Review*, 52 (December 1958), 979.

9. Wilson Gee, *Social Science Research Methods* (New York: Appleton-Century-Crofts, 1950), p. 195.

10. Jenkin, *The Study of Political Theory*, pp. 1–3; A. D. Lindsay, *The Modern Democratic State* (New York: Oxford University Press, 1943), pp. 27–51; Arnold S. Kaufman, "The Nature and Functions of Political Theory," *Journal of Philosophy*, 51 (January 7, 1954), 5–22; Alfred Cobban, "The Decline of Political Theory," *Political Science Quarterly*, 68 (September 1953), 335; Harry Eckstein, *rapporteur,* "Political Theory and the Study of Politics: A Report of a Conference,"

American Political Science Review, 50 (June 1956), 480–81; Harold D. Lasswell and Abraham Kaplan, *Power and Society: A Framework for Political Inquiry* (New Haven: Yale University Press, 1950), esp. pp. xi–xiii.

11. For example, see Charles Frankel, *The Case for Modern Man* (New York: Harper, 1955).

12. Doubts about the utility of a historical study of the thoughts of political theorists of the past have been expressed by Robert A. Dahl, "Political Theory: Truth and Consequences," *World Politics*, 11 (October 1958), 89; and by Hans Morgenthau, "Power as a Political Concept," in Roland Young, ed., *Approaches to the Study of Politics* (Evanston: Northwestern University Press, 1958), p. 71. For a more extended discussion of the question see Charles S. Hyneman, *The Study of Politics* (Urbana: University of Illinois Press, 1959), pp. 193–210.

13. A. R. M. Murray, *An Introduction to Political Philosophy* (London: Cohen & West, 1953), p. 22.

14. *Ibid.*, pp. 1–23. Cf. H. M. Magid, "An Approach to the Nature of Political Philosophy," *Journal of Philosophy*, 52 (January 20, 1955), 29–42; Leo Strauss, "What Is Political Philosophy?" *Journal of Politics*, 19 (August 1957), 343–68.

15. Robert K. Merton, *Social Theory and Social Structure* (Glencoe: Free Press, 1957), p. 114.

16. Social Science Research Council, Committee on Historiography, Bulletin 64, *The Social Sciences in Historical Study* (New York: SSRC, 1954), pp. 25–26.

17. Cf. Carl G. Hempel, *Fundamentals of Concept Formation* (Chicago: University of Chicago Press, 1952), p. 46.

18. Karl R. Popper, *The Open Society and Its Enemies* (Princeton: Princeton University Press, 1950), pp. 444–53; Karl R. Popper, *The Poverty of Historicism* (London: Routledge & Kegan Paul, 1957), p. 151. Cf. Klaus Knorr, "Theories of Imperialism," *World Politics*, 4 (April 1952), 402–3.

19. Merton, *Social Theory and Social Structure*, pp. 87–88.

20. Cf. Richard C. Snyder, H. W. Bruck, and Burton Sapin, *Decision-Making as an Approach to the Study of International Politics* (Princeton: Princton University, Organizational Behavior Section, 1954), pp. 7–13; William A. Glaser, "The Types and Uses of Political Theory," *Social Research*, 22 (Autumn, 1955), 287.

21. Herbert A. Simon and Allen Newell, "Models: Their Uses and Limitations," in Leonard D. White, ed., *The State of the Social Sciences* (Chicago: University of Chicago Press, 1956), pp. 67–69.

22. Melvin H. Marx, "The General Nature of Theory Construction," in Melvin H. Marx, ed., *Psychological Theory* (New York: Macmillan, 1951), p. 6. Cf. Frank A. Logan *et al.*, *Behavior Theory and Social Science* (New Haven: Yale University Press, 1955); and P. D. Marchant, "Theory and Practice in the Study of International Relations," *International Relations*, 1 (April 1955), 101–2.

23. Eckstein, "Political Theory and the Study of Politics," p. 481.

24. "The Nonsense Fight Over Scientific Method: A Plea for Peace," *Journal of Politics*, 18 (August 1956), 567.

25. Samuel H. Beer, Adam B. Ulam, *et al.*, *Patterns of Government* (New York: Random House, 1958), pp. 3–4.

26. *Philosophy of Science*, p. 78.

27. *Ibid.*, pp. 31–32.

28. Ernest Nagel and Carl G. Hempel, "Symposium: Problems of Concept and Theory Formation in the Social Sciences," in American Philosophical Association, Eastern Division, Vol. 1, *Science, Language, and Human Rights* (Philadelphia: University of Pennsylvania Press, 1952), p. 46.

29. *Sovereign Reason* (Glencoe: Free Press, 1954), p. 29. Cf. Campbell, *What Is Science?* pp. 81, 89; Kurt P. Tauber, "Science and Politics: A Commentary," *World Politics*, 4 (April 1952), 437.

30. Cf. David Easton, *The Political System* (New York: Alfred A. Knopf, 1953), pp. 55–57; Jenkin, *The Study of Political Theory*, p. 93; Merton, *Social Theory and Social Structure*, pp. 96–101.

31. Dahl, "Political Theory: Truth and Consequences," p. 95.

32. This statement, and the elaboration of it in the remainder of the paragraph, are based largely on Philipp Frank, *Philosophy of Science* (Englewood Cliffs: Prentice-Hall, 1957), pp. 348–60.

33. Cf. Knorr, "Theories of Imperialism," p. 402. For a discussion of some high-level theories, notably Marxist theories and evolutionary theory reflected in Social Darwinism, see P. D. Marchant, "Determinist Theories in International Relations," *International Relations*, 1 (October 1956), 251–58.

34. Cf. Bernard Crick, *The American Science of Politics, Its Origins and Conditions* (Berkeley and Los Angeles: University of California Press, 1959).

35. Cf. Karl W. Deutsch, "Higher Education and the Unity of Science," in Conference on Science, Philosophy, and Religion, Ninth Symposium, *Goals for American Education* (New York: Harpers, 1950), pp. 104 ff.

36. Arturo Rosenblueth and Norbert Wiener, "The Role of Models in Science," *Philosophy of Science*, 12 (October 1945), 316; Paul Meadows, "Models, System, and Science," *American Sociological Review*, 22 (February 1947), 3–9.

37. Cf. Harold D. Lasswell, *Power and Personality* (New York: Norton, 1948), p. 21.

38. May Brodbeck, "Models, Meaning, and Theories," in Llewellyn Gross, ed., *Symposium on Sociological Theory* (Evanston: Row, Peterson, 1959), p. 379.

39. *Ibid.*, p. 381.

40. Herbert A. Simon and Allen Newell, "Models: Their Uses and Limitations, in White, *The State of the Social Sciences*, p. 66. Cf. Ernest R. Hilgard and Daniel Lerner, "The Person: Subject and Object of Sci-

ence and Policy," in Daniel Lerner and Harold D. Lasswell, eds., *The Policy Sciences. Recent Developments in Scope and Method* (Stanford: Stanford University Press, 1951), pp. 28–29; Karl W. Deutsch, "Mechanism, Teleology, and Mind," *Philosophy and Phenomenological Research,* 12 (December 1951), 186.

41. For more extended statements of the functions of theory see Social Science Research Council, Committee on Historiography, Bulletin 64, *The Social Sciences in Historical Study,* p. 26; Talcott Parsons and Edward A. Shils, eds., *Toward a General Theory of Action* (Cambridge: Harvard University Press, 1951), p. 3; William J. Goode and Paul K. Hatt, *Methods in Social Research* (New York: McGraw-Hill, 1952), pp. 9–12; Easton, *The Political System,* esp. pp. 57–60.

42. James E. Conant, *Modern Science and Modern Man* (New York: Columbia University Press, 1952), pp. 54, 57.

43. Jenkin, *The Study of Political Theory,* pp. 62–64.

INTRODUCTION TO PART III

1. Roland Young, ed., *Approaches to the Study of Politics* (Evanston: Northwestern University Press, 1958).

2. D. E. Butler, *The Study of Political Behavior* (London: Hutchinson, 1958).

3. Cf. Avery Leiserson, "Problems of Methodology in Political Research," in Heinz Eulau, Samuel J. Eldersveld, and Morris Janowitz, eds., *Political Behavior, A Reader in Theory and Research* (Glencoe: Free Press, 1956), pp. 53–64; Daniel Lerner and Harold D. Lasswell, eds., *The Policy Sciences, Recent Developments in Scope and Method* (Stanford: Stanford University Press, 1951); George Simpson, *Man in Society* (Garden City: Doubleday, 1954), pp. 48–60.

CHAPTER TEN

1. Charles A. Beard, "Grounds for a Reconsideration of Historiography," in Social Science Research Council, Committee on Historiography, Bulletin 54, *Theory and Practice in Historical Study* (New York: SSRC, 1946), p. 5, footnote.

2. Louis Gottschalk, "A Professor of History in a Quandary," *American Historical Review,* 59 (January 1954), 279.

3. William O. Aydelotte, "History in a Liberal Education," *Journal of General Education,* 3 (October 1948), 1.

4. Gottschalk, "A Professor of History in a Quandary," p. 279.

5. *Ibid.*

6. Aydelotte, "History in a Liberal Education," p. 3.

7. Cf. Harvey C. Mansfield, "The Uses of History," *Public Administration Review,* 11 (Winter, 1951), 51–57.

8. Cf. Karl Popper, *The Poverty of Historicism* (London: Routledge & Kegan Paul, 1957). Karl R. Popper, *The Open Society and Its Enemies* (Princeton: Princeton University Press, 1950).

9. Michael Oakeshott, "Political Education," in Peter Laslett, ed., *Philosophy, Politics and Society* (New York: Macmillan, 1956), p. 12.
10. *Ibid.*, pp. 2, 12, 18.
11. Michael Oakeshott, "Rationalism in Politics," *Cambridge Journal*, 1 (November 1947), 88, 90.
12. *Ibid.*, 1 (December 1947), 153.
13. *Ibid.*, 1 (November 1947), 90.
14. *Ibid.*, 1 (December 1947), 153, 156.
15. Cf. George Simpson, *Man in Society: Preface to Sociology and the Social Sciences* (New York: Doubleday, 1954), p. 18 and *passim*.
16. This definition and those to follow are taken from Ely Chinoy, *Sociological Perspective: Basic Concepts and Their Application* (Garden City: Doubleday, 1954). See pp. 10–11, 20–23, 38, 51.
17. Robert S. Woodworth, *Contemporary Schools of Psychology* (New York: Ronald, 1948), pp. 4–5 and *passim*.
18. For an approach to the study of the political activity of individuals based on their perception of environmental stimuli and centered around the concepts of stimulus, organism, and response, see Robert E. Lane, *Political Life: Why People Get Involved in Politics* (Glencoe: Free Press, 1959).
19. Sir Halford Mackinder, *Democratic Ideals and Reality* (New York: Holt, 1942), p. 150.
20. Peter Winch, *The Idea of a Social Science* (New York: Humanities Press, 1958), pp. 5, 15.
21. Stephen K. Bailey, "New Research Frontiers of Interest to Legislators and Administrators," in *Research Frontiers in Politics and Government* (Washington: Brookings, 1955), p. 20.

CHAPTER ELEVEN

1. Carl J. Friedrich, *Constitutional Government and Democracy* (Boston: Little, Brown and Co., 1941), pp. 593, 594. Cf. John H. Hallowell, "Politics and Ethics," *American Political Science Review*, 38 (August 1944), 653; Ludwig Freund, "Power and the Democratic Process," *Social Research*, 15 (September 1948), 327–44; E. E. Schattschneider, "Intensity, Visibility, Direction, and Scope," *American Political Science Review*, 51 (December 1957), 933–42.
2. "Current Studies of the Decision Process: Automation versus Creativity," *Western Political Quarterly*, 8 (September 1955), 381–82. Cf. Harold D. Lasswell and Abraham Kaplan, *Power and Society; A Framework for Political Inquiry* (New Haven: Yale University Press, 1950), pp. xii–xiv.
3. Social Science Research Council, Committee on Historiography, *The Social Sciences in Historical Study*, Bulletin 64 (New York: SSRC, 1954), p. 69.
4. "An Approach to the Analysis of Political Systems," *World Politics*, 9 (April 1957), 385.

5. A. Gordon Dewey, "On Methods in the Study of Politics," *Political Science Quarterly*, 38 (December 1923), 638.

6. *The Study of International Relations* (New York: Appleton-Century-Crofts, 1955), pp. 130–35; "Political Science and World Stabilization," *American Political Science Review*, 44 (March 1950), 1–13.

7. Quincy Wright, "Political Science and World Stabilization," *American Political Science Review*, 44 (March 1950), 8.

8. For a discussion of a possible extension of the traditional realm of inquiry, see Robert A. Dahl, "Business and Politics: A Critical Appraisal of Political Science," *American Political Science Review*, 53 (March 1959), 1–34.

9. See Charles B. Hagan, "The Group in a Political Science," in Roland Young, ed., *Approaches to the Study of Politics* (Evanston: Northwestern University Press, 1958), p. 46.

10. Cf. the discussion of "The American Approach to War," in Robert E. Osgood, *Limited War* (Chicago: The University of Chicago Press, 1957), pp. 28–45.

11. Cf. Herbert A. Simon, *Administrative Behavior* (2d ed.; New York: Macmillan, 1957), pp. 100–102; Stephen K. Bailey, "New Research Frontiers of Interest to Legislators and Administrators," in *Research Frontiers in Politics and Government* (Washington, D.C.: Brookings, 1955), p. 13.

12. Bailey, *loc. cit.*

13. Cf. Foster H. Sherwood, "The Role of Public Law in Political Science," in Young, *Approaches to the Study of Politics*, pp. 86–96.

14. Cf. Vernon Van Dyke, *International Politics* (New York: Appleton-Century-Crofts, 1957), pp. 300–305.

15. Frederick M. Watkins, *The State as a Concept of Political Science* (New York: Harper, 1934), p. 83. Cf. G. E. G. Catlin, *The Science and Method of Politics* (New York: Knopf, 1927), esp. pp. 139–42.

16. William A. Robson, *The University Teaching of Social Sciences: Political Science* (Paris: UNESCO, 1954), pp. 17–18.

17. Hans J. Morgenthau, *Politics Among Nations* (New York: Knopf, 1954), pp. 26–27.

18. Charles P. Kindleberger in William T. R. Fox, ed., *Theoretical Aspects of International Relations* (Notre Dame: University of Notre Dame Press, 1959), p. 79.

19. Cf. Herbert A. Simon, "Notes on the Observation and Measurement of Political Power," *Journal of Politics*, 15 (November 1953), 500–516.

20. Harold D. Lasswell, *World Politics and Personal Insecurity* (New York: Whittlesey House, 1935), p. 3.

21. *The Political System*, p. 146.

22. David B. Truman, *The Governmental Process* (New York: Knopf, 1951), esp. pp. 29, 37, 46.

23. Hagan, "The Group in a Political Science," p. 45.

24. Arthur F. Bentley, *The Process of Government* (Chicago: University of Chicago Press, 1908), p. 211.

25. *Ibid.*, pp. 110, 117.

26. *Ibid.*, pp. 177, 179.

27. Cf. Gustav Bergmann, "Ideology," in his *The Metaphysics of Logical Positivism* (New York: Longmans, Green, 1954), p. 311.

28. Peter H. Odegard, "A Group Basis of Politics: A New Name for an Ancient Myth," *Western Political Quarterly*, 11 (September 1958), 701; Stanley Rothman, "Systematic Political Theory: Observations on the Group Approach," *American Political Science Review*, 54 (March 1960), 15–33.

29. In Young, *Approaches to the Study of Politics*, pp. 363–82. Cf. Peter H. Rossi, "Community Decision Making," *Administrative Science Quarterly*, 1 (March 1957), 415–43.

30. See, for example, Alexander L. George and Juliette L. George, *Woodrow Wilson and Colonel House: A Personality Study* (New York: John Day, 1956).

31. Harold D. Lasswell, *Power and Personality* (New York: Norton, 1948), esp. pp. 59–93.

32. Donald R. Matthews, *The Social Background of Political Decision-Makers* (Garden City: Doubleday, 1954); John R. Schmidhauser, "The Justices of the Supreme Court: A Collective Portrait," *Midwest Journal of Political Science*, 3 (February 1959), 1–57; Harold D. Lasswell, Daniel Lerner, and C. Easton Rothwell, *Comparative Studies of Elites: An Introduction and Bibliography* (Stanford: Stanford University Press, 1952).

33. Cf. C. Wright Mills, *The Power Elite* (New York: Oxford, 1956).

34. Floyd Hunter, *Community Power Structure; A Study of Decision Makers* (Chapel Hill: University of North Carolina Press, 1953); reviewed by Herbert Kaufman and Victor Jones, "The Mystery of Power," *Public Administration Review*, 14 (Summer, 1954), 205–12.

35. Earl Latham, *The Group Basis of Politics* (Ithaca: Cornell University Press, 1952).

36. Stephen K. Bailey, *Congress Makes a Law* (New York: Columbia University Press, 1950).

37. For a classification and review of studies of decision making by voters, see Samuel J. Eldersveld, "Theory and Method in Voting Behavior Research," *Journal of Politics*, 13 (February 1951), 70–87.

38. Richard C. Snyder, "A Decision-Making Approach to the Study of Political Phenomena," in Young, *Approaches to the Study of Politics*, pp. 3–38; Richard C. Snyder, H. W. Bruck, and Burton Sapin, *Decision-Making as an Approach to the Study of International Politics* (Princeton: Princeton University, Organizational Behavior Section, 1954). Cf. Ward Edward, "The Theory of Decision-Making," *Psychological Bulletin*, 51 (July 1954), 380–417; Bruno Leoni, "The Meaning of 'Political' in Political Decisions," *Political Studies*, 5 (October 1957), 225–39; Joseph Frankel, "Towards a Decision-Making Model in Foreign Policy," *Political Studies*, 7 (February 1959), 1–11; Paul Wasserman with Fred S. Silander, *Decision-Making: An Annotated Bibliography* (Ithaca, N.Y.: Cornell

University, Graduate School of Business and Public Administration, 1958).

39. Simon, *Administrative Behavior*, p. xxx. Cf. Inter-university Case Program, *ICP Case Series*, No. 1– . (University, Ala.: Universtiy of Alabama Press, 1951———.)

40. Cf. J. D. Williams, *The Compleat Strategyst, Being a Primer on the Theory of Games of Strategy* (New York: McGraw-Hill, 1954); Richard C. Snyder, "Game Theory and the Analysis of Political Behavior," in *Research Frontiers in Politics and Government*, pp. 70–103; Thomas C. Schelling, "The Strategy of Conflict: Prospectus for a Reorientation of Game Theory," *Journal of Conflict Resolution*, 2 (September 1958), 203–64; Morton A. Kaplan, *System and Process in International Politics* (New York: Wiley, 1957); Martin Shubik, *Readings in Game Theory and Political Behavior* (Garden City: Doubleday, 1954).

41. Cf. John Dewey, *Theory of Valuation, International Encyclopedia of Unified Science*, Vol. II, No. 4 (Chicago: University of Chicago Press, 1939).

42. Cf. Charles S. Hyneman, *The Study of Politics* (Urbana: University of Illinois Press, 1959), pp. 100–113, 165–73. Herbert A. Simon, *Administrative Behavior*, pp. xxxi–xxxii, 66. On the definition of the concept *objective*, see Snyder, Bruck, and Sapin, *Decision-Making as an Approach to the Study of International Politics*, p. 51.

CHAPTER TWELVE

1. Cf. David B. Truman, "The Impact on Political Science of the Revolution in the Behavioral Sciences," in *Research Frontiers in Politics and Government*, pp. 202–31; "The Implications of Research in Political Behavior," *American Political Science Review*, 46 (December 1952), 1003–9; Dwight Waldo, *Political Science in the USA: A Trend Report* (UNESCO, 1956), pp. 21–23.

2. James G. Miller, "Toward a General Theory for the Behavioral Sciences," *American Psychologist*, 10 (September 1955), 514.

3. *Ibid.* See also Ludwig von Bertalanffy, "General System Theory," in Ludwig von Bertalanffy and Anatol Rapoport, eds., *General Systems, Yearbook of the Society for the Advancement of General Systems Theory* (Ann Arbor, Mich.: Society for General Systems Research, 1956———), Vol. I, 1956, pp. 1–10.

4. R. C. Buck, "On the Logic of General Behavior Systems Theory," in Herbert Feigl and Michael Scriven, eds., *Minnesota Studies in the Philosophy of Science*, Vol. I, *The Foundations of Science and the Concepts of Psychology and Psychoanalysis* (Minneapolis: University of Minnesota Press, 1956), pp. 223–38.

5. Herbert A. Simon and Allen Newell, "Models: Their Uses and Limitations," in Leonard D. White, ed., *The State of the Social Sciences* (Chicago: The University of Chicago Press, 1956), p. 77.

6. Stanley H. Hoffmann, "International Relations, The Long Road to Theory," *World Politics*, 11 (April 1959), 356.

7. Cf. Charles A. McClelland, "Systems and History in International Relations: Some Perspectives for Empirical Research and Theory," in Ludwig von Bertalanffy and Anatol Rapoport, eds., *General Systems, Yearbook of the Society for General Systems Research*, Vol. III, 1958, pp. 221–47. See also David Easton, "An Approach to the Analysis of Political Systems," *World Politics*, 9 (April 1957), 383–400.

CHAPTER THIRTEEN

1. Harold and Margaret Sprout, *Man-Milieu Relationship Hypotheses in the Context of International Politics* (Princeton: Center of International Studies, 1956); Harold and Margaret Sprout, "Environmental Factors in the Study of International Politics," *Journal of Conflict Resolution*, 1 (December 1957), 309–28. Cf. Joseph Frankel, "Towards a Decision-Making Model in Foreign Policy," *Political Studies*, 7 (February 1959), 1–11.

2. Quoted from Alexander Gray, *The Socialist Tradition: Moses to Lenin* (New York: Longmans, Green, 1946), pp. 302–4.

3. Alfred G. Meyer, *Marxism: The Unity of Theory and Practice* (Cambridge: Harvard University Press, 1954), p. 15.

4. *Ibid.*, p. 14.

5. R. S. Peters, *The Concept of Motivation* (New York: Humanities Press, 1958), pp. 52–94.

6. Alfred Adler, *The Practice and Theory of Individual Psychology* (New York: Harcourt, Brace, 1929); Karen Horney, *Neurosis and Human Growth* (New York: Norton, 1950); Erich Fromm, *Escape from Freedom* (New York: Rinehart, 1941). Cf. Ruth L. Munroe, *Schools of Psychoanalytic Thought* (New York: Dryden, 1955).

7. John Dollard *et al., Frustration and Aggression* (New Haven: Yale University Press, 1939); T. H. Pear, ed., *Psychological Factors of Peace and War* (London: Hutchinson, 1950); E. F. M. Durbin and John Bowlby, *Personal Aggressiveness and War* (New York: Columbia University Press, 1939); H. J. Eysenck, *The Psychology of Politics* (New York: Praeger, 1954). Cf. Richard Christie, "Eysenck's Treatment of the Personality of Communists," *Psychological Bulletin*, 53 (November 1956), 411–30; Elton B. McNeil, "Psychology and Aggression," *Journal of Conflict Resolution*, 3 (September 1959), 195–293.

8. See especially his *Power and Personality*. Cf. Nathan Leites, "Psycho-Cultural Hypotheses About Political Acts," *World Politics*, 1 (October 1948), 102–19; Daniel Bell, "Ten Theories in Search of Reality: The Prediction of Soviet Behavior in the Social Sciences," *World Politics*, 10 (April 1958), 327–65.

9. Karl Mannheim, *Ideology and Utopia* (New York: Harcourt, Brace, 1936), pp. 4, 49, 69, 71. Cf. William A. Glaser, "The Types and Uses of

Political Theory," *Social Research*, 22 (Autumn, 1955), 275–96; P. D. Marchant, "Determinist Theories in International Relations," *International Relations*, 1 (October 1956), 251–58; Charles Frankel, *The Case for Modern Man* (New York: Harper, 1956), pp. 117–45.

10. Gustav Bergmann, *The Metaphysics of Logical Positivism* (New York: Longmans, Green, 1954), p. 310.

11. Some of the works cited earlier in connection with explanation in terms of reasons and in connection with the discussion of rules are relevant here; e.g., Nathan Leites, *A Study of Bolshevism* (Glencoe: Free Press, 1953). Cf. Herbert McClosky, "Conservatism and Personality," *American Political Science Review*, 52 (March 1958), 27–45.

12. E. H. Carr, *The Twenty Years' Crisis* (London: Macmillan, New York: St. Martin's, 1949), pp. 11–21.

CHAPTER FOURTEEN

1. Richard Robinson, *Definition* (Oxford: Clarendon, 1950), pp. 98, 180, 186–88; Charles S. Hyneman, *The Study of Politics* (Urbana: University of Illinois Press, 1959), pp. 57–58.

2. Cf. Kenneth W. Thompson, "Theories and Problems of Foreign Policy," in Roy C. Macridis, ed., *Foreign Policy in World Politics* (Englewood Cliffs: Prentice-Hall, 1958), p. 351.

3. Bernard R. Berelson, Paul F. Lazarsfeld, and William N. McPhee, *Voting: A Study of Opinion Formation in a Presidential Campaign* (Chicago: University of Chicago Press, 1954), p. 323.

4. Cf. Thomas C. McCormick and Roy G. Francis, *Methods of Research in the Behavioral Sciences* (New York: Harper, 1958), esp. Chaps. 5–8; Marie Jahoda *et al.*, *Research Methods in Social Relations* (New York: Dryden, 1951), Part One, "Basic Processes," Part Two, "Selected Techniques"; Leon Festinger and Daniel Katz, eds., *Research Methods in the Behavioral Sciences* (New York: Dryden, 1953).

5. Clyde Kluckhohn, "Cultural Anthropology," in Lynn White, ed., *Frontiers of Knowledge in the Study of Man* (New York: Harper, 1956), p. 39. For other comments on the limitations of quantitative methods, see Hans J. Morgenthau, "Power as a Political Concept," in Roland Young, ed., *Approaches to the Study of Politics* (Evanston: Northwestern University Press, 1958), pp. 69 ff.

6. Cf. Bernard Berelson, *Content Analysis in Communication Research* (Glencoe: Free Press, 1952), esp. pp. 112–34.

7. "The Policy Orientation," in Daniel Lerner and Harold D. Lasswell, eds., *The Policy Sciences. Recent Developments in Scope and Method* (Stanford: Stanford University Press, 1951), p. 5.

8. *The Study of Political Theory* (Garden City: Doubleday, 1955), pp. 15–21.

9. Max Black, *Critical Thinking* (2d ed.; New York: Prentice-Hall, 1952), p. 5.

10. Morris R. Cohen and Ernest Nagel, *An Introduction to Logic and Scientific Method* (New York: Harcourt, Brace, 1934), pp. 278–79;

Black, *Critical Thinking, passim*; Hans Reichenbach, *The Rise of Scientific Philosophy* (Berkeley and Los Angeles: University of California Press, 1951), pp. 215–49.

11. Cf. David E. Apter, "A Comparative Method for the Study of Politics," *The American Journal of Sociology*, 64 (November 1958), 221–37; Roy C. Macridis, *The Study of Comparative Government* (Garden City, N.Y.: Doubleday, 1955), esp. pp. 1–6.

12. Cf. Ernest S. Griffith, "The Methods and Problems of Research," in Ernest S. Griffith, ed., *Research in Political Science* (Chapel Hill: University of North Carolina Press, 1948), pp. 211–17.

13. James B. Conant, *Science and Common Sense* (New Haven: Yale University Press, 1951), pp. 43–50.

14. Cohen and Nagel, *An Introduction to Logic and Scientific Method*, p. 192.

15. Hyneman, *The Study of Politics*, p. 76.

CHAPTER FIFTEEN

1. Hans Reichenbach, *The Rise of Scientific Philosophy* (Berkeley and Los Angeles: University of California Press, 1951), pp. 27–49, 229–49. Cf. Olaf Helmer and Nicholas Rescher, "On the Epistemology of the Inexact Sciences," *Management Science*, 1 (October 1959), 25–52.

2. Jacob Bronowski, *The Common Sense of Science* (Cambridge: Harvard University Press, 1953), p. 70.

3. Norman Campbell, *What Is Science?* (New York: Dover Publications, 1952), p. 27.

4. Carl J. Friedrich, "Political Philosophy and the Science of Politics," in Roland Young, ed., *Approaches to the Study of Politics* (Evanston: Northwestern University Press, 1958), pp. 174–75. Alfred Jules Ayer, *Language, Truth and Logic* (New York: Dover Publications, n.d.), p. 100.

5. Morris R. Cohen and Ernest Nagel, *An Introduction to Logic and Scientific Method* (New York: Harcourt, Brace, 1934), p. 394.

6. Cf. the definition by A. Wolf quoted by Wilson Gee, *Social Science Research Methods* (New York: Appleton-Century-Crofts, 1950), pp. 156–57.

7. Philipp Frank, *Philosophy of Science* (Englewood Cliffs: Prentice-Hall, 1957), p. 42.

8. James B. Conant, *Science and Common Sense* (New Haven: Yale University Press, 1951), p. 24.

9. *Ibid.*, pp. 219–20.

10. R. G. Collingwood, *The Idea of History* (Oxford: Clarendon, 1946), p. 9. Cf. the discussion of science and scientific method in Charles S. Hyneman, *The Study of Politics* (Urbana: University of Illinois Press, 1959), Chapters V and IX.

11. "Political Philosophy in the Twentieth Century: An Appraisal of Its Contribution to the Study of Politics," in Young, *Approaches to the Study of Politics*, p. 209.

12. Quincy Wright, *A Study of War,* Vol. 2, Appendix XXV, "The Application of Scientific Method to Social Studies" (Chicago: University of Chicago Press, 1942), pp. 1355–64. Morris R. Cohen, "Reason in Social Science," in Herbert Feigl and May Brodbeck, eds., *Readings in the Philosophy of Science* (New York: Appleton-Century-Crofts, 1953), pp. 663–74. Marion J. Levy, "Some Basic Methodological Difficulties in Social Science," *Philosophy of Science,* 17 (October 1950), 287–301.

13. Social Science Research Council, Committee on Historiography, Bulletin 54, *Theory and Practice in Historical Study* (New York: SSRC, 1946), pp. 138–39.

14. Bernard Brodie, "Scientific Progress and Political Science," *Scientific Monthly,* 85 (December 1957), 315–19.

15. *Ibid.*

16. For example, see Raymond W. Mack and Richard C. Snyder, "The Analysis of Social Conflict—Toward an Overview and Synthesis," *Journal of Conflict Resolution,* 1 (June 1957), 212–48.

17. David G. Smith, "Political Science and Political Theory," *American Political Science Review,* 51 (September 1957), 735. Cf. Collingwood, *The Idea of History,* pp. 166–70.

18. Smith, "Political Science and Political Theory," p. 737. Cf. Arnold A. Rogow, "Comment on Smith and Apter: Or, Whatever Happened to the Great Issues?" *American Political Science Review,* 51 (September 1957), 763–75.

19. William A. Robson, *The University Teaching of Social Sciences: Political Science* (Paris: UNESCO, 1954), p. 108. In contrast, see Dwight Waldo, *Perspectives on Administration* (University, Ala.: University of Alabama Press, 1956), pp. 1–25.

20. Cf. Lewis White Beck, *Philosophic Inquiry* (New York: Prentice-Hall, 1952), p. 155.

21. Conant, *Science and Common Sense,* p. 294.

22. Glencoe: Free Press, 1957.

23. *A Preface to Morals* (New York: Macmillan, 1929), p. 260.

24. For a criticism of the assumption that it is desirable, in so far as possible, to make the study of politics scientific, see Hans J. Morgenthau, *Scientific Man vs. Power Politics* (Chicago: University of Chicago Press, 1946). And for a criticism of Morgenthau's position, see Ernest Nagel, *Logic Without Metaphysics* (Glencoe: Free Press, 1956), pp. 377–82. Also see Bernard Crick, "The Science of Politics in the United States," *The Canadian Journal of Economics and Political Science,* 20 (August 1954), 308–20.

INDEX

Index

Abstraction: defined, 62; and reification, 63; and models, 105–6
Adler, Alfred, 171, 225 n.6
Aleksandrov, Georgi, 69
Analysis: analytical, defined, 69; as a method, 179–80
Analytic, as the definitional or logical, 9
Anderson, William, 213 n.13
Approach(es): defined, ix, 34, 114; types, ix–x, 33–35; historical, 14–17, 116–22; economic, 123–24, 166–70; sociological, 124–27; psychological, 127–28, 170–72; geographic, 128–29, 164–66; philosophical, 129–30; significance, 130; focusing on struggle over public issues, 131–35; institutional, 135–38; legal, 138–40; power, 140–44; decision making, 149–54; ends-means analysis, 154–57; behavioral, 158–60; systems theory, 160–62; and causal theories, 163–78; Marxist, 167–70; Freudian, 170–71; ideological, 172–77
Apter, David E., 227 n.11
Attitudes, 23–24, 26–27
Aydelotte, William O., 119, 120
Ayer, A. J.: quoted, 10; cited, 209 nn. 2,3, 227 n.4

Bailey, Stephen K., 130, 222 nn.11,12, 223 n.36
Barton, Allen H., 71
Beale, Howard K., 211 n.14
Beard, Charles A., 116
Beck, Lewis White, 216 nn.1,7, 228 n.20
Becker, Carl, 214 n.8
Beer, Samuel H., 101
Behavioralism, as an approach, 158–60, 204–5
Bell, Daniel, 225 n.8
Bentley, Arthur F., 147–49

Berelson, Bernard R., 217 n.3, 226 nn.3,6
Bergmann, Gustav: quoted, 83, 88, 101; his conception of law, 85–87; on ideologies, 174–75; cited, 210 n.1, 213 n.5, 217 n.2, 223 n.27
Black, Max, 226 nn.9,10
Bowlby, John, 225 n.7
Brecht, Arnold, 95, 209 nn.2,2, 210 n.8, 211 n.13, 213 n.18
Brodbeck, May, 107, 219 n.38
Brodie, Bernard, 228 n.14
Bronowski, Jacob, 71, 77, 192
Bryce, Lord James, 56
Buck, R. C., 224 n.4
Butler, D. E., 220 n.2

Campbell, Norman R.: quoted, 88, 192; cited, 215 n.8, 216 n.1, 217 n.2, 218 n.29
Carr, E. H., 177–78
Catlin, George E. G., 216 n.11, 222 n.15
Cause: and effect, 4; and explanation, 27–29
Chinoy, Ely, 125–26
Christie, Richard, 225 n.7
Chronicles, 15
Classification, classify, 20, 62, 71–73
Clausewitz, 141
Cobban, Alfred, 46, 217 n.10
Cohen, Morris R.: quoted, 19, 60, 73, 84, 186; cited, 215 n.8, 216 n.1, 217 n.2, 218 n.29
Colligation, 16–17
Collingwood, R. G., viii, 195, 228 n.17
Conant, James B.: quoted, 108, 195; cited, 204, 214 n.6, 227 n.13, 228 n.21
Concept(s): defined, 62; and abstraction, 63; and reification, 63; functions, 64–65; and theories, 95–98
Conditions: and consequences, 4; and explanation, 38–39; necessary and sufficient, 39